BLUE RIBBON
CANNING

AWARD-
WINNING
RECIPES

JAMS, PRESERVES,
PICKLES, SAUCES & MORE

The Taunton Press

✳ Dedication ✳
In loving memory of my parents, Lee and Mary Amendt, who always believed in me and encouraged me to follow my dreams.

The Taunton Press, Inc., 63 South Main Street, PO Box 5506, Newtown, CT 06470-5506
email: tp@taunton.com

Editor: Carolyn Mandarano
Copy Editor: Li Agen
Indexer: Heidi Blough
Jacket/Cover design: Rita Sowins / Sowins Design
Interior design and layout: Rita Sowins / Sowins Design
Photographer: Andrew Purcell, except p. 115 (courtesy *Fountain Valley Living Magazine* and p. 174 (Steve Dropkin)
Food Stylist: Carrie Purcell
Prop Stylist: Paige Hicks

The following names/manufacturers appearing in *Blue Ribbon Canning* are trademarks:
Ball®, C&H®, Chambord™, ClearJel®, Cointreau®, Fleischmann's®, Gedney®, Grand Marnier®, Jack Daniels®, Mrs. Dash®, Spam®, Sure-Jell®, Tabasco®, Tilt-a-Whirl™

Library of Congress Cataloging-in-Publication Data
Amendt, Linda J., author.
  Blue ribbon canning : award-winning recipes / Linda J. Amendt.
    pages cm
  Includes index.
  ISBN 978-1-62710-769-3
1. Canning and preserving. I. Title. II. Title: Canning.
  TX601.A4668 2015
  664'.0282--dc23
                            2014049305
Printed in the United States of America
10 9 8 7 6 5 4 3 2

ACKNOWLEDGMENTS

I want to thank everyone who had a hand in making this book a reality.

A special thank you to the following people:

To Culinary Coordinator Michelle Johnson, and the amazing and dedicated California's Kitchen staff and Friends of the Fair volunteers at the California State Fair: Sabrina, Pam, Joyce, Mary Ann, Catherine, and Will—you are all part of my special "fair family." To Nancy Emelio and Stephanie Jurkowski, for your continued friendship, and in fond memory of the late Willie Garrett, who championed the open judging format at the California State Fair.

To Culinary Coordinator Renee Fontes and the wonderful staff at the OC Fair: Richard, Kim, and Julie—you make judging an absolute delight.

To Iris Dimond for your many years of friendship, encouragement, and excellent judging skills at the California State Fair.

To "Your Produce Man" Michael Marks and Julie Marks for your friendship and the outstanding job you both do emceeing the competition judging at the California State Fair.

To my good friend Eunice Preku, for all your encouragement and our wonderful, spirit-renewing "breakfast therapy" get-togethers.

To my fantastic editor, Carolyn Mandarano, for your excellent work, understanding, and friendship, and to the entire team at The Taunton Press—you all rock!

To my terrific literary agent, Linda Konner, for your expertise, professional guidance, and friendship—you're the best!

To all the fairs, fair coordinators, and fair staff across the country who helped connect me with your blue ribbon canners. Without your assistance, this book would not have been possible.

To all my friends I have met through fair competition—thank you for the opportunity to compete against you and the privilege to judge your wonderful canning and baking entries.

—Linda J. Amendt

The following contributors provided jars of their blue ribbon canned goods for use in the recipe photos.

Linda J. Amendt	Valerie J. Fong	The Romero Family
Brenda D. Bustillos	Jay Grantier	Shirley Rosenberg
Nancy Charron	Alan Gravenor	
Carolyn DeMarco	Anna Mayerhofe	

CONTENTS

✳ Introduction ✳

Canning and canning competitions are wonderful and delicious food traditions enjoyed and treasured by many generations. State, county, regional, and community fairs are woven into the fabric of our national heritage. As canners, we are all tied together into one community through our love of canning, the thrill of competing at fairs, and the joy of sharing our canning creations with family and friends.

Home canning is seeing a huge resurgence. What was once a necessity to preserve food for the long, hard winter, canning has become a popular hobby and even a year-round way of life for new generations. No longer the domain of grandmothers with large gardens, canners now come in all ages and from all backgrounds. You will find a wealth of canners in every state and every community, ranging in age from young children to seniors. Many people find canning a relaxing and enjoyable activity. We also like the satisfaction of preparing the canned goods ourselves and knowing what is in the food we feed to our families.

Behind every blue ribbon and special award earned at a fair is a skillful home canner with a unique and engaging story. Throughout these pages, you will take an award-winning recipe tour of the country, experiencing the joys of canning and meeting many amazing and talented blue ribbon winners.

You will visit with individuals, husbands and wives, multiple generations of canners in one family, and young canners who are rising stars in the youth canning divisions. From rural canners to those who live on small family farms or have large gardens to urban canners living in midsize towns and big cities, they are all here. You will also meet inspiring people who have overcome personal challenges to pursue their interest in canning and competing at fairs. Along with their delicious blue ribbon recipes, you will get to know the canners and share in their personal love-of-canning story.

For many years, fair competitions were seen as a closed world, with lots of inside politics and all the top awards going to longtime competitors. This is no longer true. Yes, many fairs were dominated by small groups of competitors, primarily older women, who would walk off with the majority of the awards. New entrants sometimes had to work their way up the ladder before winning major awards. However, those times are long past. There are plenty of first-time exhibitors taking home blue ribbons and special awards at fairs in every state. Many are surprised when they visit the fair and see ribbons hanging on their jars. The reason they are winning is the quality, care, and love they put into their entries. Nothing beats the joy and excitement of winning your first ribbon, and if that ribbon is blue, you'll be walking on air.

Fair canning competitions are not only a fun and exciting part of the canning community but they also play a very big role in educating both new and experienced canners. One of the most important things fairs do is to encourage safe canning and the use of modern canning techniques. When you read the rules for fair canning competitions, you will see very specific requirements for jar sizes, headspace (the amount of space in the top of the jar), processing methods and times, and jar labeling. At first, some of this may seem overwhelming or confusing, but every rule has a purpose. They encourage entrants to use home canning and food preservation practices approved by the United States Department of Agriculture (USDA). Exhibitors who follow safe canning practices and produce quality canned products are rewarded with those coveted ribbons. Those who don't will go home disappointed.

I had such a delightful time getting to know all of these remarkable canners, and I know you will, too. So turn the pages and join us in the kitchen on our canning journey. You'll meet some great people and have a lot of fun along the way. Let's get canning!

* Ingredients *

The quality of the ingredients you use for putting up preserves, jams, pickles, sauces, vegetables, and all things canned has a direct effect on the outcome of the finished product. Ingredients play an important role in determining the intense flavor, appropriate texture, and vibrant color that are characteristic of great canned foods. Everything from the fruits and vegetables to the sugar, vinegar or lemon juice, herbs, and any other ingredients and flavorings will all have an impact on your results. When canning, always use the best and freshest ingredients available. Don't skimp on quality or you may be disappointed with the results.

Produce

Fruits and vegetables are the primary ingredients in canning recipes. They provide the main source of flavor and help determine the texture of the finished product. The flavor and texture of your canned items will only be as good as the flavor and texture of the fruits and vegetables you put into them, so start with produce that is in season and at its peak of ripeness. Avoid using fruits or vegetables that are underripe, which have a mild flavor and very firm texture, or are overripe, which can have an "off" flavor and soft texture. Whenever possible, choose produce as soon as possible after harvest—while some fruits and vegetables last longer than others, all are at their peak within 12 to 24 hours after being picked.

Be sure the fruits and vegetables you choose are free of bruises and blemishes. Bruised or damaged fruit may contain harmful bacteria that could contaminate your canned item. Soft fruit can also affect the texture of a jam or marmalade and may prevent the spread from setting.

Sugar

Sugar serves many purposes in canning and is an essential ingredient in preserving fruit, no matter what type of canned item you're making. Sugar obviously adds sweetness, but it also acts as a preservative in canned fruits, pickles, and soft spreads by inhibiting the growth of microorganisms in the jars during storage. Sugar also enhances the flavor of fruit, helps fruit maintain both its shape and texture, and aids in the gel formation that allows a spread to set. Don't reduce the amount of sugar called for in a soft spread recipe—not only will it prevent the spread from setting, but it can also allow yeasts and molds to grow in sealed jars.

Pectin

Pectin is a water-soluble carbohydrate and natural thickening and gelling agent found in the tissues of all fruits. Some fruits, such as apples, grapes, gooseberries, and cranberries, have a naturally high level of pectin, while others, such as strawberries, cherries, pears, and pineapple, have a low pectin content. Pectin develops as fruit ripens, and the highest levels of pectin are found in fruit that is slightly underripe. The pectin found in fruit that is significantly underripe or fruit that is overripe will not form a strong gel.

Commercial pectins are made from tart apples or the peels of citrus fruit, both of which contain high amounts of natural pectin. Packaged pectin is available in both powdered and liquid forms; these are made differently, so are not interchangeable in recipes. Powdered and liquid pectins require different proportions of fruit, sugar, and acid in order to set. Be sure to use the specific type of pectin and package size called for in the recipe.

Using commercial pectins to make soft spreads like jams, jellies, and marmalades has several advantages. Instead of needing to use a significant amount of underripe fruit in spreads, commercial pectin allows you to use fully ripe fruit with the best flavor. The amount of cooking time is also significantly reduced, so the fruit retains a stronger flavor. Pectin allows you to make spreads with any fruit combination of varying pectin levels. Additionally, the same amount of fruit will produce a higher yield of finished spread with commercial pectin because the fruit doesn't need to cook down as much in order to set.

Acid

Acid plays several important roles in canning. First, it helps inhibit bacterial growth in canned products during storage, which can happen if the acid level is too low. The correct acidity level is essential to ensuring safe water bath processing and storage for canned goods that are high in acid, such as jams, jellies, fruits, and pickles. Products that have low acid levels, such as vegetables, must be processed in a pressure canner to make them safe for shelf storage. Reducing the amount of acid may make the preserve unsafe for shelf-storage after processing, so always follow the

ADDING BUTTER TO PRESERVES

Unsalted butter may be added to jams, marmalades, preserves, and conserves to help reduce the amount of foaming that occurs when the fruit mixture boils. This reduces the time spent skimming foam from the top of the jam in the pot before ladling it into the jars. Butter can cause jellies to turn cloudy, so it is not recommended that butter be added to juice mixtures when making jellies.

recipe's specified amount of acid. Lemon juice and vinegar are the two most common types of acid used in canning recipes.

A sufficient amount of acid, in the correct ratio to the fruit, sugar, and pectin, must be present for a soft spread to gel or set. If there is too little acid, the spread will remain thin and runny. If there is too much acid, the spread will set up firmer and, during storage, some liquid may separate from the gel, a process known as syneresis, or "weeping." Weeping is evident by a thin puddle of liquid on the top surface of the spread in the jar or a layer of liquid between the side of the jar and the spread.

✳ LEMON JUICE ✳

For fruits that don't have enough natural acid to set the spread, like ripe peaches, the acid is usually provided by freshly squeezed lemon juice. A small amount of freshly squeezed lemon juice is added to some spread recipes to enhance the flavor of the fruit and also to help protect the color of lighter fruits and prevent them from darkening during storage. Freshly squeezed lime juice can also be used to raise the acidity level of some fruit mixtures to improve the texture and brighten the flavor of the jam or other spread. If a recipe calls for bottled lemon juice or lime juice, do not substitute fresh juice. Bottled lemon and lime juice have a consistent acidity level needed to safely can some recipes containing low-acid fruits, such as tomatoes and figs.

✳ VINEGAR ✳

Vinegar is used in making pickles and relishes to raise the acidity level to a level high enough to permit processing in a water bath canner. Only commercially prepared vinegars with a minimum acidity level of 5% should be used for canning; check the ingredient statement on the bottle label for the acidity level. White vinegar, cider vinegar, or wine vinegar may be used, depending on the recipe and the desired result. Commercially made herb and fruit vinegars may overpower the flavor of the produce and should be used cautiously. Homemade vinegars have an unknown acidity content and shouldn't be used in canning recipes.

Herbs

Fresh herbs add a wonderful aromatic flavor to many types of preserves, from savory soft spreads to sauces and pickles. Fresh herbs have a stronger flavor than dried herbs. Choose young, tender fresh herbs with dark green color and undamaged leaves. For the strongest flavor, prepare the herbs just before you are ready to use them.

HOW TO TOAST NUTS

Position a rack in the center of the oven and heat the oven to 350°F. Line a baking sheet with foil and evenly spread the chopped nuts over the foil in a single layer. Bake the nuts for 5 minutes, stirring halfway through baking so the nuts will toast evenly and to prevent browning. Remove the nuts from the pan and let cool completely on paper towels.

Nuts and Dried Fruits

A variety of nuts and some dried fruits, such as raisins, currants, cranberries, and apricots, can be used to make conserves, which are fruit spreads containing nuts and usually dried fruit and are similar in texture to jams. Coconut is a popular addition to spreads with a tropical flair. Nuts used in spreads need to be very fresh. Stale or rancid nuts will give the conserve an unpleasant flavor. Always taste nuts before using them to make sure they are fresh. Nuts may be toasted to bring out their flavor and to accentuate their crunchy texture.

Wine and Liqueurs

Jams, marmalades, and other preserves flavored with wine and liqueurs have become quite popular. While liqueurs can greatly enhance the flavor of the fruit and give the preserves a warm, full-bodied flavor, they should be added in small quantities so that the flavor is subtle. A common mistake made by many canners is adding too much liqueur and overpowering the fresh flavor of the fruit. Wines and liqueurs are flammable and alcohol vapors can be ignited by open flames, so use caution when adding wine or a liqueur to a pan of preserves.

* Canning *
Equipment

Using the appropriate type and size of home canning equipment, including jars and lids, water bath and pressure canners, pots and pans, and utensils, will help ensure that you produce beautiful, delicious, and safe canned foods.

Home Canning Jars and Lids

Modern canning jars with two-piece lids make home canning safe and easy. Canning jars are sold in boxes of a dozen jars that also include the lids and screw bands, and come in a variety of sizes and shapes with both standard and wide-mouth jar openings.

Old-fashioned canning jars sealed with rubber-like gaskets and screw-on one-piece lids are no longer considered safe for home canning, and the United States Department of Agriculture (USDA) does not endorse their continued use. This also applies to jars with wire-bail-attached glass lids and rubber seals; these types of jars should not be used for home canning. Newer one-piece canning lids also are available, but their use is not currently endorsed by the USDA, and jars sealed with these one-piece lids are not permitted in fair competitions.

❋ CANNING JARS ❋

USDA-approved home canning jars are made of molded heat-tempered glass and are the only containers currently recommended for safe home canning. The jars have a wide rim and screw threads that are designed to work with two-piece metal vacuum lids and screw bands. Canning jars come in a variety of sizes and shapes ranging from 4-ounce, 8-ounce, and 12-ounce jars used for making jams, jellies, and other soft spreads to pint and quart jars used for canning fruits, vegetables, pickles, relishes, and most sauces. Half-gallon jars are only approved for canning apple and grape juices.

You can buy canning jars at grocery stores, hardware stores, home improvement stores, and many other retail outlets. Canning jars can be reused, but new lids must be purchased for each use.

Don't use any jars that are not specifically manufactured for home canning, including mayonnaise jars, commercial jam and jelly jars, fruit jars, condiment jars, peanut butter jars, and baby food jars, even if home canning lids and rings appear to fit them. Commercial jars are not heat-tempered like home canning jars, nor are they sturdy enough to stand up to heat processing in a water bath or pressure canner. The rim surface on these types of jars is also narrower than the jar rim of home canning jars. This significantly increases the chance the seals will fail during storage.

Jars manufactured specifically for freezer canning should not be used for canning preserves that will be processed in a water bath canner or pressure canner. Freezer jars are not tempered to withstand the high heat in the canner and may shatter during processing.

❋ CANNING LIDS AND SCREW BANDS ❋

The lid closures for canning jars consist of two pieces—a flat metal lid and a metal screw band. After the jars are filled, the lid is applied and the band is screwed on to hold the lid in place during processing in a water bath or pressure canner.

The underside of the metal lid has a protective food-safe coating that won't react with the acids in canned foods. There is a raised channel around the underside of the outer edge of the lid that is filled with a sealing compound, which is specially formulated for use in home canning to form a tight seal between the lid and the jar during processing. The flat metal lids are designed for one-time use only and cannot be reused. A new lid must be used each time you seal a jar. While the compound on unused lids has a projected shelf life of up to five years, it is best to purchase new lids each canning season to ensure the effectiveness of the sealing compound.

The screw band is designed to hold the lid firmly in place during processing and until the jar cools and the lid compound forms a solid seal between the lid and jar rim. After the jars have cooled completely, the screw bands should be removed for storage. The screw bands are designed to match the screw threads on the canning jars. It is important to use lids and screw bands made by the same manufacturer as the canning jars to ensure a proper fit and tight seal. Screw bands can be reused if they are in good condition and not rusty.

Water Bath Canner

A water bath canner, also called a boiling water canner, is an essential piece of equipment for canning high-acid preserves, such as jams, pickles, and most fruits. It is used to process and seal jars after they have been filled and the lids applied. Years ago, water bath processing of filled jars was optional, but that is no longer the case for safety reasons and is now required when canning any high-acid food.

To make the jar contents safe for storage, the jars need to be heated in boiling water for a specified amount of time. During processing, the contents reach an internal temperature high enough to kill any potential bacteria that could cause contamination. Water bath processing will also deactivate enzymes, molds, and yeasts that could cause the preserves to deteriorate over time. To learn how to process high-acid foods in a water bath canner, see p. 34.

A water bath canner consists of a large stockpot with a lid and a rack in the bottom to hold the jars. The rack allows the hot water to circulate around and under the jars so the contents will heat evenly. You can either purchase a water bath canner specially made for the job or you can put one together yourself. Commercially made canners have racks designed to hold a certain number of jars. I find these racks awkward to use, so instead of purchasing a water bath canner, I have assembled my own. I use a 20-quart stainless steel stockpot with a glass lid and a round wire cake cooling rack in the bottom. The rack holds the jars level and allows the water to circulate under the jars during processing. The stockpot is also tall, so there is plenty of room to hold even quart jars, cover the jars with 2 inches of water, and still have plenty of room to allow the water to boil without boiling over.

If you want to assemble your own water bath canner, you will need a large stockpot, preferably stainless steel, with a tight-fitting lid. It needs to be deep enough to allow for a rack in the bottom, plus the height of the jars, 1 to 2 inches of water above the top of the jars, plus another $1\frac{1}{2}$ to 2 inches of height to keep the water from boiling over.

Pressure Canner

A pressure canner is a piece of equipment specifically designed to process low-acid canned foods and seal the jars for safe storage. During processing, pressurized steam inside the canner brings the contents of the jars up to a temperature high enough to kill any bacteria spores that may be in the food.

The canner consists of a large, heavy-duty stainless steel pot with a locking lid that is clamped down to create a tight seal. A rack in the bottom of the pot securely holds and separates the jars during processing. A gauge measures the pressure inside the canner so the pressure can be maintained and adjusted as the jars are processed.

There are two basic types of pressure canners available for home canning: weighted-gauge canners and dial-gauge canners. Both work equally well for processing low-acid foods. Carefully read and follow the manufacturer's instructions that come with the canner.

Pressure canners should not be confused with pressure cookers—they are not the same piece of equipment and are not interchangeable. The internal pressure cannot be accurately regulated in a pressure cooker. Only a pressure canner specifically designed for home canning can be used to safely process low-acid foods.

Pots and Pans

A large stockpot, preferably 8 quarts, is needed for preparing many types of preserves. This size allows enough room for cooking the preserves without boiling over and enough surface area to permit the proper evaporation of some of the liquid when making jams and soft spreads. The pot should be made of heavy-gauge stainless steel with a thick bottom and a tight-fitting lid. Stainless steel is a nonreactive material, so it is an excellent choice for making all kinds of canned foods. Some metals, such as aluminum, can have a chemical reaction with the acid in some fruits and other acidic ingredients, such as lemon juice and vinegar. A heavy pot will distribute the heat evenly and prevent hot spots that can cause the preserves to burn during cooking.

A small stainless steel saucepan is ideal for heating the canning jar lids and keeping them hot until you are ready to cover and seal the jars.

Measuring Cups and Spoons

Using the appropriate types of measuring cups for measuring the different ingredients in recipes for preserved foods recipes is crucial to successful canning.

❋ LIQUID MEASURING CUPS ❋

Standard glass liquid measuring cups work well for measuring fruit, vegetables, juice, vinegar, water, and other liquid ingredients. I recommend glass measuring cups rather than plastic, as plastic can absorb strong flavors from ingredients such as chile peppers, onions, or liqueurs.

❋ DRY MEASURING CUPS ❋

A set of plastic or metal dry measuring cups, in graduated sizes, with flat rims are best for measuring sugar and other dry ingredients. It is very important that you use measuring cups designed specifically for dry ingredients in order to get an exact measure. The top of this type of measuring cup is flat so that you can use a straight knife or other utensil with a straight edge, such as a spatula or bowl scraper, to level the ingredient even with the top edge. When using a dry measure, always spoon the ingredient into the measuring cup; if you dip the cup into the ingredient, the ingredient will be compacted in the cup, so the measure will not be accurate. Dry measuring cups are also handy for measuring nuts and dried fruits.

❋ MEASURING SPOONS AND GLASSES ❋

A set of measuring spoons in graduated sizes is important for measuring small quantities of ingredients. While not essential, small measuring glasses are handy for measuring small quantities of liquid ingredients.

Other Canning Tools

In addition to standard kitchen utensils, a few specific canning tools will make preparing and processing canned foods much easier and faster.

❋ CANNING FUNNEL ❋

A canning funnel is a specially designed wide-mouth metal or plastic funnel that sits securely in the top of a canning jar and makes filling the jars easier and neater.

❋ LID WAND ❋

A lid wand is a tool with a magnet on one end and is used to remove warmed lids from the bottom of the pan of hot water when sealing jars. Kitchen tongs may also be used to retrieve hot lids from the water.

❋ JAR LIFTER ❋

A jar lifter is a special set of tongs designed to easily and safely lift jars into and out of a water bath or pressure canner. The lifter securely grips the neck of the jar while you move the jar between the counter and the hot water in the canner.

❋ KITCHEN TIMER ❋

An accurate kitchen timer is an absolute must for home canning, especially when making jams, jellies, and other soft spreads and to monitor the processing time.

❋ ZESTER ❋

A zester is a nifty little kitchen tool with four to six holes that quickly and easily removes the colored zest from citrus fruits in thin, uniform strips perfect for making premium marmalades. I use one for making all of my marmalades.

❋ FOOD MILL ❋

In home canning, a food mill is used to remove seeds and skins from tomatoes for sauces, to remove seeds from berries for seedless spreads, and to purée fruits for butters.

❋ CHEESECLOTH OR JELLY BAG ❋

Cheesecloth is used to line a sieve to strain the fruit pulp from the juice when making jellies and to strain spices from syrups for pickles. A cloth jelly bag may also be used to strain fruit juice. Jelly bags with metal stands are frequently sold in stores carrying home canning supplies.

❋ PLASTIC KNIFE OR CHOPSTICK ❋

A small plastic knife or plastic chopstick works great to coax any trapped bubbles out of jars before processing. Commercial bubble freers come with some canning utensil sets and also can be purchased separately, but they are rather large and bulky to use for many types of preserves. Don't use a metal knife or spoon because the metal can scratch the inside of the jar, which may result in the jar cracking or breaking during heat processing or cooling.

STANDARD KITCHEN EQUIPMENT USED IN CANNING

» Bowls for holding measured sugar and other ingredients

» Colander for draining rinsed fruits and vegetables

» Cooling racks or towels for cooling hot jars after processing

» Cutting boards for preparing fruits and vegetables

» Fine-mesh sieve for straining liquid ingredients and mixtures

» Flat-bottomed pan or bowl for crushing fruit for making jams and conserves

» Hot pads or trivets for hot pans

» Ladle for spooning hot preserves and liquids into jars

» Large slotted spoon for draining blanched fruits and vegetables

» Long-handled large metal spoon for stirring preserves

» Paper towels for wiping jar rims after filling

» Paring knife and chef's knife for peeling and chopping fruits and vegetables

» Potato or vegetable masher for crushing chopped fruit

» Pot holders or mitts to protect your hands when moving hot pans

» Vegetable peeler for peeling potatoes, carrots, and other root vegetables

* Canning * Techniques

Creating attractive, delicious canned goods with award-winning quality doesn't happen by accident. Skilled home canners follow some important preparation methods to produce outstanding preserves. These techniques can be mastered easily by home canners of any experience and skill level.

Review the Recipe and Assemble Ingredients and Equipment

The first step in successful canning is to review the recipe. Be sure you understand the canning procedures and that you have all of the ingredients and equipment on hand and ready to use.

Prepare Jars, Lids, and Screw Bands

Canning jars, lids, and screw bands require some basic preparation before being used. Preparing these items correctly will help form a strong seal between the lid and the jar rim.

✳ INSPECTING JARS, LIDS, AND SCREW BANDS ✳

Inspect all canning jars, lids, and screw bands for any visible signs of damage. Check the jars for scratches, cracks, or bubbles in the glass or any other flaws that may weaken the jars and cause them to break during processing. Run your finger around the rim of the jars and feel for any nicks, chips, rough spots, or uneven rims that will prevent the lids from properly sealing to the jar rims and discard any damaged items.

Always use new flat lids specifically designed for canning. Examine the lids to make sure they are not scratched, dinged, or warped, and that the food-safe coating on the underside of the lid isn't damaged. Scratches can rust during storage, and warped or bent lids won't seal properly. Check that the sealing compound around the edge of the lid is applied evenly and that there are no gaps or thin spots. Any gap in the sealing compound will prevent a tight seal and can cause the seal to fail during storage.

The screw bands can be reused if they are in good condition, but bands with any rust or corrosion should be discarded. Warped or dented bands shouldn't be used as they may not hold the lids securely on the jars during processing and cooling.

✳ WASHING AND HEATING JARS ✳

Canning jars need to be washed before each use. I like to wash my canning jars in the dishwasher because the dishwasher washes, rinses, dries, and heats the jars in one process, leaving me free to get the rest of the canning equipment ready and prepare and measure the ingredients. Keep the dishwasher door shut and locked to keep the jars hot until you need them to reduce the chance of the jars breaking when they're filled with hot preserves. If your dishwasher has a plate-warming feature, use it to keep jars hot while making several batches of preserves.

You can also wash the jars by hand in hot, soapy water and then rinse them well under hot running water to remove all of the soap. Hand-washed jars should be submerged in a pot of hot water to keep them hot until ready to use to reduce the chance of the jars breaking when filled with hot preserves.

Jars that will be processed for 10 minutes or more in a water bath canner and jars that will be processed in a pressure canner after filling do not need to be sterilized after washing. However, jars that are processed by the water bath method for less than 10 minutes need sterilizing before being filled. To sterilize jars, submerge them in a pot of hot water, bring to a boil, and boil for 10 minutes, adding 1 minute of additional time for each 1,000 feet of elevation above sea level where you're processing. When ready to fill, remove one sterilized jar from the hot water, fill, wipe the jar rim, apply the lid and screw band, and then place in the water bath canner before removing the next sterilized jar from the hot water.

Home canning jars are not designed to be used with dry heat, so never use the oven or microwave to keep jars hot while waiting to be filled. The dry heat of the oven can weaken jars and significantly increase the chance of them breaking during heat processing in a water bath or pressure canner.

❋ WASHING AND HEATING LIDS ❋

Wash the flat lids in hot soapy water, rinse well, and drain.

Place the lids in a pan of hot water and heat for 10 minutes to soften the sealing compound. When softened, the sealing compound on the lid will mold itself to the rim of the jar and form a tight seal as the jars cool after processing. Do not boil the lids—boiling will damage the sealing compound and cause the seals to fail during storage. Because of an increase in seal failures resulting from canners boiling the lids instead of heating them, one major canning lid manufacturer has recently changed their lid preparation instructions to omit the heating step. Follow the manufacturer's instructions that come with the canning lids.

❋ WASHING SCREW BANDS ❋

Quickly wash the screw bands in hot soapy water and rinse well. Thoroughly dry the screw bands to prevent rusting and set aside until needed.

Prepare and Measure Ingredients

Care needs to be taken when measuring and preparing ingredients for canning. Accuracy is essential to creating quality preserves and ensuring a finished product with a balanced flavor and the proper consistency.

❊ PREPARING PRODUCE ❊

The preparation of the produce for canning recipes has a direct impact on the quality of the finished product. To create a great preserve, you need to use care as you handle and prepare the fruit and vegetables you will be canning.

* Use fruits and vegetables when they are in season and at the peak of ripeness. For the freshest flavor and best texture, use the produce as soon after harvest as possible.

* Fruits and vegetables should be at room temperature before preparing recipes. Cold produce may alter the cooking time and the finished texture of the preserve. The denser the produce, the longer it can take to cook when cold.

* Produce can deteriorate quickly when wet, so rinse fruits and vegetables just before you use them. Wash most produce by gently rinsing under cool running water and drain it well. Spread the produce out on paper towels or a clean kitchen towel and gently blot dry. Citrus fruits, cucumbers, and root vegetables should be lightly scrubbed with a very soft fruit or vegetable brush, then rinsed and dried.

* Prepare and measure the ingredients according to the recipe instructions. Only prepare enough produce for one canning batch or recipe at a time. The produce can deteriorate if prepared too far in advance.

* Cut fruits and vegetables into pieces that are uniform in size, shape, and thickness to give your preserves a consistent texture and attractive appearance.

PEELING PEACHES, APRICOTS, AND TOMATOES

There are a few fruits and vegetables you should peel in order for your preserves to have the best texture. These include peaches, apricots, and tomatoes. To make short work of peeling these ingredients, slash a small X on the bottom of the fruit, then gently drop them, a few at a time, into a pan of boiling water. Let them soak in the water for 30 to 60 seconds, or until the peels on the peaches or apricots start to release or the skins on the tomatoes just start to split. Quickly remove the fruit from the boiling water with a slotted spoon and immediately plunge it into a large bowl or pan of ice water. Let the fruit sit in the ice water for 1 to 2 minutes to stop the cooking process. When the fruit is cool enough to handle, use a small sharp paring knife to remove the peel or skin.

✳ ACCURATELY MEASURING INGREDIENTS ✳

The accurate measurement of fruit, sugar, and other ingredients in preserves plays a key role in the outcome of the finished product. Using the correct types of measuring cups for different ingredients is very important.

For measuring ingredients such as fruits, vegetables, juice, and vinegar, use glass measuring cups that are made for measuring liquid ingredients. Level off the top of the fruit and read the markings at eye level.

For dry ingredients like sugar, use measuring cups with flat rims that are specifically designed for measuring dry ingredients. These measuring cups allow you to spoon or pour the dry ingredient into the cup and use a knife or utensil with a straight edge to scrape the excess off the top of the cup to get an accurate measurement.

Use graduated measuring spoons for measuring small portions of both liquid and dry ingredients. Small glass measuring glasses may also be used for measuring small quantities of liquids.

Filling Jars

Before filling jars, carefully remove the number of hot canning jars you need from the dishwasher and set the jars upright on a towel or heatproof cutting board on the counter. Or, using a jar lifter, remove the jars from the pot of hot water, carefully pouring the water inside the jars back into the pan, and place them upside down on a towel for a minute to drain out the remaining water. Turn the jars upright.

Hot canning jars should always be placed on a paper or cloth towel, cutting board, or wire rack. If placed directly on a cold countertop, such as tile or granite, hot jars can break from the sudden change in temperature to the bottom of the jar. When jars are filled with hot preserves, the temperature contrast between the heat of the preserves and the cold of the countertop can also cause jars to break.

A wide-mouth funnel made specifically for canning is an indispensable tool for filling canning jars. Set the funnel in the top of a jar and use a ladle to transfer the hot preserves from the pan to the jar, leaving the correct headspace. For raw pack preserves, arrange the fruit or vegetables in the jar, then place the funnel in the jar and ladle the hot covering liquid into the jars to the appropriate height.

Keep the ladle close to the funnel and fill the jars quickly to prevent air bubbles from forming and becoming trapped in the jars as you fill them. Small air bubbles trapped in jars of spreads and relishes are a cosmetic issue. However, large air bubbles are a problem because they can create air pockets in a spread, relish, or

PREPARING HOT AND SWEET PEPPERS

When working with chile peppers, handle the peppers with care. Chile peppers contain strong oils that can cause chemical burns on your skin, in your mouth, and in your eyes. Always wear latex, plastic, or rubber gloves when seeding and chopping hot peppers to avoid direct contact between your skin and the peppers. Do not wipe your hands across your face or rub your eyes while working with hot peppers.

The seeds and pith are the hottest part of a chile pepper. Remove them for a milder flavor and leave them in when you want more heat. The white or light-colored ribs on the inside of peppers are very fibrous and can become quite tough when cooked, affecting both the flavor and texture of a preserve. The white ribs should be removed from the peppers after seeding and before chopping.

---

sauce where bacteria could grow. These large air bubbles should be removed before closing the jar. It is common for air bubbles to become trapped in jars of fruits, vegetables, and pickles as you add the liquid to the jars, and these bubbles also need to be removed before applying the lid.

To remove trapped air bubbles, slide a thin-bladed plastic knife or plastic chopstick down into the jar to create a path for the air bubbles to rise to the surface. Be careful not to trap additional air in the jar as you remove the knife. For jars of fruits, vegetables, and pickles, after removing air bubbles, you may need to add more liquid to bring the headspace back up to the correct level.

The jar yield given in a canning recipe is an approximation and should be used as a guide when filling jars. The actual number of jars you get from a batch of preserves may vary. The size, density, and juice content of the produce, and how much the preserve boils down during cooking, all have an effect on the final quantity.

✳ HEADSPACE ✳

Headspace is the specific amount of space, or air gap, you need to leave between the top of the preserve and the top edge of the jar. No more, no less. During processing, the contents of the jar expand and air is forced out under the lid. As the jar starts to cool, a vacuum is created inside the jar, pulling the lid tight against the rim of the jar. When the lid compound cools, it becomes hard and forms a tight seal between the lid and the jar.

It is extremely important to closely follow the headspace requirements for home canning. This is a matter of canning safety. Extensive testing has been done to determine the appropriate amount of headspace to leave inside jars to produce the best seal and make the preserves safe for shelf storage.

If too much headspace is left in the top of the jar, the air won't fully vent from the jar during processing. This will prevent a strong vacuum from forming in the jar and the lid won't pull down tightly against the jar rim to create a solid seal. This weak vacuum means that the seal will be more likely to fail during storage and allow contaminants to enter the jar. Too much headspace in the jar will also cause the top of the preserves to darken and discolor during storage. Jar yields can vary from one batch to another. Never attempt to stretch a batch of preserves to match the number of jars indicated in the recipe by leaving a larger headspace in the jars. The larger headspace may make the jars unsafe for shelf storage.

If there is too little headspace left in the jar, then some of the preserve or liquid may be forced out between the lid and the rim of the jar during processing. Any food particles trapped between the lid compound and the jar rim will result in a jar with a weak seal. These trapped food particles will create a pathway for bacteria to enter the jar, and the weakened seal will likely fail during storage. Until you gain a good eye for determining headspaces, which will come with experience, use a ruler to be sure your headspace measurements are accurate.

✳ WIPE JAR RIMS ✳

After filling the jars, use a clean damp paper towel to remove any spilled preserves or liquid from the rim of the jar and the jar screw threads. Any food residue left on the rim of the jars may prevent a firm bond between the lid and jar rim and cause a weak seal. Drips left on the screw threads of the jar can prevent the screw band from pulling the lid down snug against the jar rim. I always use paper towels for this job because cloth towels can leave behind small fibers on the jar rim.

Never use a kitchen sponge to wipe down the jar rims. Sponges can harbor a host of bacteria that can easily be transferred to the jars and contaminate the preserves.

✳ APPLY LIDS AND SCREW BANDS ✳

Use a magnetic lid wand or kitchen tongs to carefully remove the heated lids, one at a time, from the pan of hot water. Center the lids on the jars with the sealing compound centered on the jar rims.

Place a screw band on each jar and screw the band down onto the jar threads. With your fingers, screw the band down until resistance is met, and then increase the pressure until the band is fingertip tight. Don't use force to tighten the screw band—overtightening can prevent the jars from venting air and forming a vacuum during heat processing, which can lead to seal failure. It can also cause the jars to break inside the canner, or while removing the jars from the canner, because of the pressure buildup inside the jars.

During processing, the compound on the flat lid will soften and form a partial seal with the rim of the canning jar. The softened compound will allow air to escape from the jar during processing, but prevent water from entering the jar. With the temperature change that occurs after the jar is removed from the canner, a vacuum will form inside the jar that will pull the lid down tight against the jar rim— you will hear the lid pop when this happens. As the jar continues to cool, the compound will harden and form a permanent seal holding the lid firmly in place. After 24 hours, when the compound has hardened and the seal is complete, the screw band should be removed from the jar to prevent rusting.

Screw bands may loosen slightly during processing. This is normal and you should never retighten the screw bands after processing. When the jars come out of the canner, the compound on the lids will be hot and very soft. If you retighten the screw band, you could force the compound out from between the lid and the jar rim. This will break the seal or result in a very weak seal, which could fail during storage.

Making Soft Spreads

There are two basic methods for making jams, jellies, and other soft spreads—the short-boil method and the long-boil method. The two methods yield spreads with significantly different characteristics, including different flavors and textures. The short-boil method produces spreads that have a softer texture and a flavor closer to that of fresh fruit, while spreads made by the long-boil method can range from very soft to firm and have a definite cooked fruit flavor.

✳ **SHORT-BOIL METHOD** ✳

In the short-boil method, commercial packaged pectin is added to the fruit and sugar mixture to create spreads with a bright, tantalizing flavor and tender texture. The short-boil method dramatically decreases the amount of cooking time needed to make soft spreads. Soft spread recipes using commercial pectin are formulated

Headspace Allowances for Canning per USDA	
HEADSPACE	TYPE OF PRESERVE
¼ inch	jams, jellies, marmalades, conserves, preserves, and butters
½ inch	fruits, juices, pickles, relishes, sauces, and salsas
1 inch	vegetables and most other pressure-canned low-acid foods

to work with the natural pectin of fully ripe fruit. Because the fruit is cooked for a shorter period of time in short-boil spreads, the fruit retains more of its intense natural color and flavor.

There are two types of commercial packaged pectin—powdered pectin and liquid pectin. With powdered pectin, the pectin and fruit are combined first, brought to a boil, and then the sugar is added. With liquid pectin, the fruit and sugar are combined, brought to a boil, and then the pectin is added. In both cases, after all the ingredients are combined, the mixture is boiled and stirred for 1 minute and then removed from the heat. It is a quick and easy way to make spreads that yield excellent results.

❊ LONG-BOIL METHOD ❊

In the long-boil method, the fruit is combined with the sugar and then boiled for several minutes. Some fruits are high in natural pectin while others contain very little pectin. It is often necessary to use a high percentage of underripe fruit, which contains more pectin than ripe fruit, in order to get the spread to set. Fruits with a low pectin content require a longer cooking time as the spread gels more through a process of evaporation of juice than the pectin setting. If cooked too long, the spread can become gummy or sticky.

Because the spread must cook for a period of time over moderately high heat in order to evaporate enough liquid to help thicken the mixture, there is a greater risk that the fruit in the bottom of the pan may scorch if not closely watched. The extended cooking time can also cause the sugar to caramelize and the spread to take on a molasses-like flavor and color.

Making quality spreads with the long-boil method takes some practice and skill. Because these spreads set through a combination of evaporation of liquid and activation of pectin to create a gel, there is a tendency to overcook the spread to get it to set. The hazard of overcooking a spread is that it can set up very firm or sticky.

When cooking jams and jellies using the long-boil method, cook the fruit and sugar mixture until thick and glossy and it reaches the jellying point, also known as the setting point, of 220°F measured on a canning or candy thermometer. Watch the temperature carefully—spreads heated above 220°F can set up too firm.

Jellying Point for Jams, Jellies, and Other Soft Spreads

When cooking soft spreads by the long-boil method, boil the mixture until it reaches the following temperature on a canning or candy thermometer for your altitude.

Sea Level	1,000 ft.	2,000 ft.	3,000 ft.	4,000 ft.	5,000 ft.	6,000 ft.	7,000 ft.	8,000 ft.
220°F	218°F	216°F	214°F	212°F	211°F	209°F	207°F	205°F

* Processing * Canning Jars

Even though sugar and acid act as preservatives in jars of jams, other soft spreads, fruits, pickles, relishes, and sauces, molds and bacteria can still grow inside the jars and cause these products to spoil if not properly processed. It used to be thought that filling sterilized jars with hot preserves and turning the jars upside down for a few minutes was sufficient to seal the jars and prevent mold growth. This is no longer the case. To prevent mold and bacteria growth, the USDA and the Cooperative Extension Service strongly advise that all high-acid foods be processed in a water bath canner and all low-acid foods be processed in a pressure canner to ensure the safety of the canned product.

Heat Processing

Heat processing of home-canned foods is necessary to destroy any microorganisms that could cause the food to spoil during storage. Processing also vents air from inside the jars, which creates a vacuum and allows a tight seal to form between the lid and the jar. Processing filled jars for the correct length of time, and following approved guidelines will ensure that the product is safe to store on the shelf and maintain maximum flavor, color, and texture.

Heat processing in a water bath canner is the approved and recommended method for destroying microorganisms and sealing jars of all canned foods that are high in acid. In addition to soft spreads, this is also the method used to process jars of fruit, fruit juices, tomato products to which lemon juice or vinegar has been added to increase the acid content, pickles, and many sauces. Foods that are low in acid, such as vegetables, must be processed in a pressure canner.

✳ WATER BATH PROCESSING ✳

When you process filled jars of jam, fruit, and other high-acid preserves in a water bath, the jars are submerged in boiling water long enough for all the food inside the jar to reach a temperature high enough to kill any harmful bacteria, mold spores, or yeasts that may be present in the jarred food. The boiling water bath also pulls air out of the jar, creating a vacuum inside the jar and a tight seal between the lid and the jar rim, preventing any bacteria from entering the processed jar.

✳ PRESSURE CANNER PROCESSING ✳

Jars of vegetables and other low-acid foods must be processed in a pressure canner. During pressure canner processing, the contents of the jar are brought to a high enough temperature to kill any bacteria or other contaminants that may be present in the food. The canning process also creates a vacuum in the jars and produces a tight seal between the lid and jar. Pressure canner processing makes low-acid preserves safe for shelf storage.

Altitude Adjustments for Heat Processing

Water boils at 212°F at sea level. As altitude increases, water boils at a lower temperature, which means it is less effective at killing bacteria. To compensate for the lower boiling point, water bath processing times need to be increased as altitude increases. When pressure canning at altitudes above 2,000 feet, you will need to increase the pounds of pressure used for safe processing.

Altitude Adjustments for Water Bath Processing

ALTITUDE IN FEET	INCREASE PROCESSING TIME BY
1,001 to 3,000	5 minutes
3,001 to 6,000	10 minutes
6,001 to 8,000	15 minutes
8,001 to 10,000	20 minutes

Altitude Adjustments for Pressure Canner Processing

ALTITUDE IN FEET	DIAL-GAUGE PRESSURE CANNER	WEIGHTED-GAUGE PRESSURE CANNER
Up to 2,000	11 pounds	10 pounds
2,001 to 4,000	12 pounds	15 pounds
4,001 to 6,000	13 pounds	15 pounds
6,001 to 8,100	14 pounds	15 pounds
8,001 to 10,000	15 pounds	15 pounds

The processing times listed in the recipes are based on an altitude of 1,000 feet or less for water bath canning and an altitude of 2,000 feet or less for pressure canning. If you live at a higher altitude, adjust your processing time as indicated above.

Storing Preserves

The screw bands should be removed from the jars after the jars are sealed and the contents have cooled completely. The purpose of the screw band is to hold the lid securely in place during processing. Once the jars have cooled and the lid is securely attached to the jar, the band is not needed for storage of the jars. Screw bands left on the jars may rust during storage. When giving a jar of a preserves as a gift or entering it in a fair competition, always put a new screw band on the jar.

To keep the jars safe during storage, it is best to place them on stable shelves with a raised front rail or pack the jars in sturdy boxes. Never stack canning jars on top of each other for storage. The weight of the top jar pressing down on the lid of the bottom jar can cause the seal to fail on the lower jar.

Jars of preserves should be stored in a cool, dark, dry location to preserve the color, flavor, and texture of the canned item. If left in a warm environment, canned foods can deteriorate faster and lose their intense flavor. Exposure to light for an extended period of time speeds up oxidation and can cause the color, as well as the flavor, to fade. Moist locations can cause the lids to rust. Locations that are both warm and moist can damage the seal and encourage the growth of mold.

The ideal temperature range for storing jars of home-canned foods, and the one recommended by the USDA, is between 50°F and 70°F. Jars stored at temperatures higher than 70°F may deteriorate faster. If you are fortunate to have a basement or cellar, these are ideal locations for storing home-canned preserves. Other good locations for storing jar boxes include the back of a pantry, on the floor or lower shelves of an interior closet, or under a bed.

For the best overall quality, use home-canned foods within a year after canning. While a well-canned preserve should remain safe to eat as long as the jar seal remains intact and the product shows no visible signs of spoilage, the appearance and flavor of the food will deteriorate over time.

Unsafe Canning Methods

There are several old-fashioned, outdated home canning methods that used to be considered acceptable canning practice but have been scientifically proven to be unsafe. Unfortunately, these unsafe methods are still being used today by some home canners. Any preserve made using these methods should be considered at high risk for contamination or spoilage and unsafe to eat.

❊ OPEN-KETTLE METHOD ❊

The theory behind open-kettle canning, also known as the inversion method, was that any bacteria or organisms in the food were killed when the mixture was boiled. The preserve was poured into sterilized jars, the rims wiped down, and a lid and screw band applied. The jars were then inverted (turned upside down) for 5 to 10 minutes. When the jars were turned back upright, the lid would pull down as a vacuum was created inside the jar. Because the preserve was considered sterile, it was thought that contaminants would not grow inside the jar.

In actuality, open-kettle canning carries many serious health risks. Bacteria and mold spores can enter the jar or contaminate the preserve before the jar is closed.

Even if the jars appear to seal by inversion, the seals will be weak and likely to fail during storage. The temperature of the food inside the jar is rarely hot enough to kill any contaminants that may have entered the jar while it was being filled and closed. In addition, the air has not been exhausted from inside the jars to create a strong vacuum and the jar retains enough oxygen to allow the growth of mold or other contaminants. Inverting the jars is not an acceptable substitute for water bath processing of high-acid foods.

✳ INVERTING JARS AFTER PROCESSING ✳

Some home canners still cannot let go of the notion that jars need to be inverted, even after the jars have been water bath processed. This is a dangerous practice. Inverting jars after water bath processing can weaken the seal and allow the preserve to seep between the jar and lid. Bacteria and mold can then enter and grow inside the jar, contaminating the contents.

✳ OTHER UNSAFE CANNING METHODS ✳

Other unsafe and outdated methods of canning include attempting to process and seal the filled jars in the oven, microwave, or dishwasher. There is no way to control the temperature of the contents of the jars with these hazardous methods. There is also a high risk of the jars shattering. None of these methods will properly seal jars and all are considered unsafe and very dangerous.

A Final Word on Food Safety

Bacteria and other microorganisms can be found in all foods and live on surfaces in your kitchen. It is important to eliminate as many of these contaminants as possible when preparing home-canned foods. Store-bought and home-grown fruits and vegetables should be rinsed in cool clear water before canning. Always wash your hands before handling food, and make sure that your cooking utensils and work surfaces are clean.

You can't take shortcuts or skip steps when canning and expect to produce a safe product. Follow the instructions and approved safety procedures and you will create beautiful, delicious, and safe-to-eat preserved foods you can enjoy throughout the year and will be proud to share with family and friends.

STEP-BY-STEP WATER BATH CANNING GUIDE

1. Wash canning jars and keep hot until ready to use.

2. Wash the lids and screw bands in hot, soapy water and rinse well. Dry thoroughly and set aside.

3. Fill the water bath canner pot two-thirds full of water. Place on the stovetop, cover, and heat over medium-high heat.

4. Prepare and measure the ingredients according to the recipe.

5. Place the flat lids in a small pan of hot water. Cover and keep the lids hot off the heat for 10 minutes or until ready to use. Do not boil the lids. **(A)**

6. Prepare and cook the preserves according to the recipe.

7. Place the hot jars upright on a towel or a heatproof cutting board.

8. Fill the jars, leaving the headspace indicated in the recipe. **(B)**

9. Wipe the jar rims and threads with a clean, damp paper towel.

10. Place the hot lids on the jars and apply the screw bands until fingertip-tight. Do not overtighten the bands. **(C)**

11. Position the rack in the water bath canner.

12. Using a jar lifter, carefully load the jars into the canner. Make sure the jars do not touch the sides of the canner and leave 1 inch of space between the jars. Make sure the water level is at least 1 to 2 inches above the tops of the jars. Add more hot water, if necessary. **(D) (E)**

13. Cover the canner and bring the water to a boil over high heat. Reduce the heat to maintain a gentle boil during processing.

14. Start the timer after the water reaches a boil. Check the canner periodically to make sure the water is still boiling. If the boiling stops, return the water to a boil, reset the timer for the full amount of time, and resume processing the jars. Adjust the processing time for altitudes above 1,000 feet (see p. 31).

15. When the processing time is complete, turn off the heat and remove the lid from the canner. Using a jar lifter, remove the jars from the canner and set the jars on a cooling rack or cloth towel, spacing at least 1 inch apart. Do not retighten the screw bands. Cool, undisturbed, for 12 to 24 hours to allow the seals to set. **(F)**

16. Check the seals on the cooled jars by pressing down in the center of each lid. If the lid is depressed and does not move when pressed, the jar is sealed. Unsealed jars should be stored in the refrigerator and the contents used within a few days. **(G)**

17. Remove the screw bands. Keeping the jars upright, gently wash in warm soapy water, rinse well, and dry thoroughly. Label if desired. **(H, I)**

A

B

C

D

E

F

G

H

I

STEP-BY-STEP PRESSURE CANNING GUIDE

1. Wash canning jars and keep hot until ready to use.

2. Wash the lids and screw bands in hot, soapy water and rinse well. Dry thoroughly and set aside.

3. Position the rack in the pressure canner. Fill a dial-gauge canner with 3 inches of water or a weighted-gauge canner with 5 inches of water, or the amount recommended by the manufacturer. Place on the stovetop and start heating over low heat.

4. Prepare and measure the ingredients according to the recipe.

5. Place the flat lids in a small pan of hot water. Cover and keep the lids hot off the heat for 10 minutes until ready to use. Do not boil the lids. **(A)**

6. Prepare and cook the preserves according to the recipe.

7. Place the hot jars upright on a towel or a heatproof cutting board.

8. Fill the jars, leaving the headspace indicated in the recipe. **(B) (C) (D)**

9. Wipe the jar rims and threads with a clean, damp paper towel.

10. Place the hot lids on the jars, and apply the screw bands until fingertip-tight. Do not overtighten the bands. **(E)**

11. Using a jar lifter, carefully load the jars into the canner. Make sure the jars do not touch the sides of the canner and leave 1 inch of space between the jars. **(F) (G)**

12. Place the lid on the canner and lock it in place. For a dial-gauge canner, leave the petcock open. For a weighted-gauge canner, leave the weighted gauge off the vent. Increase the heat to medium high. When steam begins to escape from the petcock or vent, set a timer for 10 minutes. **(H)**

13. After the canner has vented for 10 minutes, close the petcock or place the weighted gauge on the vent. It will take about 5 minutes for the canner to come up to pressure.

14. Start the timer when the canner reaches the processing pressure indicated in the recipe. Adjust the heat as needed to maintain the correct pressure, or slightly above, for the entire processing time. Adjust the processing time for altitudes above 2,000 feet (see p. 31).

15. When the processing time is complete, turn off the heat. Let the canner cool and depressurize until the gauge reads 0 before opening the petcock or removing the weighted gauge from the vent. Let the canner vent steam for 2 minutes before unlocking and removing the lid from the canner. Allow the jars to cool in the canner for 5 minutes.

(continued on p. 39)

16. Using a jar lifter, remove the jars from the canner and set on a cooling rack or cloth towel, spacing at least 1 inch apart. Do not retighten the screw bands. Cool, undisturbed, for 12 to 24 hours to allow the seals to set. **(I)**

17. Check the seals on the cooled jars by pressing down in the center of each lid. If the lid is depressed and does not move when pressed, the jar is sealed. Unsealed jars should be stored in the refrigerator and the contents used within a few days. **(J)**

18. Remove the screw bands. Keeping the jars upright, gently wash in warm soapy water, rinse well, and dry thoroughly. Label if desired. **(K, L)**

* Jams *

A well-made homemade jam has a vibrant color and intense flavor that can't be matched by any store-bought variety. The easiest type of soft spread to prepare, jams are made from chopped and crushed fruit that is cooked with sugar until the fruit becomes softened and translucent. Adding pectin to the jam speeds up the cooking process, allowing the jam to retain more of the natural flavor and color of the fresh fruit.

Jams have a thick texture—thicker than preserves but not as firm as jellies. You should be able to effortlessly spoon jam out of its jar, and it should mound up in the spoon and hold its shape, yet the jam should spread easily. The jam shouldn't be runny and there should be no separation of the juice and fruit.

Preparing Fruit for Jams

Preparing fruit for making jam is simple and straightforward. Gently rinse the fruit under cool running water to remove any dirt or dust. Spread it out on paper towels or clean kitchen towels in a single layer and gently blot the fruit dry. Wash berries just before using and handle them carefully as they are fragile and damage easily. Sturdier fruits, such as apples and citrus, can sit at room temperature for a while after washing without deteriorating. Peel and pit stone fruits, core and peel apples and pears, and hull or stem berries. Fruit should always be peeled because the peels or skins become tough and gummy when cooked.

Cut the peeled fruit into small pieces and then gently crush with a potato or vegetable masher, one layer at a time to ensure the fruit is evenly crushed, in a flat-bottomed pan or bowl. You want to end up with lots of smaller crushed pieces of fruit. Transfer the fruit to a measuring cup before adding more fruit and crushing the next layer. Avoid getting carried away with the masher—you do not want to purée the fruit. Puréeing the fruit releases too much juice and will make the spread soft and runny. The jam also will be more likely to fail to set. The exception to puréeing is when making a seedless berry jam, where the process of removing the seeds creates a smooth berry pulp.

Preventing Floating Fruit

Fruit that floats to the top in jars of jams can be caused by cutting it into pieces that are too large and not crushing it enough. Pieces that are too large or have not been crushed won't release the air trapped inside the fruit cells. As the jam cools, the air-filled fruit will separate from the jam mixture and rise to the top of the jar before the spread sets. To prevent floating fruit, be sure to cut the fruit into small pieces and then gently crush them to release the air from the fruit cells. This also allows the fruit to absorb more sugar, making the pieces heavier and reducing the chance that it will separate from the juice and float to the top of the jars.

Salsa Jam

CONTRIBUTOR: LINDA J. AMENDT, CALIFORNIA

MAKES ABOUT FIVE 8-OUNCE JARS

2 cups peeled, seeded, and chopped Roma or other plum-type tomatoes (8 to 10 medium tomatoes)

⅔ cup chopped red onions

⅔ cup canned tomato sauce

3 tablespoons seeded and finely chopped jalapeño peppers

3 tablespoons freshly squeezed lime juice

1½ teaspoons finely grated lime zest

¼ teaspoon Tabasco® or other hot pepper sauce

5 cups granulated sugar

1 pouch (3 ounces) liquid pectin

SERVING SUGGESTION

To create special appetizers for your next party, spread softened goat cheese or cream cheese on crackers or crostini and top with a small spoonful of this zesty jam.

In addition to winning multiple blue ribbons and two Best of Show awards, this festive jam also earned the first-place award in the Sure-Jell® Jam Competition at the California State Fair, where the judges declared it "an A+ jam!"

1. In an 8-quart stainless steel stockpot, combine the tomatoes, onions, tomato sauce, and jalapeños. Bring to a boil over medium heat, stirring constantly. Reduce the heat and simmer gently for 5 minutes, stirring frequently to prevent sticking. Add the lime juice, lime zest, and Tabasco, then gradually stir in the sugar.

2. Heat the mixture over medium-low heat, stirring constantly, until the sugar is completely dissolved. Increase the heat to medium high and bring to a full rolling boil, stirring constantly. Stir in the pectin. Return the mixture to a full rolling boil, stirring constantly. Boil for 1 minute, stirring constantly.

3. Remove the pot from heat and skim off any foam. Let the jam cool in the pot for 5 minutes, stirring occasionally.

4. Ladle the jam into hot jars, leaving ¼-inch headspace. Remove any air bubbles. Wipe the jar rims and threads with a clean, damp paper towel. Apply hot lids and screw bands.

5. Process 4-ounce, 8-ounce, and pint jars in a water bath canner for 10 minutes (see p. 34 for instructions). Remove from the water bath canner and let cool for 12 to 24 hours. Check the seals and remove the screw bands. Store jars in a cool, dry, dark place for up to 1 year.

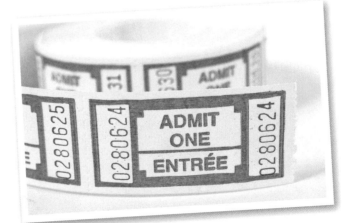

Strawberry Kiwi Jam

CONTRIBUTOR: GEORGE YATES, TEXAS

**MAKES ABOUT SIX
8-OUNCE JARS**

3 cups crushed
strawberries (3 to 4 pints
whole strawberries)

3 kiwi, peeled and diced

1 tablespoon freshly
squeezed lemon juice

1 box (1.75 ounces)
powdered pectin

5 cups granulated sugar

Strawberries and kiwi are a quintessential fruit pairing and make a beautiful and tasty jam with a tropical flair.

1. In an 8-quart stainless steel stockpot, combine the strawberries, kiwi, lemon juice, and pectin. Bring the mixture to a full rolling boil over medium-high heat, stirring constantly.

2. Add the sugar and stir until completely dissolved. Return the mixture to a full rolling boil, stirring constantly. Boil for 1 minute, stirring constantly. Remove the pot from the heat and skim off any foam.

3. Ladle the jam into hot jars, leaving ¼-inch headspace. Remove any air bubbles. Wipe the jar rims and threads with a clean, damp paper towel. Apply hot lids and screw bands.

4. Process 4-ounce, 8-ounce, and pint jars in a water bath canner for 10 minutes (see p. 34 for instructions). Remove from the water bath canner and let cool for 12 to 24 hours. Check the seals and remove the screw bands. Store jars in a cool, dry, dark place for up to 1 year.

GEORGE YATES

DALLAS, TEXAS

GEORGE YATES (1963–2014) started his canning adventures as a child by helping his grandmother in her garden and kitchen as she picked and preserved her fruits and vegetables. Before long, he was preparing his own entries for the Sheldon County Fair in Texas. After moving to Dallas, he had the great fortune to meet legendary Texas cook and canner Lillie Crowley, who provided him with valuable encouragement and canning and fair entry tips. This advice helped George win his first blue ribbon at the State Fair of Texas, which was an exciting beginning that led to collecting many more blue ribbons, magazine interviews, and an appearance on a Food Network special on canning.

During his 25 years of state and county fair competitions, George earned over 260 blue ribbons.

George made fabulous wine jellies and won a passel of blue ribbons for his entries. He so dominated the class at the State Fair of Texas that competitors begged him not to enter his red wine jellies so that they might have a chance to take home the blue ribbon.

Despite battling cancer twice, George still loved to cook and can. He also continued to participate at the State Fair of Texas, taking the time to make his entries perfect. "I get great joy from the ability to create award-winning recipes in my own kitchen, using fresh fruits and vegetables, and sharing my canning with my family and good friends." George wished more people would experience the fun and satisfaction of home canning that was so important in his life. During about 25 years of state and county fair competitions, he earned over 260 blue ribbons and many Best of Show and special awards, including five Grand Champion awards. George had the heart of a champion, yet was humble and appreciative of his accomplishments.

Blackberry Chambord Jam

CONTRIBUTOR: VALERIE J. FONG, CALIFORNIA

MAKES SIX TO SEVEN 8-OUNCE JARS OR 3 PINTS

5½ cups seedless blackberry pulp (about six 18-ounce packages blackberries, crushed and pressed through a fine-mesh sieve twice)

1 box (1.75 ounces) powdered pectin

½ teaspoon unsalted butter (optional)

7 cups granulated sugar

¼ cup Chambord™

SERVING SUGGESTION

Enjoy this jam on toasted bread, muffins, and scones. It also makes a wonderful filling for individual fruit tarts and shaped cookies or a syrup to pour over vanilla ice cream.

This delightful jam is a wonderful blend of blackberries and Chambord, a black raspberry liqueur. Chambord brings out the delicious flavor of the blackberries and creates a sweet spread for muffins and scones.

1. In an 8-quart stainless steel stockpot, combine the blackberry pulp and pectin. Add the butter, if using. Bring the mixture to a full rolling boil over medium-high heat, stirring constantly.

2. Add the sugar and stir until completely dissolved. Return the mixture to a full rolling boil, stirring constantly. Boil for 1 minute, stirring constantly.

3. Remove the pot from the heat and skim off any foam. Add the Chambord and stir until well blended. Let the jam rest for a few minutes, stirring occasionally.

4. Ladle the jam into hot jars, leaving ¼-inch headspace. Remove any air bubbles. Wipe the jar rims and threads with a clean, damp paper towel. Apply hot lids and screw bands.

5. Process 4-ounce, 8-ounce and pint jars in a water bath canner for 10 minutes (see p. 34 for instructions). Remove from the water bath canner and let cool for 12 to 24 hours. Check the seals and remove the screw bands. Store jars in a cool, dry, dark place for up to 1 year.

Cantaloupe Jam

CONTRIBUTOR: ALAN GRAVENOR, MARYLAND

MAKES ABOUT SIX
8-OUNCE JARS

7 cups peeled, chopped, and mashed cantaloupe pulp (2 to 3 large cantaloupe)

2 cups granulated sugar

2 tablespoons freshly squeezed lemon juice

1 teaspoon finely grated lemon zest

SERVING SUGGESTION

This melon jam is delicious served on biscuits or scones for breakfast. It also makes a nice fruit dip when combined with yogurt, and is very enjoyable when drizzled over vanilla ice cream.

This jam is a must for any melon lover! It is quick to make—ready in less than an hour—as there is not much prep work for the melon. It's a great way to use ripe cantaloupe.

1. Place the cantaloupe pulp in an 8-quart stainless steel stockpot. Bring to a boil over low heat, stirring constantly, and cook until smooth, 8 to 10 minutes.

2. Stir in the sugar, lemon juice, and lemon zest, stirring constantly until the sugar is dissolved. Continue boiling for 15 to 20 minutes, stirring occasionally, until the mixture begins to thicken and reaches the jelling point (220°F at sea level). Remove the pot from the heat and skim off any foam.

3. Ladle the jam into the hot jars, leaving ¼-inch headspace. Remove any air bubbles. Wipe the jar rims and threads with a clean, damp paper towel. Apply hot lids and screw bands.

4. Process 4-ounce, 8-ounce, and pint jars in a water bath canner for 10 minutes (see p. 34 for instructions). Remove from the water bath canner and let cool for 12 to 24 hours. Check the seals and remove the screw bands. Store jars in a cool, dry, dark place for up to 1 year.

> **DID YOU KNOW?**
>
> Long ago, butter sculptures at state fairs were introduced by the dairy industry to promote its products. The first one is said to date back to 1903. In 2001 at the Iowa State Fair, a life-size butter sculpture of John Wayne required 400 pounds of butter and 4 days to complete.

MIRIAM KENTNER

LYNDEN, WASHINGTON

GROWING UP IN EASTERN WASHINGTON, Miriam Kentner remembers her mom canning lots of jams, jellies, fruits, and vegetables. "Every year, when the apricots were in season, she made apricot pineapple jam. She also made pickled asparagus and plums that were beautiful in the jar."

After buying her first house in a small farm town, Miriam knew that she wanted to learn how to can and bring her jams to the county fair. "I moved into my house in January and we went out strawberry and raspberry picking as soon as the berries were ripe. My 11-year-old son picked strawberries so fast that we had to tell him to slow down. Once I got home, I had a lot of berries to make into jam."

When it came time to enter her berry jams into fair competition, Miriam searched for tips on how to tell a perfect jar of jam. "I held up my jars to the light and inspected each jar until I picked out the best two. I carefully typed out labels and placed them on the jars as directed on the entry paperwork." She took her jams to the fair and crossed her fingers.

"On the first day I could get to the fair, I rushed to the agriculture exhibit to look for my jars. I was so excited and proud when I saw that I had won first place on both my strawberry jam and raspberry jam! I was hooked on canning and competing and could hardly wait to enter again the next year."

DID YOU KNOW? Strawberries aren't true berries. They are the only fruit that wear their seeds on the outside, and technically a berry has seeds on the inside. The average strawberry has about 200 seeds on it.

Strawberry Jam

CONTRIBUTOR: MIRIAM KENTNER, WASHINGTON

**MAKES ABOUT EIGHT
8-OUNCE JARS**

4 cups granulated sugar

1½ boxes (1.75 ounces each) powdered pectin

6 cups crushed strawberries

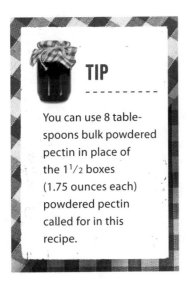

TIP

You can use 8 tablespoons bulk powdered pectin in place of the 1¹/₂ boxes (1.75 ounces each) powdered pectin called for in this recipe.

This amazingly easy strawberry jam will remind you of summer, no matter what season you eat it. The jam is so delicious but don't be tempted to double the recipe as it won't set properly. If you want to leave some bigger pieces in the jam the way Miriam does, crush up about 4 cups of berries and then slice and lightly crush the remaining berries.

1. In a small bowl, combine ¼ cup of the sugar with the pectin until thoroughly blended.

2. In an 8-quart stainless steel stockpot, combine the strawberries and pectin mixture. Bring the mixture to a full rolling boil over medium-high heat, stirring constantly.

3. Add the remaining sugar and stir until completely dissolved. Return the mixture to a full rolling boil, stirring constantly. Boil for 1 minute, stirring constantly.

4. Remove the pot from the heat and skim off any foam. Let the jam cool for 5 minutes, stirring occasionally.

5. Ladle the jam into hot jars, leaving ¼-inch headspace. Remove any air bubbles. Wipe the jar rims and threads with a clean, damp paper towel. Apply hot lids and screw bands.

6. Process 4-ounce, 8-ounce, and pint jars in a water bath canner for 10 minutes (see p. 34 for instructions). Remove from the water bath canner and let cool for 12 to 24 hours. Check the seals and remove the screw bands. Store jars in a cool, dry, dark place for up to 1 year.

Kiwi Daiquiri Jam

CONTRIBUTOR: SHIRLEY ROSENBERG, UTAH

MAKES ABOUT FOUR 8-OUNCE JARS

2 cups peeled, chopped, and crushed kiwi (10 to 12 medium kiwi)

⅔ cup unsweetened pineapple juice

⅓ cup freshly squeezed lime juice

¼ cup unsweetened flaked or shredded coconut

1 box (2 ounces) powdered pectin

¼ teaspoon unsalted butter (optional)

3 cups granulated sugar

¼ cup rum or ½ teaspoon rum extract

Few drops of green food coloring (optional)

Shirley's husband really likes kiwi, but the fruit spoils quickly, so she created this jam recipe to use it up before it went bad. Her husband loves the jam, and the judges at the Utah State Fair did, too. Shirley leaves the pulp in the lime juice to add a little more zing to the jam. If you want to bring out a nuttier flavor, toast the coconut before making the jam.

1. In an 8-quart stockpot, combine the kiwi, pineapple juice, lime juice, coconut, pectin, and butter, if using. Bring the mixture to a full rolling boil over medium-high heat, stirring constantly.

2. Add the sugar and stir until completely dissolved. Return the mixture to a full rolling boil, stirring constantly. Boil for 1 minute, stirring constantly.

3. Remove the pot from the heat and skim off any foam. Stir in the rum and food coloring, if using.

4. Ladle the jam into hot jars, leaving ¼-inch headspace. Remove any air bubbles. Wipe the jar rims and threads with a clean, damp paper towel. Apply hot lids and screw bands.

5. Process 4-ounce, 8-ounce, and pint jars in a water bath canner for 10 minutes (see p. 34 for instructions). Remove from the water bath canner and let cool for 12 to 24 hours. Check the seals and remove the screw bands. Store jars in a cool, dry, dark place for up to 1 year.

TIP

If using bulk-packaged powdered pectin, 6 level tablespoons of pectin is equal to a 2-ounce box of powdered pectin.

Strawberry Margarita Jam (recipe on p. 54) and Kiwi Daiquiri Jam

Strawberry Margarita Jam

CONTRIBUTOR: TERRY COAKLEY, CALIFORNIA

MAKES ABOUT SEVEN
8-OUNCE JARS

**3 cups crushed
strawberries (3 to 4 pints
whole strawberries)**

**⅔ cup freshly squeezed
lime juice**

½ cup tequila

**¼ cup Cointreau® or
Triple Sec**

6 cups granulated sugar

**½ teaspoon unsalted
butter (optional)**

**1 pouch (3 ounces) liquid
pectin**

If you like strawberry margaritas, you will love this jam (shown on p. 52) based on the flavors of the classic drink. What's not to like—strawberries, lime, and a little kick!

1. In an 8-quart stainless steel stockpot, combine the strawberries, lime juice, tequila, and Cointreau. Stir in the sugar and add the butter, if using. Cook the mixture over medium-low heat, stirring constantly, until the sugar is completely dissolved. Increase the heat to medium high and bring to a full rolling boil, stirring constantly.

2. Stir in the pectin. Return the mixture to a full rolling boil, stirring constantly. Boil for 1 minute, stirring constantly.

3. Remove the pot from the heat and skim off any foam. Let the jam cool in the pot for 5 minutes, stirring occasionally.

4. Ladle the jam into hot jars, leaving ¼-inch headspace. Remove any air bubbles. Wipe the jar rims and threads with a clean, damp paper towel. Apply hot lids and screw bands.

5. Process 4-ounce, 8-ounce, and pint jars in a water bath canner for 10 minutes (see p. 34 for instructions). Remove from the water bath canner and let cool for 12 to 24 hours. Check the seals and remove the screw bands. Store jars in a cool, dry, dark place for up to 1 year.

Adapted from *175 Best Jams, Jellies, Marmalades & Other Soft Spreads,* by Linda J. Amendt.

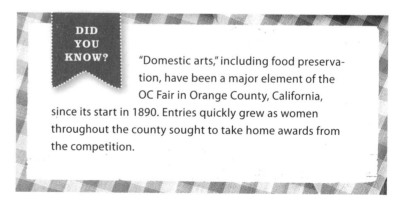

DID YOU KNOW? "Domestic arts," including food preservation, have been a major element of the OC Fair in Orange County, California, since its start in 1890. Entries quickly grew as women throughout the county sought to take home awards from the competition.

Strawberry Banana Jam

CONTRIBUTOR: BETH WALLACE, ARKANSAS

**MAKES ABOUT EIGHT
8-OUNCE JARS**

1 cup mashed ripe
bananas (about
2 medium bananas)

1 tablespoon freshly
squeezed lemon juice

4 cups crushed
strawberries (4 to 5 pints
whole strawberries)

1 box (1.75 ounces)
powdered pectin

7 cups granulated sugar

This pretty jam combines two flavors that pair together beautifully, strawberry and banana, and has become a favorite jam of Beth's granddaughter.

1. In an 8-quart stockpot, combine the bananas and lemon juice. Add the strawberries and stir to combine. Stir in the pectin.

2. Bring the mixture to a full rolling boil over medium-high heat, stirring constantly. Add the sugar and stir until completely dissolved. Return the mixture to a full rolling boil, stirring constantly. Boil for 1 minute, stirring constantly. Remove the pot from the heat and skim off any foam.

3. Ladle the jam into hot jars, leaving ¼-inch headspace. Remove any air bubbles. Wipe the jar rims and threads with a clean, damp paper towel. Apply hot lids and screw bands.

4. Process 4-ounce, 8-ounce, and pint jars in a water bath canner for 10 minutes (see p. 34 for instructions). Remove from the water bath canner and let cool for 12 to 24 hours. Check the seals and remove the screw bands. Store jars in a cool, dry, dark place for up to 1 year.

TIP

Bananas used for making jam should be ripe—golden in color with a few flecks of brown—but not overripe. They are a low-acid fruit and overripe bananas have a very low acid content, which can keep the jam from setting and reduce the shelf-storage time.

Peach Raspberry Jam

CONTRIBUTOR: GEORGE YATES, TEXAS

**MAKES ABOUT SIX
8-OUNCE JARS**

1 quart whole
raspberries

2½ cups pitted, peeled,
and crushed peaches
(about 2½ pounds
peaches)

5 tablespoons freshly
squeezed lemon juice,
strained

6¾ cups granulated
sugar

½ teaspoon unsalted
butter (optional)

1 pouch (3 ounces) liquid
pectin

Colorful and delicious, this jam is best made when raspberries and peaches are both at the peak of ripeness.

1. Press the raspberries through a food mill or fine-mesh sieve to remove the seeds. Discard the seeds and measure out 1 cup of puréed raspberry pulp.

2. In an 8-quart stockpot, combine the peaches, raspberry pulp, lemon juice, sugar, and butter, if using. Heat the mixture over medium-low heat, stirring constantly, until the sugar is dissolved. Increase the heat to medium high and bring the mixture to a full rolling boil.

3. Stir in the pectin. Return the mixture to a full rolling boil, stirring constantly. Boil for 1 minute, stirring constantly. Remove the pot from the heat and skim off any foam.

4. Ladle the jam into hot jars, leaving ¼-inch headspace. Remove any air bubbles. Wipe the jar rims and threads with a clean, damp paper towel. Apply hot lids and screw bands.

5. Process 4-ounce, 8-ounce, and pint jars in a water bath canner for 10 minutes (see p. 34 for instructions). Remove from the water bath canner and let cool for 12 to 24 hours. Check the seals and remove the screw bands. Store jars in a cool, dry, dark place for up to 1 year.

DID YOU KNOW? The Ball Brothers Glass Manufacturing Co. began manufacturing the first glass Ball® fruit jars in 1884 in Buffalo, New York. After a fire destroyed the plant, the five Ball brothers relocated the business and their families to Muncie, Indiana. Now known as the Ball Corporation, the company established itself as the leading manufacturer of jars in the home canning industry.

Ripe Gooseberry Jam

CONTRIBUTOR: LOUISE PIPER, IOWA

**MAKES ABOUT SIX
8-OUNCE JARS**

**4 cups ripe gooseberries,
coarsely ground**

**6¾ cups granulated
sugar**

**1 pouch (3 ounces) liquid
pectin**

Ripe gooseberries have a lavender pink color and make a tasty jam because cooking them with the sugar counteracts their tartness. Be careful to remove all of the stems and blossoms from the berries. In addition to winning a blue ribbon, this jam was chosen as the 2nd Best Overall Jam winner at the Iowa State Fair.

1. In an 8-quart stainless steel stockpot, combine the gooseberries and sugar. Heat the mixture over low heat, stirring constantly, until the gooseberries release some of their juice. Gradually increase the heat to medium high and bring the mixture to a full rolling boil, stirring constantly.

2. Stir in the pectin. Return the mixture to a full rolling boil, stirring constantly. Boil for 1 minute, stirring constantly. Remove the pot from the heat and skim off any foam.

3. Ladle the jam into hot jars, leaving ¼-inch headspace. Remove any air bubbles. Wipe the jar rims and threads with a clean, damp paper towel. Apply hot lids and screw bands.

4. Process 4-ounce, 8-ounce, and pint jars in a water bath canner for 10 minutes (see p. 34 for instructions). Remove from the water bath canner and let cool for 12 to 24 hours. Check the seals and remove the screw bands. Store jars in a cool, dry, dark place for up to 1 year.

DID YOU KNOW?

Growing gooseberries was illegal in New York State in the early 1900s. The law was enacted to prevent the spread of white pine blister rust. The federal version of the law was rescinded in 1966, and New York rescinded its law in 2003. While gooseberries are still less popular than other berries, they're starting to show up more in farmers' markets and backyard gardens.

Sweet Cherry Jam

CONTRIBUTOR: LINDA J. AMENDT, CALIFORNIA

MAKES ABOUT SIX
8-OUNCE JARS

4 cups pitted and
chopped Bing cherries,
or other sweet cherries
(3 to 4 pounds cherries)

½ cup freshly squeezed
lemon juice

5 cups granulated sugar

½ teaspoon unsalted
butter (optional)

1 pouch (3 ounces) liquid
pectin

1 teaspoon pure almond
extract

Linda and her parents would go cherry picking every June and bring home between 40 and 80 pounds of ripe, sweet cherries. This jam is a family favorite and always in demand. A multiple blue ribbon and special award winner, the judges remarked, "A beautiful cherry jam. Your excellent canning skills shine through. The color, texture, and delicious Bing cherry flavor were a delight to judge. An outstanding product!"

1. In an 8-quart stainless steel stockpot, combine the cherries and lemon juice. Stir in the sugar and add the butter, if using. Heat the mixture over medium-low heat, stirring constantly, until the sugar is completely dissolved. Increase the heat to medium high and bring to a full rolling boil, stirring constantly. Stir in the pectin. Return the mixture to a full rolling boil, stirring constantly. Boil for 1 minute, stirring constantly.

2. Remove the pot from the heat and skim off any foam. Stir in the almond extract. Let the jam cool in the pot for 5 minutes, stirring occasionally.

3. Ladle the jam into hot jars, leaving ¼-inch headspace. Remove any air bubbles. Wipe the jar rims and threads with a clean, damp paper towel. Apply hot lids and screw bands.

4. Process 4-ounce, 8-ounce, and pint jars in a water bath canner for 10 minutes (see p. 34 for instructions). Remove from the water bath canner and let cool for 12 to 24 hours. Check the seals and remove the screw bands. Store jars in a cool, dry, dark place for up to 1 year.

LINDA J. AMENDT

MURRIETA, CALIFORNIA

"MY DAD, WHO GREW UP IN IOWA, would tell me stories about his mother's canning kitchen, outside on the back porch, and the cellar lined with shelves proudly filled with hundreds of her neatly arranged canning jars." Unfortunately, Linda's grandmother passed away when Linda was young, and she never had the opportunity to learn how to can from her.

As a child, Linda showed a strong interest in baking. Her mom, who made fantastic lemon meringue pies but didn't do much other baking, encouraged her to bake. In her early teen years Linda decided to learn how to can. The only thing either of her parents had ever canned was green beans, in metal cans. "When my parents were first married, the owner of a neighboring property in San Diego discovered his crop had been invaded by weeds and gave my parents the weekend to harvest as many beans as they wanted before he plowed under the field. They canned over 100 cans of green beans in 2 days!"

1,000 awards total in preserved foods and baked goods combined.

For five years, from 1996 to 2000, she was the top preserved foods competitor in California. In 1999 and 2000, she was also the top preserved foods competitor in the nation, winning blue ribbons, special awards, and sweepstakes awards at fairs across the country. Linda is proud to have been named a Lifetime Member of the Inaugural Class of the Sure-Jell Hall of Fame, honoring the best jam and jelly makers in the country.

After competing in canning competitions for 11 years, Linda was classified as a food professional when her first canning cookbook was published in 2001. No longer eligible to compete in amateur fair competitions, several fairs asked her to jump to the other side of the table, and she became a preserved foods and baked goods judge. She now enjoys judging as much as she did competing. Each year she looks forward to judging at local county fairs and the California State Fair, where she is the head preserved foods judge and part of a team conducting an open judging and discussing the merits of each entry in front of an audience of State Fair exhibitors and visitors. "I love fairs and fair competitions and am thrilled to give back to events that brought me so much fun and joy as a competitor."

For 2 years in a row, Linda was named the top preserved foods competitor in the nation.

Urged by her sister-in-law, Linda's first fair entry and blue ribbon was a cross-stitch birth sampler she made for her nephew. After successfully competing in needle arts for several years, she entered baked goods. Preserved foods entries followed a few years later. Linda earned over 400 blue ribbons and special awards for excellence in preserved foods alone and over 700 blue ribbons and special awards and nearly

Raspberry Plum Jam

CONTRIBUTOR: LINDA J. AMENDT, CALIFORNIA

**MAKES ABOUT SEVEN
8-OUNCE JARS**

2 quarts whole
raspberries

1⅔ cups pitted, peeled,
and crushed red plums
(about 2 pounds plums)

1 tablespoon freshly
squeezed lemon juice

6½ cups granulated
sugar

½ teaspoon unsalted
butter (optional)

1 pouch (3 ounces) liquid
pectin

TIP

A 12-ounce bag of
frozen unsweetened
raspberries will
yield about 1 cup
of seedless
raspberry pulp.

Combine the intense flavors of raspberries and plums and you
have one mighty tasty jam with a beautiful color. To make a
seedless jam, crush and press the raspberries through a fine-
mesh sieve before measuring. The plums tend to break down
when cooked, so this jam has a smooth texture with fewer
fruit pieces.

1. Press the raspberries through a food mill or fine-mesh sieve to
   remove the seeds. Discard the seeds and measure out 2½ cups of
   puréed raspberry pulp.

2. In an 8-quart stainless steel stockpot, combine the raspberry
   pulp, plums, and lemon juice. Stir in the sugar and add the butter, if using. Heat the mixture over medium-low heat, stirring
   constantly, until the sugar is completely dissolved. Increase the
   heat to medium high and bring to a full rolling boil, stirring
   constantly.

3. Stir in the pectin. Return the mixture to a full rolling boil, stirring constantly. Boil for 1 minute, stirring constantly.

4. Remove the pot from the heat and skim off any foam. Let the
   jam cool in the pot for 5 minutes, stirring occasionally.

5. Ladle the jam into hot jars, leaving ¼-inch headspace. Remove
   any air bubbles. Wipe the jar rims and threads with a clean,
   damp paper towel. Apply hot lids and screw bands.

6. Process 4-ounce, 8-ounce, and pint jars in a water bath canner for
   10 minutes (see p. 34 for instructions). Remove from the water
   bath canner and let cool for 12 to 24 hours. Check the seals and
   remove the screw bands. Store jars in a cool, dry, dark place for
   up to 1 year.

*Raspberry Plum Jam and
Plum Jam (recipe on p. 62)*

Plum Jam

CONTRIBUTOR: LINDA J. AMENDT, CALIFORNIA

**MAKES ABOUT EIGHT
8-OUNCE JARS**

4½ cups pitted, peeled, and crushed plums (about 5 pounds plums)

7½ cups granulated sugar

½ teaspoon unsalted butter (optional)

1 pouch (3 ounces) liquid pectin

When she was growing up, Linda's family had a Santa Rosa plum tree that was an abundant producer. The jam made from those plums was her mother's favorite. Linda also likes to make plum jam with beautiful golden-fleshed plums from the farmers' market (shown on p. 60). This recipe works with just about any variety of plum and makes a lovely sweet and tangy jam. Linda has won multiple blue ribbons and special awards with this jam, including first place in the Sure-Jell Jam Competition at the California State Fair. The judges loved the bright flavor and smooth texture created by peeling the plums.

1. In an 8-quart stainless steel stockpot, combine the plums, sugar, and butter, if using. Cook the mixture over medium-low heat, stirring constantly, until the sugar is completely dissolved. Increase the heat to medium high and bring to a full rolling boil, stirring constantly.

2. Stir in the pectin. Return the mixture to a full rolling boil, stirring constantly. Boil for 1 minute, stirring constantly.

3. Remove the pot from the heat and skim off any foam. Let the jam cool in the pot for 5 minutes, stirring occasionally.

4. Ladle the jam into hot jars, leaving ¼-inch headspace. Remove any air bubbles. Wipe the jar rims and threads with a clean, damp paper towel. Apply hot lids and screw bands.

5. Process 4-ounce, 8-ounce, and pint jars in a water bath canner for 10 minutes (see p. 34 for instructions). Remove from the water bath canner and let cool for 12 to 24 hours. Check the seals and remove the screw bands. Store jars in a cool, dry, dark place for up to 1 year.

Nectarine Jam

CONTRIBUTOR: ROMERO FAMILY, COLORADO

**MAKES ABOUT NINE
8-OUNCE JARS**

5 cups peeled, pitted,
and crushed nectarines
(about 5 pounds
nectarines)

7 tablespoons freshly
squeezed lemon juice

1 box (2 ounces)
powdered pectin

½ teaspoon unsalted
butter (optional)

7 cups granulated sugar

Nectarines are a wonderful summer fruit and this is a family favorite. No matter how many jars the Romero kids make, there never seems to be enough of this one because it goes so fast.

1. In an 8-quart stainless steel stockpot, combine the nectarines and lemon juice. Stir in the pectin and add the butter, if using. Bring the mixture to a full rolling boil over medium-high heat, stirring constantly.

2. Add the sugar and stir until completely dissolved. Return the mixture to a full rolling boil, stirring constantly. Boil for 1 minute, stirring constantly. Remove the pot from the heat and skim off any foam.

3. Ladle the jam into hot jars, leaving ¼-inch headspace. Remove any air bubbles. Wipe the jar rims and threads with a clean, damp paper towel. Apply hot lids and screw bands.

4. Process 4-ounce, 8-ounce, and pint jars in a water bath canner for 10 minutes (see p. 34 for instructions). Remove from the water bath canner and let cool for 12 to 24 hours. Check the seals and remove the screw bands. Store jars in a cool, dry, dark place for up to 1 year.

DID YOU KNOW?

The Mason jar is named for John Landis Mason, who originated and patented the design of a glass jar topped with a screw closure and gasket which formed a hermetic seal with the jar. The U. S. government issued Mason a patent on November 30, 1858, giving Mason the sole manufacturing rights on its invention for the next 14 years. In 1872 the U.S. Patent Office extended the patent for an additional 7 years. When the patent expired in 1879, other glass manufacturers were legally allowed to begin producing jars similar to Mason's design. Taking advantage of the popularity of Mason's jars, these manufacturers added wording to their jars to show that they were being manufactured according to Mason's patent.

ROXANNE & CHERYLANNE PETRUNTI

MALDEN, MASSACHUSETTS

TWIN SISTERS ROXANNE AND CHERYLANNE PETRUNTI have been canning since childhood, working alongside their mother, grandmother, great aunt, and godmother. Roxanne enjoyed canning with them and learning the family's Italian traditions and recipes. Cherrylanne has fond memories of the family going strawberry picking and then harvesting rhubarb from her great aunt's garden. They would then return home and can jars and jars of strawberry rhubarb jam.

> "Growing your own produce and then canning your garden harvest gives you such a heartwarming and rewarding feeling."

In 2004, Roxanne entered the Topsfield Fair and won her first canning ribbon. Unfortunately, she developed breast cancer and spent several years battling it until the cancer went into remission. Once she was healthy, Roxanne started canning again. "Canning took my mind off my illness. It helped me relax. I look forward to entering my jams and other canning exhibits into the fair each year." Roxanne loves giving her canned goods as thank-you gifts to family and friends as a way to pay them back for all their help and support while she was fighting cancer.

After seeing her sister's success and excitement at winning awards at the fair, Cherylanne recently decided to enter her canned goods into competition and has started bringing home her own blue ribbons. She is taking canning classes to improve her skills and looks forward to increasing her fair wins. "Growing your own produce and then canning your garden harvest gives you such a heartwarming and rewarding feeling. Giving away the jars as gifts is also very special."

Peach Amaretto Jam

CONTRIBUTOR: CHERYLANNE PETRUNTI, MASSACHUSETTS

**MAKES ABOUT SIX
8-OUNCE JARS**

**4 cups pitted, peeled, and
finely chopped peaches
(about 4 pounds peaches)**

4 cups granulated sugar

½ cup amaretto liqueur

For the holidays, especially at Christmastime, Cherylanne bakes a variety of cookies with her twin sister, Roxanne. One of their family's favorites is the Italian Venetian Rainbow cookies. Traditionally apricot or raspberry jam is used between the cookie layers. Instead, she uses this Peach Amaretto Jam, as amaretto is a favorite flavor in her family. She also uses this jam in thumbprint cookies.

1. In an 8-quart stainless steel stockpot, combine the peaches and sugar. Bring the mixture to a boil over medium-high heat, stirring constantly. Reduce the heat to medium low to low and simmer gently, stirring constantly, until the jam is thick and reaches the jellying point (220°F at sea level), about 15 minutes.

2. Remove the pot from the heat and skim off any foam. Stir in the amaretto.

3. Ladle the jam into hot jars, leaving ¼-inch headspace. Remove any air bubbles. Wipe the jar rims and threads with a clean, damp paper towel. Apply hot lids and screw bands.

4. Process 4-ounce, 8-ounce, and pint jars in a water bath canner for 10 minutes (see p. 34 for instructions). Remove from the water bath canner and let cool for 12 to 24 hours. Check the seals and remove the screw bands. Store jars in a cool, dry, dark place for up to 1 year.

DID YOU KNOW? Over 3,200 fairs are held in North America each year. They provide industrial exhibits, demonstrations, and competitions aimed at the advancement of livestock, horticulture, and agriculture with special emphasis placed on educational activities such as 4-H and similar youth development programs.

Spiced Blueberry Jam

CONTRIBUTOR: ROXANNE M. PETRUNTI, MASSACHUSETTS

MAKES ABOUT SEVEN 8-OUNCE JARS

6 cups whole blueberries, lightly crushed

1 box (2 ounces) powdered pectin

2 tablespoons freshly squeezed lemon juice

1 teaspoon ground cinnamon

¼ teaspoon ground ginger

¼ teaspoon ground nutmeg

5 cups granulated sugar

A great way to start Christmas morning is with a family favorite. For a special treat, Roxanne makes homemade blueberry pancakes and tops them with this jam and warm maple syrup.

1. In an 8-quart stainless steel stockpot, combine the blueberries, pectin, lemon juice, cinnamon, ginger, and nutmeg. Bring the mixture to a full rolling boil over medium-high heat, stirring constantly.

2. Add the sugar and stir until completely dissolved. Return the mixture to a full rolling boil, stirring constantly. Boil for 1 minute, stirring constantly. Remove the pot from the heat and skim off any foam.

3. Ladle the jam into hot jars, leaving ¼-inch headspace. Remove any air bubbles. Wipe the jar rims and threads with a clean, damp paper towel. Apply hot lids and screw bands.

4. Process 4-ounce, 8-ounce, and pint jars in a water bath canner for 10 minutes (see p. 34 for instructions). Remove from the water bath canner and let cool for 12 to 24 hours. Check the seals and remove the screw bands. Store jars in a cool, dry, dark place for up to 1 year.

DID YOU KNOW? In 1790, French Chemist Louis Nicolas Vauquelin discovered a chemical in apple cider vinegar with gelatinous properties. This substance was pectin. In 1825, Henri Braconnot, a French chemist and pharmacist, was the first person to isolate and describe pectin, although the action of pectin to thicken jams and marmalades had been known for many years. It wouldn't be until the 20th century before the structure and working properties of pectin were fully identified.

Pear Lime Jam

CONTRIBUTOR: LINDA J. AMENDT, CALIFORNIA

**MAKES ABOUT SIX
8-OUNCE JARS**

5 cups granulated sugar

1 box (1.75 ounces)
powdered pectin

4½ cups peeled, cored,
chopped, and lightly
crushed Bartlett pears
(about 4½ pounds pears)

3 tablespoons freshly
squeezed lime juice

1 tablespoon finely
grated lime zest

½ teaspoon unsalted
butter (optional)

When she received a big box of ripe Bartlett pears as a thank-you gift from a friend, Linda decided to make pear jam. But she didn't have any lemons at the time, only limes. That was a lucky turn of events—the lime juice and zest add a bright zing and complement the pear flavor, creating a delightful jam. This is now her favorite pear jam recipe.

1. In a small bowl, combine ¼ cup of the sugar with the pectin until thoroughly blended.

2. In an 8-quart stainless steel stockpot, combine the pears, lime juice, and lime zest. Stir in the pectin mixture and add the butter, if using. Bring the mixture to a full rolling boil over medium-high heat, stirring constantly.

3. Add the remaining sugar and stir until completely dissolved. Return the mixture to a full rolling boil, stirring constantly. Boil for 1 minute, stirring constantly.

4. Remove the pot from the heat and skim off any foam. Let the jam cool in the pot for 5 minutes, stirring occasionally.

5. Ladle the jam into hot jars, leaving ¼-inch headspace. Remove any air bubbles. Wipe the jar rims and threads with a clean, damp paper towel. Apply hot lids and screw bands.

6. Process 4-ounce, 8-ounce, and pint jars in a water bath canner for 10 minutes (see p. 34 for instructions). Remove from the water bath canner and let cool for 12 to 24 hours. Check the seals and remove the screw bands. Store jars in a cool, dry, dark place for up to 1 year.

Mango Raspberry Jam

CONTRIBUTOR: ROMERO FAMILY, COLORADO

**MAKES ABOUT SEVEN
8-OUNCE JARS**

3¼ cups peeled and
finely chopped mangos
(about 4 mangos)

1¼ cups crushed
raspberries (about 3 cups
whole raspberries)

2 tablespoons freshly
squeezed lemon juice

1 box (2 ounces)
powdered pectin

½ teaspoon unsalted
butter (optional)

5½ cups granulated
sugar

A lovely combination of mango and raspberries gives this
mixed-fruit jam great flavor and a beautiful color.

1. In an 8-quart stainless steel stockpot, combine the mangos, raspberries, and lemon juice. Stir in the pectin and add the butter, if using. Bring the mixture to a full rolling boil over medium-high heat, stirring constantly.

2. Add the sugar and stir until completely dissolved. Return the mixture to a full rolling boil, stirring constantly. Boil for 1 minute, stirring constantly. Remove the pot from the heat and skim off any foam.

3. Ladle the jam into hot jars, leaving ¼-inch headspace. Remove any air bubbles. Wipe the jar rims and threads with a clean, damp paper towel. Apply hot lids and screw bands.

4. Process 4-ounce, 8-ounce, and pint jars in a water bath canner for 10 minutes (see p. 34 for instructions). Remove from the water bath canner and let cool for 12 to 24 hours. Check the seals and remove the screw bands. Store jars in a cool, dry, dark place for up to 1 year.

THE ROMERO FAMILY

PUEBLO, COLORADO

THE ROMERO FAMILY didn't set out to be award-winning canners. The girls, Hannah and Kiki, began entering baked goods in the Colorado State Fair when they were around 9 and 12 years old. In 2005, the fair extended its adult award, Queen of the Kitchen, to include youth exhibitors; all youth, 18 years old and under, could vie for the new award, Princess of the Kitchen. The entry categories included many types of canned goods, baked goods, dried foods, and ethnic foods.

What began as a desire to win has turned into a love of canning for the whole family.

The next year, when Kiki was 11, she decided she wanted to compete for Princess. The girls already knew how to make everything necessary to win, except for the canning. Step in Gramme LaDean. Although LaDean's mom had canned prolifically throughout the years, LaDean had never learned how to can. Yet, wishing to help fulfill her granddaughter's dream, Gramme figured that if they could read directions, they could figure out how to can properly and learn together. She was right.

Fast forward a few years and the Romero family has earned numerous awards at the Colorado State Fair. Kiki won Princess twice, Hannah once, and brother Darian was the very first Prince of the Kitchen. Each has won hundreds of blue ribbons and taken home multiple special awards, judge's choice awards, and category sweepstakes. For each fair, they entered between 50 and 76 canned goods, plus many types of baked goods. The newest canning competitors, Nathaniel and Jeremiah, are now bringing home their own blue ribbons, with Nathaniel also winning Prince of the Kitchen. Joshua will soon be learning to can and entering the competition as well.

Over the years, Gramme has taught five of her grandchildren to can and she has high standards and expectations. She teaches the importance of proper sealing techniques, correct water levels, and time adjustments for high altitude. She urges prize-winning quality and practices for every jar canned. Each vegetable and fruit slice must be of equal size and placed perfectly in the jar. When packing corn, kernels are carefully selected for uniform size. Only the freshest and brightest fruit is used, and everything must look mouth-watering in the jars. Striving for perfection has proven successful, and the blue ribbons are the proof. What began as a desire to win has turned into a love of canning for the whole family.

Mom, Resa, says that with so many kids canning and competing at once, it's sometimes a challenge to get all the canned goods to the fair in a timely and organized manner. "It usually takes two carloads to deliver everything. It's not an easy feat! Most years, we remind the kids that it's a good thing we live in the same city as our State Fair."

Peach Vanilla Bean Jam

CONTRIBUTOR: LINDA J. AMENDT, CALIFORNIA

**MAKES ABOUT SEVEN
8-OUNCE JARS**

7 cups granulated sugar

2 whole vanilla beans

4 cups pitted, peeled, and crushed peaches (about 4 pounds peaches)

3 tablespoons freshly squeezed lemon juice

½ teaspoon unsalted butter (optional)

1 pouch (3 ounces) liquid fruit pectin

TIP

To scrape the seeds from the vanilla bean pods, hold one half of the cut-open pod with your fingers as you scrape down the length of the pod with a sharp knife, collecting the seeds on the blade.

While enjoying fresh peach cobbler topped with a scoop of vanilla bean ice cream, Linda thought this would make a great flavor combination for a jam. She was right! And the proof was in the Best of Show ribbon she found hanging on the jar. Make the vanilla bean sugar 2 days ahead of making the jam to allow time for the flavor to fully develop.

1. Place the sugar in a large bowl. Using a sharp knife, slice the vanilla beans in half lengthwise. Carefully scrape the seeds from the inside of the vanilla pods and add to the sugar. Cut the pods into 1-inch pieces and add to the sugar. Stir to distribute the seeds and pods throughout the sugar. Cover and let stand for 48 hours, stirring once a day. Sift the sugar through a fine-mesh sieve to remove the vanilla pod pieces; save in a tightly sealed container for another use.

2. In an 8-quart stainless steel stockpot, combine the peaches and lemon juice. Stir in the vanilla bean sugar and add the butter, if using. Cook the mixture over medium-low heat, stirring constantly, until the sugar is completely dissolved. Increase the heat to medium high and bring to a full rolling boil, stirring constantly.

3. Stir in the pectin. Return the mixture to a full rolling boil, stirring constantly. Boil for 1 minute, stirring constantly.

4. Remove the pot from the heat and skim off any foam. Let the jam cool in the pot for 5 minutes, stirring occasionally.

5. Ladle the jam into hot jars, leaving ¼-inch headspace. Remove any air bubbles. Wipe the jar rims and threads with a clean, damp paper towel. Apply hot lids and screw bands.

6. Process 4-ounce, 8-ounce, and pint jars in a water bath canner for 10 minutes (see p. 34 for instructions). Remove from the water bath canner and let cool for 12 to 24 hours. Check the seals and remove the screw bands. Store jars in a cool, dry, dark place for up to 1 year.

Carrot Apple Jam

CONTRIBUTOR: BETH WALLACE, ARKANSAS

**MAKES ABOUT SIX
8-OUNCE JARS**

2 Red Delicious apples,
peeled, cored, and finely
chopped or grated

2 tablespoons freshly
squeezed lemon juice

2 pounds carrots, peeled
and grated

¼ cup unsweetened
apple juice

1 box (1.75 ounces)
powdered pectin

5 cups granulated sugar

This unique jam has a grand flavor and wonderful color. Beth likes to add a dollop over the top of vegetables, particularly beans and peas; the jam also makes a good topping for biscuits.

1. In an 8-quart stockpot, combine the apples and lemon juice. Add the carrots and apple juice and stir to combine. Stir in the pectin.

2. Bring the mixture to a full rolling boil over medium-high heat, stirring constantly. Add the sugar and stir until completely dissolved. Return the mixture to a full rolling boil, stirring constantly. Boil for 1 minute, stirring constantly. Remove the pot from the heat and skim off any foam.

3. Ladle the jam into hot jars, leaving ¼-inch headspace. Remove any air bubbles. Wipe the jar rims and threads with a clean, damp paper towel. Apply hot lids and screw bands.

4. Process 4-ounce, 8-ounce, and pint jars in a water bath canner for 10 minutes (see p. 34 for instructions). Remove from the water bath canner and let cool for 12 to 24 hours. Check the seals and remove the screw bands. Store jars in a cool, dry, dark place for up to 1 year.

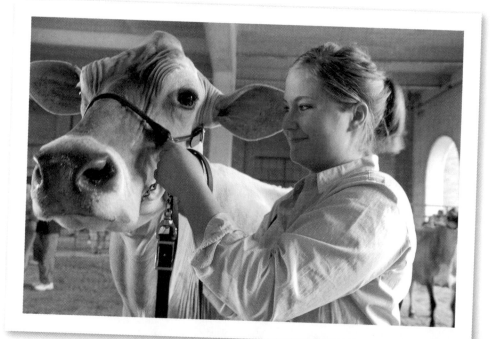

Apricot Jam

CONTRIBUTOR: LINDA J. AMENDT, CALIFORNIA

MAKES ABOUT SIX 8-OUNCE JARS

3¾ cups pitted, peeled, and crushed apricots (about 3½ pounds apricots)

6 tablespoons freshly squeezed lemon juice

5¾ cups granulated sugar

½ teaspoon unsalted butter (optional)

1 pouch (3 ounces) liquid pectin

Peeling apricots for canning recipes is not common, but it makes a big difference in this jam, giving it a silky texture and strong fruit flavor. It takes a bit of time, but the effort is worth it to create a superior jam. The exquisite flavor and texture achieved by peeling the apricots is why this jam has won special awards.

1. In an 8-quart stainless steel stockpot, combine the apricots and lemon juice. Stir in the sugar and add the butter, if using. Cook the mixture over medium-low heat, stirring constantly, until the sugar is completely dissolved. Increase the heat to medium high and bring to a full rolling boil, stirring constantly.

2. Stir in the pectin. Return the mixture to a full rolling boil, stirring constantly. Boil for 1 minute, stirring constantly.

3. Remove the pot from the heat and skim off any foam. Let the jam cool in the pot for 5 minutes, stirring occasionally.

4. Ladle the jam into hot jars, leaving ¼-inch headspace. Remove any air bubbles. Wipe the jar rims and threads with a clean, damp paper towel. Apply hot lids and screw bands.

5. Process 4-ounce, 8-ounce, and pint jars in a water bath canner for 10 minutes (see p. 34 for instructions). Remove from the water bath canner and let cool for 12 to 24 hours. Check the seals and remove the screw bands. Store jars in a cool, dry, dark place for up to 1 year.

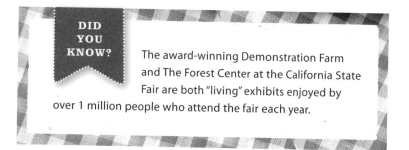

DID YOU KNOW? The award-winning Demonstration Farm and The Forest Center at the California State Fair are both "living" exhibits enjoyed by over 1 million people who attend the fair each year.

CATHIE MERRIHEW

GRAND ISLE, VERMONT

CATHIE MERRIHEW has been making jams, jellies, and pickles for nearly 30 years, and she started canning fruits and vegetables about 10 years ago. "I enjoy the creativity of canning, and I find it relaxing—turn on some good country music and I'm in my own tranquil space. I also like knowing that my family and friends are eating good food."

> "I enjoy the creativity of canning and I find it relaxing—turn on some good country music and I'm in my own tranquil space."

About 25 years ago, her mom suggested that she enter a few of her jams and pickles into a fair competition. "I was surprised when I won blue ribbons that first time, and I continue to challenge myself to enter different recipes each year." Cathie has won many blue ribbons over the years and has received 10 Judges' Favorite awards. "I collect old recipe books and flyers and use them to get ideas I can build on. My oldest find is a 1917 Farmers Bulletin from the U.S. Department of Agriculture!"

"My family has a summer place on a lake here in Vermont. I live there in the summer and I do all my canning and jamming at the 'camp.'" The kitchen is small but very user-friendly, with an old 1940s-style large white enamel sink. Cathie picks many of her own fruits for making jams and jellies, including strawberries, raspberries, and blueberries. Many of her neighbors also supply her with extra fruit from their apple, pear, and plum trees. In return, she gives them a supply of her canned products. "My local fair requires that all canning entries use types of produce grown in Vermont, so that is what I use for my canning."

Blueberry Orange Jam

CONTRIBUTOR: CATHIE MERRIHEW, VERMONT

MAKES ABOUT SIX
8-OUNCE JARS

4 cups crushed
blueberries (3 to 4 pints
whole blueberries)

Grated zest of 1 large
orange

2 tablespoons freshly
squeezed orange juice

⅓ cup powdered pectin

4 cups granulated sugar

¼ cup Triple Sec or other
orange-flavored liqueur

As she was creating this jam to use an overabundance of blueberries, on a whim Cathie added some Triple Sec to boost the orange flavor—and it worked! With the delightful blend of blueberry and orange flavors, this tasty jam earned both a blue ribbon and the Judge's Favorite award at the Champlain Valley Fair.

1. In an 8-quart stainless steel stockpot, combine the blueberries, orange zest, and orange juice. Stir in the pectin. Bring the mixture to a full rolling boil over medium-high heat, stirring constantly.

2. Add the sugar and stir until completely dissolved. Return the mixture to a full rolling boil, stirring constantly. Boil for 1 minute, stirring constantly.

3. Remove the pot from the heat and skim off any foam. Add the Triple Sec and stir until well blended.

4. Ladle the jam into hot jars, leaving ¼-inch headspace. Remove any air bubbles. Wipe the jar rims and threads with a clean, damp paper towel. Apply hot lids and screw bands.

5. Process 4-ounce, 8-ounce, and pint jars in a water bath canner for 10 minutes (see p. 34 for instructions). Remove from the water bath canner and let cool for 12 to 24 hours. Check the seals and remove the screw bands. Store jars in a cool, dry, dark place for up to 1 year.

DID YOU KNOW? The Tilt-a-Whirl™, that wildly spinning ride found at almost every fair in the country, was created by Herbert Sellner in his backyard in 1926. The ride features seven cars that rotate on a platform that raises and lowers itself. Changing centrifugal and gravitational forces on the cars make them tip and spin randomly, leading some riders to call this the "torture whirl."

Strawberry Peach Grand Marnier Jam

CONTRIBUTOR: LINDA J. AMENDT, CALIFORNIA

MAKES EIGHT TO NINE
8-OUNCE JARS

2 cups crushed
strawberries (2 to 3 pints
whole strawberries)

2 cups pitted, peeled,
and crushed peaches
(about 2 pounds peaches)

3 tablespoons freshly
squeezed lemon juice

7 cups granulated sugar

½ teaspoon unsalted
butter (optional)

1 pouch (3 ounces) liquid
pectin

⅓ cup Grand Marnier®

This Best of Show winner combines the beautiful summer flavors of strawberries and peaches with a splash of Grand Marnier, an orange-flavored liqueur. It received rave reviews from the judges, and it ranks high on the Christmas gift request list of several friends.

1. In an 8-quart stainless steel stockpot, combine the strawberries, peaches, and lemon juice. Stir in the sugar and add the butter, if using. Cook the mixture over medium-low heat, stirring constantly, until the sugar is completely dissolved. Increase the heat to medium high and bring to a full rolling boil, stirring constantly.

2. Stir in the pectin. Return the mixture to a full rolling boil, stirring constantly. Boil for 1 minute, stirring constantly.

3. Remove the pot from the heat and skim off any foam. Stir in the Grand Marnier. Let the jam cool in the pot for 5 minutes, stirring occasionally.

4. Ladle the jam into hot jars, leaving ¼-inch headspace. Remove any air bubbles. Wipe the jar rims and threads with a clean, damp paper towel. Apply hot lids and screw bands.

5. Process 4-ounce, 8-ounce, and pint jars in a water bath canner for 10 minutes (see p. 34 for instructions). Remove from the water bath canner and let cool for 12 to 24 hours. Check the seals and remove the screw bands. Store jars in a cool, dry, dark place for up to 1 year.

Raspberry Jam

CONTRIBUTOR: MIRIAM KENTNER, WASHINGTON

MAKES ABOUT EIGHT
8-OUNCE JARS

7 cups granulated sugar

1 box (1.75 ounces)
powdered pectin

6 cups fresh raspberries,
crushed (about 6 pints
whole raspberries)

After the hot summer sun goes down, bring out this fresh and flavorful raspberry jam and spread it on anything from cookies to crêpes or add it to marinades and salad dressings. It also makes a great ice cream topping. You will want to make extra batches because everybody is going to want some.

1. In a small bowl, combine ¼ cup of the sugar with the pectin until thoroughly blended.

2. In an 8-quart stainless steel stockpot, combine the raspberries and pectin mixture. Bring the mixture to a full rolling boil over medium-high heat, stirring constantly.

3. Add the remaining sugar and stir until completely dissolved. Return the mixture to a full rolling boil, stirring constantly. Boil for 1 minute, stirring constantly.

4. Remove the pot from the heat and skim off any foam. Let the jam cool for 5 minutes, stirring occasionally.

5. Ladle the jam into hot jars, leaving ¼-inch headspace. Remove any air bubbles. Wipe the jar rims and threads with a clean, damp paper towel. Apply hot lids and screw bands.

6. Process 4-ounce, 8-ounce, and pint jars in a water bath canner for 10 minutes (see p. 34 for instructions). Remove from the water bath canner and let cool for 12 to 24 hours. Check the seals and remove the screw bands. Store jars in a cool, dry, dark place for up to 1 year.

Simple Fruit Jam

CONTRIBUTOR: SARA AND MICHAEL LAUSMANN, OREGON

MAKES ABOUT EIGHT
8-OUNCE JARS

4 cups crushed or puréed
fresh fruit or berries

4 cups granulated sugar

1 box (2 ounces)
powdered pectin

½ tablespoon freshly
squeezed lemon juice

½ teaspoon unsalted
butter (optional)

Sara affectionately calls this her jam "formula" rather than her jam recipe. It can be easily adjusted for the amount of fruit you have, and it works well with any fruit—strawberries, apricots, raspberries, or whatever you have on hand. The beauty and flavor are in its simplicity and the freshness of the fruit.

1. In an 8-quart stainless steel stockpot, combine the fruit and sugar. Bring the mixture to a boil over medium heat, stirring constantly.

2. Stir in the pectin, lemon juice, and butter, if using. Return the mixture to a full rolling boil, stirring constantly. Boil for 1 minute, stirring constantly. Remove the pot from the heat and skim off any foam.

3. Ladle the jam into hot jars, leaving ¼-inch headspace. Remove any air bubbles. Wipe the jar rims and threads with a clean, damp paper towel. Apply hot lids and screw bands.

4. Process 4-ounce, 8-ounce, and pint jars in a water bath canner for 10 minutes (see p. 34 for instructions). Remove from the water bath canner and let cool for 12 to 24 hours. Check the seals and remove the screw bands. Store jars in a cool, dry, dark place for up to 1 year.

> **DID YOU KNOW?**
>
> In the early 20th century, the county or state fair was the highlight of the harvest season for many families. The whole family would spend several exciting days preparing for and traveling to the fair to exhibit their entries with pride. While the men gathered in the fair barns to compare livestock and crops, the women would compete against each other with their needlework and canning entries.

SARA & MICHAEL LAUSMANN

EUGENE, OREGON

WHEN THEIR FIRST SON WAS AN INFANT, Sara and Michael Lausmann began preparing their own baby food for him by picking the fruits and vegetables from their local farmers' market and local farms. "We stumbled across our favorite produce farm while hunting for pumpkins. Now we return to the farm every year, throughout the growing season, picking the fruit at its ripest and preserving it the very same day." They also pick fruit from the wild and throughout their neighborhood. "We have learned where and when to find the wild strawberries and huckleberries in the Cascade Mountains, and the wild black raspberries, salmonberries, and gooseberries in the Oregon Coast Range. And we know all the great neighborhood foraging spots."

> "With canning, we wanted to get back to basics, to believe in our own ability to sustain our family through our love of nature, and to challenge ourselves to become intimate with our natural surroundings."

Sara and Michael also can jams and jellies to carry them through the hard gray winters of the Pacific Northwest. "Each time we open a new jar, it's like inviting summer back into our home. Unless, of course, it's a jar of thimbleberry jam—then it's like having Christmas in a jar."

They didn't start canning to enter competitions and win blue ribbons. "We wanted to get back to basics, to believe in our own ability to sustain our family through our love of nature, and to challenge ourselves to become intimate with our natural surroundings." Sara and Michael love the process of canning and the time spent as a family, doing something together from start to finish.

When she decided to test out some of her jams in the competitive scene, Sara didn't expect much. "The day the Lane County Fair opened, we walked over after work to check our entries. Making our way through the exhibition hall we spotted the jams and jellies and started scanning for our entries." Seeing what looked like a blue ribbon hanging off an apricot jam, Sara's first thought was that someone else had used the same jar presentation. Upon closer inspection, she realized that the name on that blue ribbon was her own. "I was so surprised, elated, and excited that I cried tears of joy right there in the middle of the exhibition hall! We made such a commotion that everyone within 100 feet of us turned to look, many of them offering congratulations. We then found another blue ribbon hanging on the strawberry jam."

At the urging of Michael's father, the next stop was the Oregon State Fair. Michael took home a blue ribbon for his golden plum jelly, and Sara's strawberry jam entry was again graced with a blue ribbon.

* Jellies *

Jellies are transparent, jewel-like spreads made from the extracted juice of the fruit. A well-made jelly will be crystal clear, sparkle and shimmer in the light, and have a delightful, fresh fruit flavor. Jellies have a tender texture and are firm enough to hold their shape when cut or spooned from the jar but still quiver and spread easily.

The process of making jelly is similar to that of jam, except that jelly-making involves two processes: one to extract the juice from the fruit and the second to transform the juice into jelly. To separate the fruit pulp from the juice, the fruit mixture is strained through several layers of damp fine-knit cheesecloth or a cloth jelly bag. While jellies can take longer to make than jams, they are well worth the effort.

Pectin is frequently added to jelly recipes because few fruit juices contain enough natural pectin to create a gel on their own. The addition of pectin also substantially reduces the cooking time, which means the jelly will have a fresher flavor closer to that of the natural flavor of the fruit. Jellies made by the long-boil method, without the addition of pectin, thicken through a combination of evaporation and jelling of the natural pectin in the juice. If the jelly is cooked too long, it can turn out very firm with an unpleasant molasses-like flavor.

Extracting Juice for Jelly

The fruit used to make jellies should be peeled, pitted, and crushed or finely chopped. The peels can give the extracted juice a bitter or earthy taste, so it's best to remove them before juicing the fruit. Never purée fruit when making jellies—doing so blends the fruit pulp and juice together rather than allowing the juice to separate from the fruit pulp. Jellies made from puréed fruits will be very cloudy.

To extract the juice, gently cook the fruit until very soft to release the juice. Strain the fruit and juice through a fine-mesh sieve lined with damp, fine-knit cheesecloth or in a damp jelly bag placed over a large bowl. This process can take time and should not be rushed—the juice needs to drain slowly to prevent it from turning cloudy. If you force the juice through the cheesecloth or squeeze the jelly bag, the juice will retain tiny pieces of fruit pulp and cause the finished jelly to be opaque and cloudy instead of crystal clear. To speed the process, you can strain the fruit mixture through a fine-mesh sieve first to remove the bulk of the fruit pulp from the juice before straining through the cheesecloth. If the cheesecloth fibers become clogged with pulp, pour the unstrained fruit mixture into a container, rinse the cheesecloth or jelly bag to clean the fabric, and resume the straining process through the cleaned fabric.

Black Raspberry Jelly

CONTRIBUTOR: LAURA MILOSAVICH, COLORADO

**MAKES ABOUT EIGHT
8-OUNCE JARS**

3½ quarts whole black raspberries

1 box (1.75 ounces) powdered pectin

½ teaspoon unsalted butter (optional)

6½ cups granulated sugar

This jelly has a wonderful fresh berry taste and is great on toast, English muffins, or as a filling for cupcakes or thumbprint cookies.

1. In an 8-quart stainless steel stockpot, lightly mash the black raspberries. Add just enough water to cover the berries. Stir to combine and cover the pot. Simmer the mixture over medium heat, stirring occasionally, for about 15 minutes.

2. Remove the pot from the heat. Strain the black raspberry mixture through a fine-mesh sieve lined with several layers of damp fine-knit cheesecloth or a damp jelly bag placed over a large bowl. Discard the pulp and seeds. Measure out 4½ cups prepared black raspberry juice.

3. Rinse and dry the stockpot. In the pot, combine the 4½ cups black raspberry juice, the pectin, and butter, if using. Bring the mixture to a full rolling boil over medium-high heat, stirring constantly.

4. Add the sugar and stir until completely dissolved. Return the mixture to a full rolling boil, stirring constantly. Boil for 1 minute, stirring constantly. Remove the pot from the heat and skim off any foam.

5. Ladle the jelly into hot jars, leaving ¼-inch headspace. Remove any air bubbles. Wipe the jar rims and threads with a clean, damp paper towel. Apply hot lids and screw bands.

6. Process 4-ounce, 8-ounce, and pint jars in a water bath canner for 10 minutes (see p. 34 for instructions). Remove from the water bath canner and let cool for 12 to 24 hours. Check the seals and remove the screw bands. Store jars in a cool, dry, dark place for up to 1 year.

LAURA MILOSAVICH

PUEBLO, COLORADO

LAURA MILOSAVICH'S grandmother helped feed her family by canning produce for local farmers. They would bring bushels of fresh produce to her grandmother and she would can them. As payment, the farmers would give her grandmother half of the finished canned food. Laura grew up cooking alongside her mother and grandmother. After many years of baking and savory cooking, Laura decided to try her hand at making homemade pickles and jams. Unfortunately, by then her grandmother had passed away. "I remember how wonderful her pickles and chili sauce were, and to this day I am still trying to replicate them. My daughter loves my dill pickles, so I told her she needed to learn how to make them."

Laura has taught both her daughter and husband how to can, and they have won blue ribbons of their own.

Laura has taught both her daughter and husband how to can, and they have won blue ribbons of their own in numerous canning categories.

Over the years, Laura has earned first place in every canning category; earned numerous best of class, sweepstakes, and special awards; and was named Queen of the Kitchen three times at the Colorado State Fair. Her recipes have been featured in several local and national publications. Laura became a certified pantry judge in 2012 and has judged specialty cooking and canning contests at the Colorado State Fair. She is also an accomplished porcelain doll artist and has judged the special doll category at the Colorado State Fair.

Pomegranate Red Wine Jelly

CONTRIBUTOR: GEORGE YATES, TEXAS

MAKES ABOUT FIVE
8-OUNCE JARS

3 cups pomegranate red
wine, such as Mogen
David

1 box (1.75 ounces)
powdered pectin

4 cups granulated sugar

Wine makes great jelly. George liked to use fruit-flavored wines, and pomegranate red wine is one of his favorites for making jelly. The judges liked it, too.

1. In an 8-quart stainless steel stockpot, combine the wine and pectin. Bring the mixture to a full rolling boil over medium-high heat, stirring constantly, and boil for 1 minute, stirring constantly.

2. Add the sugar and stir until completely dissolved. Return the mixture to a full rolling boil, stirring constantly. Boil for 1 minute, stirring constantly. Remove the pot from the heat and skim off any foam.

3. Ladle the jelly into hot jars, leaving ¼-inch headspace. Remove any air bubbles. Wipe the jar rims and threads with a clean, damp paper towel. Apply hot lids and screw bands.

4. Process 4-ounce, 8-ounce, and pint jars in a water bath canner for 10 minutes (see p. 34 for instructions). Remove from the water bath canner and let cool for 12 to 24 hours. Check the seals and remove the screw bands. Store jars in a cool, dry, dark place for up to 1 year.

DID YOU KNOW?

George Ferris invented the Ferris wheel and presented his idea for the giant rotating wheel at the World's Columbian Exposition of 1893 in Chicago. His ride cost $380,000 and was 264 feet tall with a wheel diameter of 250 feet. Each car held 60 people. The ride, which cost 50 cents, was one of the most popular attractions at the World's Fair.

Rhubarb–Red Raspberry Jelly

CONTRIBUTOR: LOUISE PIPER, IOWA

MAKES ABOUT SEVEN
8-OUNCE JARS

4 pounds rhubarb

1 quart whole red
raspberries

4 cups granulated sugar

2 pouches (3 ounces
each) liquid pectin

When she makes jellies, Louise packages up any leftover juices and freezes them. Sometimes she'll make extra juice on purpose so she can blend flavors and create her own combination jellies. This is one of her original—and favorite—jelly recipes.

1. Cut the rhubarb into 1-inch pieces. Using a food processor, grinder, or a blender, finely grind the rhubarb. Place three layers of damp fine-knit cheesecloth in a large bowl. Spoon the ground rhubarb into the center of the cheesecloth. Tie the ends of the cheesecloth together and hang over a large bowl until the dripping stops. Or spoon the rhubarb into a damp jelly bag and let drain. Discard the pulp. Measure out 3 cups rhubarb juice.

2. Thoroughly crush the raspberries. Place three layers of damp fine-knit cheesecloth in a large bowl. Spoon the crushed raspberries into the center of the cheesecloth. Tie the ends of the cheesecloth together and hang over a large bowl until the dripping stops. Or spoon the raspberries into a damp jelly bag and let drain. Discard the pulp and seeds. Measure out ¾ cup raspberry juice.

3. In an 8-quart stainless steel stockpot, combine the rhubarb juice, raspberry juice, and sugar. Bring the mixture to a full rolling boil over medium-high heat, stirring constantly.

4. Stir in the entire contents of both pectin pouches. Return the mixture to a full rolling boil, stirring constantly. Boil for 1 minute, stirring constantly. Remove the pot from the heat and quickly skim off any foam.

5. Immediately ladle the jelly into hot jars, leaving ¼-inch headspace. Wipe the jar rims and threads with a clean, damp paper towel. Apply hot lids and screw bands.

6. Process 4-ounce, 8-ounce, and pint jars in a water bath canner for 10 minutes (see p. 34 for instructions). Remove from the water bath canner and let cool for 12 to 24 hours. Check the seals and remove the screw bands. Store jars in a cool, dry, dark place for up to 1 year.

Wild Grape Jelly

CONTRIBUTOR: DONNA WREN, MASSACHUSETTS

MAKES ABOUT NINE 8-OUNCE JARS

5 pounds wild grapes or Concord grapes

2 cups water

1 box (1.75 ounces) powdered pectin

7 cups granulated sugar

The Wren family is pretty traditional when it comes to grape jelly. Donna has made this jelly with other kinds of grapes, such as Muscat, but everyone always gravitates back to the dark purple Concord. Wild grapes in their area of Massachusetts are generally "fox grapes," of which Concord grapes are a cultivar. These wild grapes are a little smaller and have a more concentrated flavor, which translates to a richer jelly.

1. In an 8-quart stainless steel stockpot, combine the grapes and water. Bring the mixture to a simmer over medium heat and cook until the grapes soften and the skins start to burst, about 5 minutes. Using a vegetable masher or a large spoon, crush the grapes, then continue to simmer until the grapes are very soft and break down, at least another 5 minutes.

2. Remove the pot from the heat. Strain the mixture through a fine-mesh sieve lined with several layers of damp fine-knit cheesecloth or a damp jelly bag placed over a large bowl. Measure 5 cups of grape juice. If you do not get 5 cups of juice, add enough water to make 5 cups.

3. Rinse and dry the stockpot. In the pot, combine the grape juice and pectin. Bring the mixture to a full rolling boil over medium-high heat, stirring constantly.

4. Add the sugar and stir until completely dissolved. Return the mixture to a full rolling boil, stirring constantly. Boil for 1 minute, stirring constantly. Remove the pot from the heat and skim off any foam.

5. Ladle the jelly into hot jars, leaving ¼-inch headspace. Remove any air bubbles. Wipe the jar rims and threads with a clean, damp paper towel. Apply hot lids and screw bands.

6. Process 4-ounce, 8-ounce, and pint jars in a water bath canner for 10 minutes (see p. 34 for instructions). Remove from the water bath canner and let cool for 12 to 24 hours. Check the seals and remove the screw bands. Store jars in a cool, dry, dark place for up to 1 year.

DONNA WREN

ARLINGTON, MASSACHUSETTS

DONNA WREN admits she is not much of a gardener. But she is a forager. "I have a place memory for foods. When I drive by a particular street, I remember that a friend on that road has grapes. I think of blueberries when I go by the hill where they grow, no matter the time of year. My family is mostly used to my craziness, especially when I drag them out of bed early to go pick berries before it gets too hot." Donna knows where all the good local spots are for blackberries, elderberries, blueberries—you name it. "Preserving the food preserves the memory of the experience of getting the food. Going strawberry picking with a friend. Foraging for wild blueberries and coming across a deer. I am also a collector, and canning is a way of collecting unusual ingredients, much like a prized butterfly." She makes it a point to try to preserve paw paws, black locust flowers, elderberries, Muscat grapes, and any other ingredient with limited availability.

"Preserving the food preserves the memory of the experience of getting the food."

"Canning was not really something my mother did. Once, when my grandmother came to visit, our crabapple tree was covered in fruit. She insisted upon making crabapple jelly. Well, we had jars and jars and jars of it. We were still finding jars in the storage room years later!" But, to Donna, canning

seemed like fun, so she later tried it herself. "It feels great to make recipes handed down from both of my grandmothers."

She has also dabbled in fermentation. "My husband calls me a food fundamentalist— I like to go back to the original techniques when I can. We've brewed beer together, and I've made cheese and yogurt and sausage, and anything else that seems like a skill worth knowing." Donna blogs about her experiences, partly as a way to write down recipes that she has tried, maybe altered a bit, or made up herself. "Sometimes my blog posts have a funny story to tell. Failure is particularly funny, and I have my fair share!"

Mint Jelly

CONTRIBUTOR: LINDA J. AMENDT, CALIFORNIA

MAKES ABOUT SIX
8-OUNCE JARS

3½ cups firmly packed chopped fresh mint leaves

4½ cups water

¼ cup strained freshly squeezed lemon juice

A few drops of green and blue food coloring

6½ cups granulated sugar

2 pouches (3 ounces each) liquid pectin

SERVING SUGGESTION

If you love the flavor combination of chocolate and mint, try spreading a thin layer of warmed mint jelly on chocolate cake layers before frosting.

You can use any variety of mint to make jelly, but Linda likes to use a combination of spearmint and lemon mint leaves for a strong mint flavor that pairs well with food.

1. In a 4-quart stainless steel stockpot, over medium-high heat, combine the mint leaves and water and bring to a boil. Remove the pot from the heat, cover, and let stand for 30 minutes.

2. Strain the mint pulp and juice through a fine-mesh sieve. Discard the pulp. Rinse the sieve and line with four layers of damp fine-knit cheesecloth. Strain the juice through the cheesecloth two times, rinsing the cheesecloth between each straining. Refrigerate the juice for several hours or overnight. Slowly pour the juice into another container, being careful to leave the sediment behind. Discard the sediment. For crystal-clear juice, strain the juice through a damp coffee filter, if desired.

3. Measure out 3½ cups of mint juice. Stir in the lemon juice. Add a few drops of food coloring to reach the desired shade of green. The color will lighten after the addition of the sugar.

4. In an 8-quart stainless steel stockpot over medium heat, combine the mint juice and sugar, stirring constantly until the sugar is completely dissolved. Increase the heat to medium high and bring to a full rolling boil, stirring constantly. Stir in both pouches of pectin. Return the mixture to a full rolling boil, stirring constantly. Boil for 1 minute, stirring constantly.

5. Remove the pot from the heat and quickly skim off any foam.

6. Immediately ladle the jelly into hot jars, leaving ¼-inch headspace. Wipe the jar rims and threads with a clean, damp paper towel. Apply hot lids and screw bands.

7. Process 4-ounce, 8-ounce, and pint jars in a water bath canner for 10 minutes (see p. 34 for instructions). Remove from the water bath canner and let cool for 12 to 24 hours. Check the seals and remove the screw bands. Store jars in a cool, dry, dark place for up to 1 year.

Raspberry Jelly

CONTRIBUTOR: LINDA J. AMENDT, CALIFORNIA

**MAKES ABOUT EIGHT
8-OUNCE JARS**

3½ quarts fresh or
frozen whole raspberries,
crushed

7½ cups granulated
sugar

2 pouches (3 ounces
each) liquid pectin

TIP

If using frozen ber-
ries, measure the
berries while still
frozen, then thaw
and crush.

Raspberry jelly is one of Linda's favorite flavors of jellies. This one is also very fragrant, and it has won many blue ribbons, special awards, and Best of Show. Because you can use either fresh or frozen raspberries in this recipe, you can make raspberry jelly throughout the year.

1. Place the crushed raspberries in an 8-quart stainless steel stockpot and bring to a boil over medium-high heat. Reduce the heat, cover, and simmer for 5 minutes. Remove the pot from the heat and let stand for 30 minutes.

2. Strain the raspberry pulp and juice through a fine-mesh sieve. Discard the pulp and seeds. Rinse the sieve and line with four layers of damp fine-knit cheesecloth. Strain the juice through the cheesecloth two times, rinsing the cheesecloth between each straining. Refrigerate the juice for several hours or overnight. Slowly pour the juice into another container, being careful not to disturb the sediment in the bottom of the container. Discard the sediment. For crystal-clear juice, strain the juice through a damp coffee filter, if desired. Measure out 4 cups of raspberry juice.

3. In an 8-quart stainless steel stockpot, over medium heat, combine the raspberry juice and sugar, stirring constantly until the sugar is completely dissolved. Increase the heat to medium high and bring to a full rolling boil, stirring constantly. Stir in both pouches of pectin. Return the mixture to a full rolling boil, stirring constantly. Boil for 1 minute, stirring constantly.

4. Remove the pot from the heat and quickly skim off any foam.

5. Immediately ladle the jelly into hot jars, leaving ¼-inch headspace. Wipe the jar rims and threads with a clean, damp paper towel. Apply hot lids and screw bands.

6. Process 4-ounce, 8-ounce, and pint jars in a water bath canner for 10 minutes (see p. 34 for instructions). Remove from the water bath canner and let cool for 12 to 24 hours. Check the seals and remove the screw bands. Store jars in a cool, dry, dark place for up to 1 year.

Crabapple Jelly

CONTRIBUTOR: CATHIE MERRIHEW, VERMONT

MAKES ABOUT ELEVEN 8-OUNCE JARS

5 pounds crabapples

5 cups water

⅓ cup powdered pectin

1 package (3 to 4 ounces) mulling spices

9 cups granulated sugar

Sweet and spicy, this jelly is a Merrihew family favorite. Mulling spices can be purchased at most apple orchards or online. The package contains about 2 tablespoons of fragrant spices including cinnamon sticks, whole or broken cloves, and nutmeg pieces, and comes with a small cloth bag to hold them.

1. Cut the crabapples in half and remove the stems and blossom ends. Do not peel. Place the apples in an 8-quart stainless steel stockpot and add the water. Bring to a boil over medium-high heat, stirring occasionally. Reduce the heat, cover, and simmer, stirring occasionally, until the apples are soft, 30 to 40 minutes. Using a vegetable masher or the back of a large spoon, gently crush the cooked apples, then cover and cook for another 5 to 7 minutes. Remove the pot from the heat.

2. Strain the apple mixture through a fine-mesh sieve lined with several layers of damp fine-knit cheesecloth. Strain again and measure out 7 cups of clear crabapple juice. Rinse out the stockpot.

3. In the stockpot, combine the crabapple juice and pectin. Add the bag of mulling spices then bring the mixture to a full rolling bowl over medium-high heat, stirring constantly.

4. Add the sugar and stir until completely dissolved. Return the mixture to a full rolling boil, stirring constantly. Boil for 1 minute, stirring constantly. Remove the pot from the heat, skim off any foam, and remove the spice bag.

5. Ladle the jelly into hot jars, leaving ¼-inch headspace. Remove any air bubbles. Wipe the jar rims and threads with a clean, damp paper towel. Apply hot lids and screw bands.

6. Process 4-ounce, 8-ounce, and pint jars in a water bath canner for 10 minutes (see p. 34 for instructions). Remove from the water bath canner and let cool for 12 to 24 hours. Check the seals and remove the screw bands. Store jars in a cool, dry, dark place for up to 1 year.

Cranberry Jelly

CONTRIBUTOR: LINDA J. AMENDT, CALIFORNIA

**MAKES ABOUT SIX
8-OUNCE JARS**

**5 cups fresh or frozen
whole cranberries**

4½ cups water

6 cups granulated sugar

**1 pouch (3 ounces) liquid
pectin**

SERVING SUGGESTION

Cranberry jelly can be
served on toast or along-
side meat or poultry
dishes. Put it out on your
Thanksgiving breakfast
table, too.

Cranberries make a lovely red jelly with a tangy flavor. If you
don't want to make your own juice, use bottled unsweetened
100% cranberry juice and not cranberry juice cocktail, which
can unbalance the recipe and prevent the jelly from setting.

1. In a 4-quart stainless steel stockpot over medium-high heat,
   combine the cranberries and water and bring to a boil. Reduce
   the heat, cover, and boil gently for 15 minutes, or until all of the
   berries have popped their skins and turned soft. Remove the pot
   from the heat and let stand for 1 hour.

2. Strain the cranberry pulp and juice through a fine-mesh sieve. Discard the pulp and seeds. Rinse the sieve and line with four layers of
   damp fine-knit cheesecloth. Strain the juice through the cheesecloth two times, rinsing the cheesecloth between each straining.
   Refrigerate the juice for several hours or overnight. Slowly pour
   the juice into another container, being careful not to disturb the
   sediment in the bottom of the container. Discard the sediment.
   For crystal-clear juice, strain the juice through a damp coffee
   filter, if desired. Measure out 4 cups of cranberry juice.

3. In an 8-quart stainless steel stockpot, over medium heat, combine the cranberry juice and sugar, stirring constantly until the
   sugar is completely dissolved. Increase the heat to medium high
   and bring to a full rolling boil, stirring constantly. Stir in the
   pectin. Return the mixture to a full rolling boil, stirring constantly. Boil for 1 minute, stirring constantly. Remove the pot
   from the heat and quickly skim off any foam.

4. Immediately ladle the jelly into hot jars, leaving ¼-inch headspace. Wipe the jar rims and threads with a clean, damp paper
   towel. Apply hot lids and screw bands.

5. Process 4-ounce, 8-ounce, and pint jars in a water bath canner for
   10 minutes (see p. 34 for instructions). Remove from the water
   bath canner and let cool for 12 to 24 hours. Check the seals and
   remove the screw bands. Store jars in a cool, dry, dark place for
   up to 1 year.

Blackberry Jelly

CONTRIBUTOR: LAURA MILOSAVICH, COLORADO

**MAKES ABOUT EIGHT
8-OUNCE JARS**

**4 cups whole
blackberries**

4 cups water

**1 box (1.75 ounces)
powdered pectin**

**½ teaspoon unsalted
butter (optional)**

**4½ cups granulated
sugar**

This is a wonderful jelly to use on top of pancakes, toast, or waffles. It is also perfect for a PB&J sandwich. For a decadent treat, smear it on blue cheese-topped crostini.

1. In an 8-quart stainless steel stockpot, lightly mash the blackberries. Stir in the water, cover the pot, and simmer over medium heat, stirring occasionally, for about 15 minutes. Remove the pot from the heat.

2. Strain the blackberry mixture through a fine-mesh sieve lined with several layers of damp fine-knit cheesecloth or a damp jelly bag. Discard the pulp and seeds. Measure out 3¾ cups blackberry juice. If necessary, add up to ½ cup water to the juice to obtain the exact measurement.

3. In an 8-quart stainless steel stockpot, combine the blackberry juice, pectin, and butter, if using. Bring the mixture to a full rolling boil over medium-high heat, stirring constantly.

4. Add the sugar and stir until completely dissolved. Return the mixture to a full rolling boil, stirring constantly. Boil for 1 minute, stirring constantly. Remove the pot from the heat and skim off any foam.

5. Ladle the jelly into hot jars, leaving ¼-inch headspace. Remove any air bubbles. Wipe the jar rims and threads with a clean, damp paper towel. Apply hot lids and screw bands.

6. Process 4-ounce, 8-ounce, and pint jars in a water bath canner for 10 minutes (see p. 34 for instructions). Remove from the water bath canner and let cool for 12 to 24 hours. Check the seals and remove the screw bands. Store jars in a cool, dry, dark place for up to 1 year.

Gooseberry Jelly

CONTRIBUTOR: MELINDA REESE, VIRGINIA

**MAKES ABOUT SIX
8-OUNCE JARS**

3 pounds gooseberries
(about 6 quarts)

1 package (1.75 ounces)
powdered pectin

5½ cups granulated
sugar

Gooseberries are light green berries about the size of a quarter. One year, Melinda's grandmother gave her some gooseberries that had pink lines radiating out from the base. She made gooseberry jelly that had a beautiful pink color instead of the traditional light green.

1. Remove and discard the gooseberry stems and crush the berries.

2. Place the crushed gooseberries in an 8-quart stainless steel stockpot. Slowly heat the berries over medium heat, stirring frequently, until the juices begin to flow and the berries come to a boil. Reduce the heat; cover and simmer for 15 minutes, stirring occasionally. Remove the pot from the heat.

3. Line a fine-mesh sieve with several layers of damp fine-knit cheesecloth and strain the gooseberry mixture into a large bowl; or strain it through a damp jelly bag. Discard the pulp and seeds. Measure out 4 cups of gooseberry juice. If necessary, add up to ½ cup water to the juice to obtain the exact measurement.

4. In the same 8-quart stockpot, combine the gooseberry juice and pectin. Bring the mixture to a full rolling boil over medium-high heat, stirring constantly.

5. Add the sugar and stir until completely dissolved. Return the mixture to a full rolling boil, stirring constantly. Boil for 1 minute, stirring constantly. Remove the pot from the heat and skim off any foam.

6. Ladle the jelly into hot jars, leaving ¼-inch headspace. Remove any air bubbles. Wipe the jar rims and threads with a clean, damp paper towel. Apply hot lids and screw bands.

7. Process 4-ounce, 8-ounce, and pint jars in a water bath canner for 10 minutes (see p. 34 for instructions). Remove from the water bath canner and let cool for 12 to 24 hours. Check the seals and remove the screw bands. Store jars in a cool, dry, dark place for up to 1 year.

Pear Jelly

CONTRIBUTOR: BETH WALLACE, ARKANSAS

MAKES ABOUT SIX
8-OUNCE JARS

This jelly has a unique flavor, is very pretty, and is delicious served with hot buttered biscuits or as part of a cheese plate.

4 cups pear juice (see the tip below)

2 tablespoons freshly squeezed lemon juice

1 box (1.75 ounces) powdered pectin

5 cups granulated sugar

1. In an 8-quart stainless steel stockpot, combine the pear juice, lemon juice, and pectin. Bring the mixture to a full rolling boil over medium-high heat, stirring constantly.

2. Add the sugar and stir until completely dissolved. Return the mixture to a full rolling boil, stirring constantly. Boil for 1 minute, stirring constantly. Remove the pot from the heat and skim off any foam.

3. Ladle the jelly into hot jars, leaving ¼-inch headspace. Remove any air bubbles. Wipe the jar rims and threads with a clean, damp paper towel. Apply hot lids and screw bands.

4. Process 4-ounce, 8-ounce, and pint jars in a water bath canner for 10 minutes (see p. 34 for instructions). Remove from the water bath canner and let cool for 12 to 24 hours. Check the seals and remove the screw bands. Store jars in a cool, dry, dark place for up to 1 year.

TIP

To make pear juice, combine 6 pounds peeled, cored, and finely chopped or crushed Bartlett pears and 2 cups water in an 8-quart stainless steel stockpot. Over medium-high heat, bring the mixture to a boil. Reduce the heat, cover, and simmer gently for 5 minutes. Remove the pan from the heat and skim off any foam. Let stand, covered, for 20 minutes. Strain the pear pulp and juice through a fine-mesh sieve. Discard the pulp. Rinse the sieve and line with four layers of damp fine-knit cheesecloth. Strain the juice into a large bowl, then rinse the cheesecloth and strain again.

Transfer the juice to a pitcher. Cover and refrigerate overnight. Carefully pour off the juice without disturbing the sediment in the bottom of the container. Makes 4 cups juice.

BETH WALLACE

GREENBRIER, ARKANSAS

BETH WALLACE has been canning and entering fair competitions for over 45 years. Her mother taught her how to can, and the two of them competed against each other in fair canning competitions for many years. Competing in state, county, and district fair competitions, Beth has won hundreds of blue ribbons. In 2013, she won 70 blue ribbons and 7 Best of Show awards.

The vegetables Beth cans for her blue ribbon entries come from her abundant garden. "I enjoy making jam and jelly. One of my best awards was winning the Sure-Jell award and being inducted into the Sure-Jell Hall of Fame." She is also a master food preserver, has attended several fair judging classes, taught a fair judging class, and has judged preserved foods at many county fairs.

Beth is passing on the family canning tradition to her grandson and granddaughter. They especially like to make jelly. The competitive bug has also been passed down—both of her grandchildren like entering fair competitions and are winning many blue ribbons and Best of Show awards of their own. Both used their canning skills for 4-H projects, and her granddaughter won the state record book award with her food preservation project.

Habanero Pineapple Jelly

CONTRIBUTOR: JAY GRANTIER, GEORGIA

- -

**MAKES SIX TO SEVEN
8-OUNCE JARS**

5 to 6 habanero peppers,
seeded, deribbed, and
coarsely chopped

2 red bell peppers,
seeded, deribbed, and
coarsely chopped

1 orange bell pepper,
seeded, deribbed, and
coarsely chopped

1 can (8 ounces) juice-
packed pineapple tidbits,
drained

1 cup white vinegar

1 box (1.75 ounces)
powdered pectin

Juice of 1 lemon

4 cups granulated sugar

This Georgia National Fair Best in Show winner is one of Jay's favorites and is by far the most popular among his friends.

1. In a blender or food processor, combine the habanero peppers, red and orange bell peppers, and drained pineapple tidbits. Process until very finely chopped.

2. In an 8-quart stainless steel stockpot, combine the pepper mixture and vinegar and bring to a boil over medium-high heat, stirring frequently. Reduce the heat and boil for 5 minutes, stirring frequently.

3. Add the pectin and lemon juice to the pepper mixture. Bring the mixture to a full rolling boil over medium-high heat, stirring constantly.

4. Add the sugar and stir until completely dissolved. Return the mixture to a full rolling boil, stirring constantly. Boil for 1 minute, stirring constantly. Remove the pot from the heat and skim off any foam.

5. Ladle the jelly into hot jars, leaving ¼-inch headspace. Remove any air bubbles. Wipe the jar rims and threads with a clean, damp paper towel. Apply hot lids and screw bands.

6. Process 4-ounce, 8-ounce, and pint jars in a water bath canner for 10 minutes (see p. 34 for instructions). Remove from the water bath canner and let cool for 12 to 24 hours. Check the seals and remove the screw bands. Store jars in a cool, dry, dark place for up to 1 year.

Raspberry Blackberry Jelly

CONTRIBUTOR: LINDA J. AMENDT, CALIFORNIA

**MAKES ABOUT EIGHT
8-OUNCE JARS**

**2 quarts fresh or frozen
whole raspberries,
crushed**

**1½ quarts fresh
or frozen whole
blackberries, crushed**

**7½ cups granulated
sugar**

**2 pouches (3 ounces
each) liquid pectin**

TIP

If using frozen
berries, measure
them while still
frozen, then thaw
and crush.

Whenever she has an abundance of berries, Linda freezes them to use later for making jelly. She first made this jelly when she had leftover berry juice after canning both raspberry and blackberry jellies.

1. In an 8-quart stainless steel stockpot combine the raspberries and blackberries. Bring to a boil over medium-high heat, then reduce the heat, cover, and simmer for 5 minutes. Remove the pot from the heat and let stand for 30 minutes.

2. Strain the berry pulp through a fine-mesh sieve. Discard the pulp and seeds. Rinse the sieve and line with four layers of damp fine-knit cheesecloth. Strain the juice through the cheesecloth two times, rinsing the cheesecloth between each straining. Refrigerate the juice for several hours or overnight. Slowly pour the juice into another container, being careful not to disturb the sediment in the bottom of the container. Discard the sediment. For crystal-clear juice, strain the juice through a damp coffee filter, if desired. Measure out 4½ cups of berry juice.

3. In an 8-quart stainless steel stockpot, over medium heat, combine the berry juice and sugar, stirring constantly until the sugar is completely dissolved. Increase the heat to medium high and bring to a full rolling boil, stirring constantly. Stir in both pouches of pectin. Return the mixture to a full rolling boil, stirring constantly. Boil for 1 minute, stirring constantly.

4. Remove the pot from the heat and quickly skim off any foam.

5. Immediately ladle the jelly into hot jars, leaving ¼-inch headspace. Wipe the jar rims and threads with a clean, damp paper towel. Apply hot lids and screw bands.

6. Process 4-ounce, 8-ounce, and pint jars in a water bath canner for 10 minutes (see p. 34 for instructions). Remove from the water bath canner and let cool for 12 to 24 hours. Check the seals and remove the screw bands. Store jars in a cool, dry, dark place for up to 1 year.

Apple Jelly

CONTRIBUTORS: SANDRA BEASLEY, HANNAH BEASLEY, MARIA BEASLEY,
RUTH BEASLEY, AND LYDIA BEASLEY, NORTH CAROLINA

**MAKES ABOUT SIX
8-OUNCE JARS**

4 cups unsweetened
apple juice

1 box (2 ounces)
powdered pectin

¼ teaspoon unsalted
butter (optional)

5 cups granulated sugar

The Beasley family loves biscuits for any meal of the day. And they especially like them slathered with apple jelly. This fun and easy recipe allows them to make jelly year-round so they never have to worry about running out. Bring on the biscuits!

1. In an 8-quart stainless steel stockpot, combine the apple juice, pectin, and butter, if using. Bring the mixture to a full rolling boil over medium-high heat, stirring constantly.

2. Add the sugar and stir until completely dissolved. Return the mixture to a full rolling boil, stirring constantly. Boil for 1 minute, stirring constantly. Remove the pot from the heat and skim off any foam.

3. Ladle the jelly into hot jars, leaving ¼-inch headspace. Remove any air bubbles. Wipe the jar rims and threads with a clean, damp paper towel. Apply hot lids and screw bands.

4. Process 4-ounce, 8-ounce, and pint jars in a water bath canner for 10 minutes (see p. 34 for instructions). Remove from the water bath canner and let cool for 12 to 24 hours. Check the seals and remove the screw bands. Store jars in a cool, dry, dark place for up to 1 year.

THE BEASLEY FAMILY

PFAFFTOWN, NORTH CAROLINA

CANNING SINCE 2000, SANDRA BEASLEY is raising a family of blue ribbon canners. Her family began canning as a result of participating in their community fair. The first year, Sandra and her two oldest daughters, Hannah and Maria, all entered baked goods, and Sandra entered some art pieces. When they visited the Dixie Classic Fair that same year, Sandra talked with Betty Frindle, who ran the canning department. "She was a great canning enthusiast and encouraged me to work on canning with my girls. That next year I worked hard to learn as much as I could about canning, and my father purchased a pressure canner for us. He wanted us to make him some homemade pickles and that was a great deal for us! I made a few entries, and to my utter surprise, I won Judges' Choice and the Ball Soft Spread award for my orange marmalade." Sandra admired all of the other competitors' entries and was inspired to explore canning even more.

"It is a blessing to know my family has healthy food to eat."

Every year, the family picks strawberries and blueberries at a local patch. They also have a friend who owns a farm and generously lets them pick some of his vegetables, and their own little family garden and grapevines yield enough produce to can some of the harvest. "The children became interested in canning as well, so I began working with them. You should see our little kitchen that, at one point, held even our oldest son—for a total of six people, all canning. I had to work out a schedule of who did what when. My own canning had to wait until the little ones were in bed or before they arose in the morning. And did the house ever get hot!"

For Sandra, the most rewarding part about canning is knowing that her children know how to preserve good food safely. "Have we ever had fun with all those strawberries to wash and cap, corn shucking with corn silk everywhere, and sticky jam and berry juice all over the floor!" Sandra, Hannah, Maria, Ruth, and Lydia Beasley have each brought home a bunch of blue ribbons, and every one of them has won at least one special award for their excellent canning entries.

Sandra says, "I enjoy preserving freshly harvested food that lasts until the next growing season, as well as having that special food set aside and ready to eat. I also like continuing the legacy of Great-Great Grandma Robb and Great Grandma Mary Wilcox. I remember admiring Great Grandma's canned goods in her cellar when we'd visit, and it is a blessing to know my family has healthy food to eat."

Honey Jelly

CONTRIBUTOR: MILDRED RINGHAUSEN, ILLINOIS

MAKES ABOUT FOUR
8-OUNCE JARS

3 cups honey

1 cup water

1 pouch (3 ounces) liquid pectin

TIP

Clover honey or orange blossom honey are wonderful choices to use for making this delightful jelly.

This sweet, blue ribbon jelly stays on a biscuit for a delicious "no mess" treat.

1. In a large saucepan, combine the honey and water, then bring to a full rolling boil over medium-high heat, stirring constantly.

2. Stir in the pectin. Return the mixture to a full rolling boil, stirring constantly. Boil for 1 minute, stirring constantly.

3. Remove the pan from the heat and quickly skim off any foam.

4. Immediately ladle the jelly into hot jars, leaving ¼-inch headspace. Wipe the jar rims and threads with a clean, damp paper towel. Apply hot lids and screw bands.

5. Process 4-ounce, 8-ounce, and pint jars in a water bath canner for 10 minutes (see p. 34 for instructions). Remove from the water bath canner and let cool for 12 to 24 hours. Check the seals and remove the screw bands. Store jars in a cool, dry, dark place for up to 1 year.

MILDRED RINGHAUSEN

HARDIN, ILLINOIS

MILDRED RINGHAUSEN first learned to can as a child, helping her mother put up food for the family of eight. As an adult, she started canning again in the 1980s and has been entering fair competitions since 1990. In addition to the Illinois State Fair, Mildred also participates in the Missouri State Fair and the Clay County Fair in Missouri. She has also won blue ribbons for her tatting, crocheting, knitting, and embroidery.

> Mildred cans in the same kitchen used by her husband's grandmother and processes her canning jars in the same reliable pressure canner used by her mother and grandmother.

Mildred and her husband, Dwight, are the third generation to live in his family's centennial farm. She cans in the same kitchen used by her husband's grandmother and processes her canning jars in the same reliable pressure canner used by her mother and grandmother. Serving quality food to loved ones and the pleasure of displaying her canned products in the kitchen are the most enjoyable parts of canning for Mildred.

An avid cookbook collector and cook, Mildred's favorite competitive canning experience was winning a blue ribbon, Best of Division silver tray, and a First Champion purple rosette for her Basketweave Carrot Coins (see the recipe on p. 152). "I first saw my mother can carrots using the basketweave, or brick, pattern when I was 4 or 5 years old. I was so impressed that the memory has stayed with me all these years." It was her husband who encouraged Mildred to can the carrots in the special pattern and enter them in the fair competition. "My mother was my idol, and she was very creative. She won a blue ribbon for carrots canned in this basketweave pattern some 60 years ago, so she must be smiling down from heaven at my Best of Division award from the Illinois State Fair."

Wine Jelly

CONTRIBUTOR: LINDA J. AMENDT, CALIFORNIA

**MAKES ABOUT SEVEN
8-OUNCE JARS**

4 cups wine

6 cups granulated sugar

2 pouches (3 ounces each) liquid pectin

Linda likes to use Cabernet Sauvignon, Chardonnay, or White Zinfandel wine to make this jelly and has won multiple blue ribbons and special awards with each varietal. She has also won blue ribbons using Merlot and Sauvignon Blanc wines, and even Champagne. Her dad's favorite was the Cabernet Sauvignon jelly. Any full-bodied wine works well in this jelly. The key is to not let the wine boil; otherwise, the jelly may take on an unpleasant flavor.

1. In an 8-quart stainless steel stockpot, combine the wine and sugar. Heat the wine over medium heat to just below simmering, stirring constantly until the sugar is completely dissolved. Tiny bubbles will form on the bottom of the pan, but not rise to the surface. Do not allow the wine to boil. Remove the pot from the heat.

2. Stir in the entire contents of both pectin pouches until thoroughly combined. Quickly skim off any foam.

3. Immediately ladle the jelly into hot jars, leaving ¼-inch headspace. Wipe the jar rims and threads with a clean, damp paper towel. Apply hot lids and screw bands.

4. Process 4-ounce, 8-ounce, and pint jars in a water bath canner for 10 minutes (see p. 34 for instructions). Remove from the water bath canner and let cool for 12 to 24 hours. Check the seals and remove the screw bands. Store jars in a cool, dry, dark place for up to 1 year.

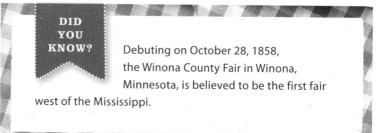

DID YOU KNOW? Debuting on October 28, 1858, the Winona County Fair in Winona, Minnesota, is believed to be the first fair west of the Mississippi.

Lavender Jelly

CONTRIBUTOR: JAY GRANTIER, GEORGIA

MAKES FIVE TO SIX
8-OUNCE JARS

3½ cups water

¾ cup dried culinary
lavender flowers

¼ cup freshly squeezed
lemon juice

1 box (1.75 ounces)
powdered pectin

4 cups granulated sugar

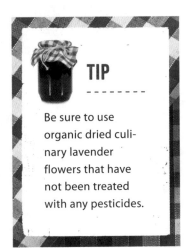

TIP

Be sure to use organic dried culinary lavender flowers that have not been treated with any pesticides.

This recipe was inspired by a trip Jay took to France a few years ago. The jelly has a delicate rose color.

1. In a large saucepan over medium-high heat, bring the water to a boil. Remove the pan from the heat and stir in the dried lavender flowers. Cover and let steep for 30 minutes.

2. Strain the lavender liquid through a fine-mesh sieve lined with several layers of damp fine-knit cheesecloth. Discard the lavender flowers.

3. In an 8-quart stainless steel stockpot, combine the lavender liquid, lemon juice, and pectin. Bring the mixture to a full rolling boil over medium-high heat, stirring constantly.

4. Add the sugar and stir until completely dissolved. Return the mixture to a full rolling boil, stirring constantly. Boil for 1 minute, stirring constantly. Remove the pot from the heat and skim off any foam.

5. Ladle the jelly into hot jars, leaving ¼-inch headspace. Remove any air bubbles. Wipe the jar rims and threads with a clean, damp paper towel. Apply hot lids and screw bands.

6. Process 4-ounce, 8-ounce, and pint jars in a water bath canner for 10 minutes (see p. 34 for instructions). Remove from the water bath canner and let cool for 12 to 24 hours. Check the seals and remove the screw bands. Store jars in a cool, dry, dark place for up to 1 year.

* Marmalades & Preserves *

Marmalades and preserves have many admirers for their intense flavor and beautiful appearance with fruit tantalizingly suspended in a tender, shimmery jelly. They are also the two most challenging preserves to perfect. Once you understand the preparation techniques, you will be making top-notch marmalades and preserves, too.

Making Marmalades

A marmalade is a sweet and tangy spread made from citrus fruit. It normally contains both small chopped pieces of citrus along with thin strips of the colored outer peel of the citrus. Both the fruit and peel are evenly suspended in a shimmering, translucent jelly that will hold its shape and mound up in a spoon. The texture of marmalade is similar to that of jam. Marmalades can be made with a variety of citrus fruits, a combination of two or more citrus fruits, and by using both citrus and other fruits.

There are two keys to making an exceptional marmalade. The first is to use only the outer colored portion of the peel of the citrus, known as the zest. The white portion of the peel, called the pith, is very fibrous and will give the finished marmalade a bitter, unpleasant flavor. Zest should be cut into very thin strips, not thick strips or large chunks. Large strips of cooked peel can be very tough and difficult to chew and will detract from the texture of the spread. I use a handheld zesting tool to quickly and easily remove several thin, uniform strips of zest from the citrus fruit with each stroke. A vegetable peeler can be used to remove only the outer colored portion of the peel and then the zest can be sliced very thin with a sharp knife.

The second step to creating a great marmalade is to cut away the fibrous membrane that surrounds each citrus fruit section. The white membrane is tough and chewy, and becomes even tougher when cooked. It detracts from both the flavor and texture of the marmalade. Although it is more work, taking the time to remove the membrane from the sections before chopping the fruit will produce a marmalade with an intense citrus flavor and tender texture. It is well worth the effort.

To separate the fruit sections from the membrane, after removing the zest, slice the top and bottom off of the citrus. Place the citrus on a cutting board, cut side down, and use a sharp knife to cut the peel from the citrus in thick strips. Be sure to remove all of the white pith from the outside of the citrus. Holding the peeled citrus in your hand, carefully use a small paring knife to cut between the citrus sections and the membrane. Discard the membrane, remove any seeds from the sections, and chop the citrus sections.

Making Preserves

The crowning jewel of soft spreads, perfect preserves contain brightly colored translucent fruit with intense flavor that is tender and glistens, making them completely irresistible. When it comes to elegance, preserves are hard to beat!

The distinguishing characteristic of a quality preserve is the beautiful pieces of fruit distributed throughout the jar. Preserves are made with small whole fruit or larger fruits that have been cut into uniformly sized pieces. During the cooking process, dissolved sugar penetrates the fruit cells, giving the fruit pieces a luminous, shimmering appearance. The cooked fruit holds its shape and the pieces are evenly suspended in a soft jelly or very thick syrup.

While preserves have traditionally been made from only one kind of fruit, as with jams, mixed fruit preserves are rapidly gaining in popularity among home canners. One, two, or even three fruits can be used together in a preserve to create a unique flavor combination.

❋ PREVENTING FLOATING FRUIT ❋

As with jams, floating fruit in preserves is a common problem for many home canners. To help prevent floating fruit, choose fully ripe fruit—underripe fruit is more likely to float. Also, use fruit that is not overly juicy. Fruit that is very juicy creates a high jelly-to-fruit ratio, making the finished preserve softer, significantly increasing the chances the fruit pieces will float to the top. Letting the fruit and sugar mixture stand for a while before cooking allows the fruit to absorb more sugar, making it heavier and less likely to float.

Orange Marmalade

CONTRIBUTORS: SANDRA BEASLEY AND HANNAH BEASLEY, NORTH CAROLINA

**MAKES ABOUT SEVEN
8-OUNCE JARS**

4 medium oranges

2 medium lemons

2½ cups water

⅛ teaspoon baking soda

1 box (2 ounces)
powdered pectin

6½ cups granulated
sugar

This recipe has been a Beasley family favorite for years. Ever since Hannah was a toddler, only orange marmalade would do on her biscuit! It was also Sandra's first blue ribbon winner and won the Judges' Choice award at the Dixie Classic Fair.

1. Using a soft scrub brush, thoroughly scrub the oranges and lemons, then rinse well and dry. Using a vegetable peeler or paring knife, remove only the outer colored portion of the peel in strips. Slice the peel into very thin strips of uniform size. Using a knife, peel the oranges and lemons, removing all of the outer white pith and membrane. Cut the fruit sections away from the white membrane and remove any seeds. Discard the membrane and seeds. Chop the orange and lemon sections, reserving the juices.

2. In an 8-quart stainless steel stockpot, combine the orange and lemon peel, water, and baking soda, and bring to a boil over medium heat. Reduce the heat and simmer, covered, for 20 minutes, stirring occasionally.

3. Add the chopped oranges and lemons and the reserved juice to the pot with the cooked peel. Simmer, covered, for 10 minutes.

4. Remove the cover and slowly stir in the pectin. Increase the heat to medium high and bring to a full rolling boil, stirring constantly. Add the sugar and stir until completely dissolved. Return the mixture to a full rolling boil, stirring constantly. Boil for 1 minute, stirring constantly. Remove the pot from the heat and skim off any foam.

5. Ladle the marmalade into hot jars, leaving ¼-inch headspace. Remove any air bubbles. Wipe the jar rims and threads with a clean, damp paper towel. Apply hot lids and screw bands.

6. Process 4-ounce, 8-ounce, and pint jars in a water bath canner for 10 minutes (see p. 34 for instructions). Remove from the water bath canner and let cool for 12 to 24 hours. Check the seals and remove the screw bands. Store jars in a cool, dry, dark place for up to 1 year.

Strawberry Lemon Marmalade

CONTRIBUTOR: SHEILA BUSTILLOS, TEXAS

**MAKES FIVE TO SIX
8-OUNCE JARS**

2 to 4 lemons

2 cups water

4 cups blended or
crushed strawberries
(4 to 5 pints whole
strawberries)

1 box (2 ounces)
powdered pectin

6 cups granulated sugar

Everyone who tries this marmalade loves it. Maybe it's because of the sweet-sour flavor from the berries and fresh lemon, or because it's delicious spread on anything—or eaten straight from the jar. Sheila uses a hand mixer to blend the fruit, which makes for a thicker and creamier marmalade. If you enjoy a marmalade with pieces of fruit and that spreads more like a preserve, crush the strawberries instead.

1. Using a soft scrub brush, thoroughly scrub the lemons, then rinse well and dry. Using a zester, remove only the outer colored portion of the lemon peel in thin strips. Or use a paring knife to remove the peel and then slice it into very thin strips. Measure out ¼ cup. Squeeze one of the lemons and measure out 1 tablespoon of juice.

2. In an 8-quart stainless steel stockpot, combine the lemon peel and water. Bring the mixture to a boil over medium-high heat and boil until the peel is softened, about 5 minutes. Drain off and discard the liquid.

3. Add the strawberries and lemon juice to the boiled peel and mix well. Stir in the pectin until well combined. Bring the mixture to a full rolling boil over medium-high heat, stirring constantly.

4. Add the sugar and stir until completely dissolved. Return the mixture to a full rolling boil, stirring constantly. Boil for 1 minute, stirring constantly. Remove the pot from the heat and skim off any foam.

5. Ladle the marmalade into hot jars, leaving ¼-inch headspace. Remove any air bubbles. Wipe the jar rims and threads with a clean, damp paper towel. Apply hot lids and screw bands.

6. Process 4-ounce, 8-ounce, and pint jars in a water bath canner for 10 minutes (see p. 34 for instructions). Remove from the water bath canner and let cool for 12 to 24 hours. Check the seals and remove the screw bands. Store jars in a cool, dry, dark place for up to 1 year.

SHEILA BUSTILLOS

DENTON, TEXAS

SHEILA BUSTILLOS has fond memories of her grandpa, who was a baby during the Great Depression. Something significant she learned from her grandpa was the importance and excitement of canning food. "He passed down his joy for canning to my mother, and now it's been passed down to me. For me, canning helps create a happy mental space where I revere family and friends who have passed and treasure family and friends in my present. I love to can alone, yet I would much rather can with someone."

"Jams, jellies, sauces, stews, vegetables—you name it, I can can it."

Sheila grows her own produce, but admits she doesn't have much of a green thumb. In addition to canning food she's grown herself, Sheila also cans produce she picks at local farms and seasonal fruits and vegetables from local grocery stores. "Jams, jellies, sauces, stews, vegetables—you name it, I can can it." She once canned hundreds of 4-ounce jars of jams and jellies for a friend's wedding reception, as gifts for the guests. "I love canning in Texas—hot days spent over a hot stove. Mostly, I think about how excited friends and family get when I hand them a jar of the latest thing I've canned."

After canning her own food for about 6 years, she started teaching canning classes with local community groups in San Marcos, Texas, and with Natural Grocers in Denton, Texas. Sheila enjoys meeting others who love to can and learned that people who grow their own produce are a small minority in her classes. Thrifty shoppers, fans of farmers' markets, and those who like to know exactly what is in their food are all attending her classes and learning to can.

Orange Jack Marmalade

CONTRIBUTOR: TERRY COAKLEY, CALIFORNIA

MAKES ABOUT FIVE 8-OUNCE JARS

12 to 14 medium Valencia oranges

¼ cup freshly squeezed lemon juice

⅛ teaspoon baking soda

5 cups granulated sugar

½ teaspoon unsalted butter (optional)

1 pouch (3 ounces) liquid pectin

¼ cup Jack Daniels, or other Tennessee whiskey

DID YOU KNOW?

You can buy a barrel filled with Jack Daniels from the company for the bargain price of about $10,000! Not only do you get 240 bottles of whiskey in that barrel, but the barrel is yours to keep too.

This wonderful marmalade earned Terry two Best of Show awards for all preserved foods entries at the Orange County Fair. Jack Daniels® is a smooth, oak-barrel-aged Tennessee whiskey. It gives this luscious orange marmalade a warm flavor and special kick. Brandy or bourbon may be substituted for the whiskey.

1. Using a zester, remove only the outer colored portion of the peel in very thin strips from 6 of the oranges. Coarsely chop the strips of peel. Or use a paring knife to remove the peel and then slice it into very thin strips and coarsely chop. Peel all of the oranges, removing all of the outer white pith. Cut the fruit sections away from the membrane and remove any seeds. Discard the pith and membrane. Finely chop the fruit, reserving the juice. Combine the fruit and enough of the juice to measure 2½ cups.

2. In an 8-quart stainless steel stockpot, combine the chopped oranges, lemon juice, and baking soda. Bring to a boil over medium-high heat, then reduce the heat, cover, and simmer gently for 8 minutes. Stir in the orange peel until well distributed. Cover and simmer for 3 minutes.

3. Gradually stir in the sugar and the butter, if using. Increase the heat to medium high and bring to a full rolling boil, stirring constantly. Stir in the pectin. Return the mixture to a full rolling boil, stirring constantly. Boil for 1 minute, stirring constantly.

4. Remove the pot from the heat and skim off any foam. Stir in the whiskey, then let cool for 5 minutes, stirring occasionally.

5. Ladle the marmalade into hot jars, leaving ¼-inch headspace. Remove any air bubbles. Wipe the jar rims and threads with a clean, damp paper towel. Apply hot lids and screw bands.

6. Process 4-ounce, 8-ounce, and pint jars in a water bath canner for 10 minutes (see p. 34 for instructions). Remove from the water bath canner and let cool for 12 to 24 hours. Check the seals and remove the screw bands. Store jars in a cool, dry, dark place for up to 1 year.

Adapted from *175 Best Jams, Jellies, Marmalades & Other Soft Spreads* by Linda J. Amendt.

TERRY COAKLEY

FOUNTAIN VALLEY, CALIFORNIA

TERRY COAKLEY decided to start canning when a plum tree in the yard went crazy with way too many plums and her husband suggested she should make jam. Not too unusual, except for the fact that Terry had lost most of her sight several years earlier and had never thought about canning. The plum jam turned out fine, so she decided to try making grape jelly. "I learned that pectin can be fickle—you could actually slice that jelly! Fortunately, my husband liked it that way; the jelly didn't ooze out of the sandwich."

> **"I made two to three batches of everything, and made everybody taste them all and help me pick the best."**

She bought some canning cookbooks and set about learning what she was doing right and how to improve her efforts. Terry kept trying different canning recipes and learned to adapt some of the preparation techniques, such as limiting the use of knives, to accommodate her limited vision. Instead of peeling peaches, plums, and some other fruits, she discovered that a grapefruit spoon does a good job of scooping the fruit out of the skin. Her husband made her a special plastic tool to accurately measure the headspace in the jars.

As she became more adept at canning, Terry's husband decided she should enter her preserves in the Orange County Fair in southern California. He kept goading her about it until she finally did. Terry thoroughly studied the entry requirements and what she needed to do to make a good impression on the judges. "I made two to three batches of everything, and made everybody taste them all and help me pick the best. I used a magnifier to make sure the headspace was clean, and to check that there wasn't any floating fruit and that you could see through my jelly. Then I took them in to the Fair and held my breath." Her careful attention to detail and remarkable canning skill paid off. The very first year she entered the fair competition, Terry won seven blue ribbons. That was all it took for her to be hooked on competing, and she continued entering the canning competition and winning blue ribbons and special awards.

After winning the overall Best of Show award in canning 3 years in a row, the OC Fair asked Terry to take a couple years off from competing, switch to the other side of the table, and become a preserved foods judge.

Red Onion Marmalade

CONTRIBUTOR: BRENDA BUSTILLOS, TEXAS

MAKES ABOUT FOUR TO FIVE
8-OUNCE JARS

1½ cups halved and thinly sliced red onions (about 2 medium onions)

½ cup finely chopped dried cranberries

¼ cup lightly packed brown sugar

¼ cup cider vinegar

2 teaspoons finely grated orange zest

2½ cups unsweetened apple juice

1 box (1.75 ounces) powdered pectin

3½ cups granulated sugar

SERVING SUGGESTION

This marmalade makes a great accompaniment or glaze for baked ham or smoked pork ribs, and also makes a great filling for a freshly baked bread product.

This special marmalade recipe is a double winner. Not only did it earn a blue ribbon for marmalade, but it was also a big hit when Brenda used it to make a sweet bread for the Texas State Fair Fleischmann's® Yeast Bake for a Cure special contest. Her Red Onion Apricot Braid won first prize and the marmalade was the key ingredient!

1. In a large skillet, over medium heat, combine the red onions, cranberries, brown sugar, and vinegar. Cook, stirring constantly, until the onions are translucent, about 10 minutes. Do not let them brown.

2. In an 8-quart stainless steel stockpot, combine the cooked onion mixture, orange zest, and apple juice. Stir in the pectin. Bring the mixture to a full rolling boil over medium-high heat, stirring constantly.

3. Add the sugar and stir constantly until completely dissolved. Return the mixture to a full rolling boil, stirring constantly. Boil for 1 minute, stirring constantly.

4. Ladle the marmalade into hot jars, leaving ¼-inch headspace. Remove any air bubbles. Wipe the jar rims and threads with a clean, damp paper towel. Apply hot lids and screw bands.

5. Process 4-ounce, 8-ounce, and pint jars in a water bath canner for 10 minutes (see p. 34 for instructions). Remove from the water bath canner and let cool for 12 to 24 hours. Check the seals and remove the screw bands. Store jars in a cool, dry, dark place for up to 1 year.

Pink Grapefruit Marmalade

CONTRIBUTOR: LINDA J. AMENDT, CALIFORNIA

MAKES ABOUT FIVE
8-OUNCE JARS

7 to 9 medium pink grapefruit

¼ cup water

⅛ teaspoon baking soda (optional)

5 cups granulated sugar

½ teaspoon unsalted butter (optional)

1 pouch (3 ounces) liquid pectin

VARIATION:
TANGERINE MARMALADE

This recipe also works very well with tangerines, mandarin oranges, or tangelos. Substitute 20 to 28 tangerines, mandarin oranges, or tangelos for the grapefruit, and remove the outer colored portion of the peel in very thin strips from 12 to 15 fruits.

Grapefruit makes a shimmering marmalade that is both sweet and tangy. Pink grapefruit produces a beautiful deep color. The darker the color of the flesh, the darker the finished color of the marmalade will be. This marmalade is also excellent made with white grapefruit (which is a little less sweet than the pink) or a combination of pink and white.

1. Using a soft scrub brush, thoroughly scrub the grapefruit, then rinse well and dry. Using a zester, remove only the outer colored portion of the peel in very thin strips from 4 of the grapefruit. Coarsely chop the strips of peel. Or use a paring knife to remove the peel and then slice it into very thin strips and coarsely chop. Measure out 1 cup. Using a knife, peel the grapefruit, removing all of the outer white pith and membrane. Cut the individual grapefruit sections away from the white membrane and remove any seeds. Discard the membrane and seeds. Chop the grapefruit sections and drain lightly, reserving the juice. Measure out 2¾ cups chopped grapefruit and add enough grapefruit juice to fill in the air gaps. Measure out an additional ½ cup of the grapefruit juice.

2. In an 8-quart stainless steel stockpot, combine the grapefruit zest, juice, water, and baking soda, if using. Bring the mixture to a boil over medium heat, then reduce the heat, cover, and simmer for 10 minutes, stirring occasionally.

3. Add the chopped grapefruit to the pot. Cover and bring to a boil, then reduce the heat and simmer for 5 minutes.

4. Uncover the pot and stir in the sugar and butter, if using. Cook the mixture over medium heat, stirring constantly, until the sugar is completely dissolved. Increase the heat to medium high and bring to a full rolling boil, stirring constantly. Stir in the pectin. Return the mixture to a full rolling boil, stirring constantly. Boil for 1 minute, stirring constantly.

5. Remove the pot from the heat and skim off any foam. Let the marmalade cool for 5 minutes, stirring occasionally.

Pink Grapefruit Marmalade and Cherry Pie Preserves (recipe on p. 126)

6. Ladle the marmalade into hot jars, leaving ¼-inch headspace. Remove any air bubbles. Wipe the jar rims and threads with a clean, damp paper towel. Apply hot lids and screw bands.

7. Process 4-ounce, 8-ounce, and pint jars in a water bath canner for 10 minutes (see p. 34 for instructions). Remove from the water bath canner and let cool for 12 to 24 hours. Check the seals and remove the screw bands. Store jars in a cool, dry, dark place for up to 1 year.

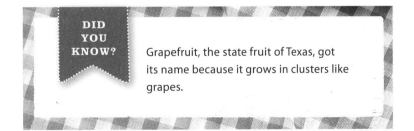

DID YOU KNOW? Grapefruit, the state fruit of Texas, got its name because it grows in clusters like grapes.

Apricot Orange Marmalade

CONTRIBUTOR: ROBIN TARBELL-THOMAS, IOWA

MAKES ABOUT SEVEN
8-OUNCE JARS

FOR THE ORANGE
MIXTURE

4 navel oranges, thinly
sliced and seeded, slices
quartered (about 2 cups)

3 lemons, thinly sliced
and seeded, slices
quartered (about
1½ cups)

6 cups water

Granulated sugar

FOR THE APRICOT
MIXTURE

4 cups water

2 cups firmly packed
dried apricots, rinsed

2 cups granulated sugar

DID
YOU
KNOW?

Every year since 1911,
the Iowa State Fair has
featured a giant butter
sculpture of a cow.

Robin prepares the apricot and orange mixtures separately and then combines them to finish the marmalade. Use this marmalade to glaze a holiday ham or turkey to add a sweet new twist.

1. Prepare the orange mixture: In a 4-quart stainless steel stockpot, combine the quartered orange and lemon slices. Add the water, cover, and let stand for 6 to 8 hours. Bring the mixture to a boil over medium-high heat. Reduce the heat and simmer for 30 minutes, then remove the pan from the heat and let cool. Cover and let stand for another 6 to 8 hours. Measure the orange mixture and return it to the pot. Add 1 cup of sugar for each 1 cup of orange mixture. Stir well, then set aside.

2. Prepare the apricot mixture: In an 8-quart stainless steel stockpot, combine the water and apricots. Cover and let stand for 8 hours. Bring the soaked apricots and water to a boil over medium-high heat, then reduce the heat and simmer until very soft, 30 to 40 minutes. Remove the pot from the heat. Press the apricot mixture through a food mill or coarse sieve, return to the pot, then bring to a boil over medium heat, stirring frequently. Stir in the sugar. Reduce the heat and simmer gently, stirring frequently, for 40 minutes. As the mixture starts to thicken, stir constantly to prevent scorching.

3. Add the orange mixture to the apricot mixture and bring to a boil over medium heat. Reduce the heat and simmer, stirring constantly, until the marmalade reaches the jelly stage (220°F at sea level), about 20 minutes.

4. Ladle the marmalade into hot jars, leaving ¼-inch headspace. Remove any air bubbles. Wipe the jar rims and threads with a clean, damp paper towel. Apply hot lids and screw bands.

5. Process 4-ounce, 8-ounce, and pint jars in a water bath canner for 10 minutes (see p. 34 for instructions). Remove from the water bath canner and let cool for 12 to 24 hours. Check the seals and remove the screw bands. Store jars in a cool, dry, dark place for up to 1 year.

Peach and Blackberry Preserves

CONTRIBUTOR: GEORGE YATES, TEXAS

**MAKES ABOUT SIX
8-OUNCE JARS**

3 cups peeled, pitted, and roughly chopped peaches (2 to 2½ pounds peaches)

1½ cups whole blackberries

5 tablespoons freshly squeezed lemon juice, strained

7 cups granulated sugar

½ teaspoon unsalted butter (optional)

1 pouch (3 ounces) liquid pectin

The combination of peaches and blackberries makes an excellent preserve. Opening a jar of these sunny preserves can warm even the coldest winter day.

1. In an 8-quart stainless steel stockpot, combine the peaches, blackberries, lemon juice, sugar, and butter, if using. Cook over medium-low heat, stirring constantly, until the sugar is dissolved. Increase the heat to medium high and bring the mixture to a full rolling boil.

2. Stir in the pectin. Return the mixture to a full rolling boil, stirring constantly. Boil for 1 minute, stirring constantly. Remove the pot from the heat and skim off any foam.

3. Ladle the preserves into hot jars, leaving ¼-inch headspace. Remove any air bubbles. Wipe the jar rims and threads with a clean, damp paper towel. Apply hot lids and screw bands.

4. Process 4-ounce, 8-ounce, and pint jars in a water bath canner for 10 minutes (see p. 34 for instructions). Remove from the water bath canner and let cool for 12 to 24 hours. Check the seals and remove the screw bands. Store jars in a cool, dry, dark place for up to 1 year.

DID YOU KNOW? Deep-fried foods are a staple at state and county fairs, with new concoctions being invented every year. At the State Fair of Texas, deep-fried chicken has been sold to visitors since the fair first opened in 1886.

Tomato Preserves

CONTRIBUTOR: CAROLYN DEMARCO, OREGON

MAKES ABOUT SIX 8-OUNCE JARS

1 tablespoon pickling spices

One ½-inch piece fresh ginger, peeled

4 cups granulated sugar

2 medium lemons, thinly sliced and seeded

¾ cup water

2 pounds red, yellow, or green tomatoes, peeled

2 teaspoons ground cinnamon

½ teaspoon ground cloves

¼ teaspoon ground allspice

¼ teaspoon ground nutmeg

SERVING SUGGESTION

Tomato preserves are great used as a toast topping, but they really shine when used to glaze meats, especially chicken. Tomato preserves can be used on their own or in combination with barbecue sauce when roasting chicken. They can also be added to a simple pan sauce to make it complex and flavorful.

Carolyn grows tomatoes every year and usually buys boxes of them as well for her canning needs. One year when she had more tomatoes left over than she knew what to do with, she decided to try something different and make them into preserves. Besides being tasty spread on toast, these tomato preserves turned out to be a very versatile condiment for meats and sauces.

1. Tie the pickling spices and piece of ginger in a spice bag or in 2 or 3 layers of fine-knit cheesecloth tied with a string.

2. In an 8-quart stainless steel stockpot, combine the spice bag, sugar, lemon slices, and water. Bring to a boil over medium-high heat, then reduce the heat and simmer for 15 minutes.

3. Add the tomatoes and simmer until they soften and break down into chunks and the syrup thickens, 20 to 30 minutes. Remove and discard the spice bag. Stir in the cinnamon, cloves, allspice, and nutmeg. Remove the pot from the heat.

4. Ladle the preserves into hot jars, leaving ¼-inch headspace. Remove any air bubbles. Wipe the jar rims and threads with a clean, damp paper towel. Apply hot lids and screw bands.

5. Process 8-ounce and pint jars in a water bath canner for 20 minutes (see p. 34 for instructions). Remove from the water bath canner and let cool for 12 to 24 hours. Check the seals and remove the screw bands. Store jars in a cool, dry, dark place for up to 1 year.

Strawberry Preserves Supreme

CONTRIBUTOR: LINDA J. AMENDT, CALIFORNIA

MAKES ABOUT NINE
8-OUNCE JARS

9 cups whole small ripe strawberries

⅓ cup freshly squeezed lemon juice

8 cups granulated sugar

½ teaspoon unsalted butter (optional)

1 pouch (3 ounces) liquid pectin

TIP

Cut medium-size berries in half. If the strawberries you have are large, cut them into quarters. Large whole berries will not absorb enough sugar and are more likely to float in the jars.

These preserves, Linda's favorite, feature large, flavorful pieces of strawberries suspended in the tender jelly and have won 12 blue ribbons and many special awards at state and county fairs across the country. During a Best of Show judging, one of the judges exclaimed about the flavor, "Some of those strawberries are still alive!" Be sure to use ripe strawberries for the best flavor and texture and to help prevent floating fruit.

1. In a large bowl, combine the strawberries and lemon juice, stirring gently to coat the berries.

2. In an 8-quart stainless steel stockpot, alternately layer the strawberries and sugar. Cover and let stand for 4 to 5 hours.

3. Cook the strawberries over medium-low heat, stirring constantly and gently, until the sugar is completely dissolved. Stir in the butter, if using. Increase the heat to medium high and bring to a boil, then reduce the heat and boil gently for 10 minutes, stirring occasionally to prevent sticking.

4. Increase the heat to medium high again and bring the mixture to a full rolling boil, stirring constantly and gently. Stir in the pectin. Return the mixture to a full rolling boil, stirring constantly. Boil for 1 minute, stirring constantly.

5. Remove the pot from the heat and skim off any foam. Let cool for 5 minutes, stirring occasionally.

6. Ladle the preserves into hot jars, leaving ¼-inch headspace. Remove any air bubbles. Wipe the jar rims and threads with a clean, damp paper towel. Apply hot lids and screw bands.

7. Process 4-ounce, 8-ounce, and pint jars in a water bath canner for 10 minutes (see p. 34 for instructions). Remove from the water bath canner and let cool for 12 to 24 hours. Check the seals and remove the screw bands. Store jars in a cool, dry, dark place for up to 1 year.

Grandma Jenkins' Fig Preserves

CONTRIBUTOR: JAY GRANTIER, GEORGIA

**MAKES FIVE TO SIX
8-OUNCE JARS**

6 pounds fresh figs,
preferably Celestial

3 medium lemons

4 pounds granulated
sugar (about 9½ cups)

This delicious preserve was named in honor of Jay's grand-mother, and he always thinks of her fondly as he prepares the fruit and stirs the bubbling pot of thickening goodness. Living in Georgia, Jay always has an abundance of figs readily available in his backyard. If you don't have Celestial figs available in your area, use your favorite locally grown fresh figs.

1. Using a sharp knife, cut off the stem and blossom end of each fig.

2. Using a soft scrub brush, thoroughly scrub 1 lemon, then rinse well and dry. Using a paring knife, remove only the outer colored portion of the lemon peel, then cut into very thin strips; set aside. Juice all 3 lemons.

3. In an 8-quart stainless steel stockpot, combine the figs and lemon juice. Pour the sugar over the figs, cover, and let stand for about 6 hours.

4. Over medium-high heat, stirring very gently to prevent scorching, bring the fig mixture to a boil. Reduce the heat and boil, stirring frequently, for 15 minutes. Remove the pot from the heat and stir in the lemon peel. Let the mixture cool, then cover and let rest for 24 hours at room temperature.

5. The next day, bring the fig mixture to a boil over medium heat, stirring frequently and gently. Reduce the heat and simmer, stirring frequently and gently, for 5 minutes.

6. Remove the pot from the heat and skim off any foam. Let the preserves cool in the pot for 5 minutes, stirring occasionally.

7. Ladle the preserves into hot jars, leaving ¼-inch headspace. Remove any air bubbles. Wipe the jar rims and threads with a clean, damp paper towel. Apply hot lids and screw bands.

8. Process 4-ounce, 8-ounce, and pint jars in a water bath canner for 10 minutes (see p. 34 for instructions). Remove from the water bath canner and let cool for 12 to 24 hours. Check the seals and remove the screw bands. Store jars in a cool, dry, dark place for up to 1 year.

Cherry Pie Preserves

CONTRIBUTOR: LINDA J. AMENDT, CALIFORNIA

**MAKES ABOUT FIVE
8-OUNCE JARS**

5 cups pitted small
sour pie cherries (about
2 pounds)

4 cups granulated sugar

⅓ cup light corn syrup

½ teaspoon unsalted
butter (optional)

1 pouch (3 ounces) liquid
pectin

1 teaspoon pure almond
extract

These preserves are like cherry pie in a jar! Linda likes to use sour cherries when she can get them but also uses sweet cherries in this recipe. If you are using sweet cherries, simply add 2 tablespoons freshly squeezed lemon juice and increase the corn syrup to ½ cup. Both versions are proven winners.

1. In an 8-quart stainless steel stockpot, layer the cherries, 2 cups of the sugar, and the corn syrup. Let stand for 20 minutes.

2. Cook the mixture over medium-low heat, stirring frequently, until the sugar is mostly dissolved. Stir in the remaining 2 cups sugar and the butter, if using, then continue to heat, stirring until the sugar is completely dissolved.

3. Increase the heat to medium high and bring the mixture to a full rolling boil, stirring constantly. Stir in the pectin. Return the mixture to a full rolling boil, stirring constantly. Boil for 1 minute, stirring constantly.

4. Remove the pot from the heat and skim off any foam. Stir in the almond extract. Let the preserves cool in the pot for 5 minutes, stirring occasionally.

5. Ladle the preserves into hot jars, leaving ¼-inch headspace. Remove any air bubbles. Wipe the jar rims and threads with a clean, damp paper towel. Apply hot lids and screw bands.

6. Process 4-ounce, 8-ounce, and pint jars in a water bath canner for 10 minutes (see p. 34 for instructions). Remove from the water bath canner and let cool for 12 to 24 hours. Check the seals and remove the screw bands. Store jars in a cool, dry, dark place for up to 1 year.

Blackberry Preserves

CONTRIBUTOR: LINDA J. AMENDT, CALIFORNIA

**MAKES ABOUT SEVEN
8-OUNCE JARS**

7 cups whole
blackberries (if using
frozen berries, do not
thaw)

6½ cups granulated
sugar

½ teaspoon unsalted
butter (optional)

1 pouch (3 ounces) liquid
pectin

TIP

- - - - - - - -

If you live on the
West Coast and see
olallieberries, buy
some—they have a
very short growing
season. Olallieberries
are a member of the
blackberry family
and have a wonder-
fully sweet taste and
tender flesh.

These preserves have a luscious, intense flavor and are loaded with whole tender berries. Linda also makes this recipe using boysenberries, olallieberries, and even loganberries, depending on what berries are filling the vines in her backyard or are available locally. She's even won blue ribbons using frozen berries.

1. In an 8-quart stainless steel stockpot, layer the blackberries and about half of the sugar. Let stand for 30 minutes.

2. Cook the mixture over medium heat, stirring frequently, until the sugar is mostly dissolved. Stir in the remaining sugar and the butter, if using. Continue to heat and stir until the sugar is completely dissolved.

3. Increase the heat to medium high and bring the mixture to a full rolling boil, stirring constantly. Stir in the pectin. Return the mixture to a full rolling boil, stirring constantly. Boil for 1 minute, stirring constantly.

4. Remove the pot from the heat and skim off any foam. Let the preserves cool in the pot for 5 minutes, stirring occasionally.

5. Ladle the preserves into hot jars, leaving ¼-inch headspace. Remove any air bubbles. Wipe the jar rims and threads with a clean, damp paper towel. Apply hot lids and screw bands.

6. Process 4-ounce, 8-ounce, and pint jars in a water bath canner for 10 minutes (see p. 34 for instructions). Remove from the water bath canner and let cool for 12 to 24 hours. Check the seals and remove the screw bands. Store jars in a cool, dry, dark place for up to 1 year.

Jeannie's Strawberry Sunrise Preserves

CONTRIBUTOR: JAY GRANTIER, GEORGIA

MAKES SIX TO SEVEN 8-OUNCE JARS

4 pounds whole small strawberries

1 vanilla bean

2½ pounds granulated sugar (about 6 cups)

2 navel oranges

Jay's mom had a love for everything strawberry, which included everything in her kitchen—she had strawberry-decorated things everywhere. He created this recipe in her honor. She loved it and everyone else he shares it with does too—it has become his most popular preserve. Jay always keeps a few jars on hand to open for friends, which gives him an opportunity to share a story about his best friend, his mom, Jeannie.

1. In an 8-quart stainless steel stockpot, combine the strawberries and vanilla bean. Pour the sugar over top of the berries. Cover, set aside, and let macerate for 24 hours at room temperature.

2. Bring the strawberry mixture to a boil over medium-high heat, stirring frequently. Reduce the heat and boil, stirring frequently, for 5 minutes. Remove the pot from the heat, cool, cover, and let rest for 24 hours at room temperature.

3. Using a soft scrub brush, thoroughly scrub the oranges, then rinse well and dry. Finely grate the zest from 1 orange and set aside. Peel and section both oranges. Discard the peel, membrane, and seeds and roughly chop the orange segments, reserving the juice.

4. Add the orange segments and juice to the strawberry mixture. Bring the mixture to a boil over medium-high heat, stirring frequently. Reduce the heat and simmer, stirring frequently, for 20 minutes, or until the preserves reach the desired consistency. Stir in the orange zest.

5. Remove the pot from the heat and skim off any foam. Remove and discard the vanilla bean and let the preserves cool in the pot for 5 minutes, stirring occasionally.

6. Ladle the preserves into hot jars, leaving ¼-inch headspace. Remove any air bubbles. Wipe the jar rims and threads with a clean, damp paper towel. Apply hot lids and screw bands.

JAY GRANTIER

MARIETTA, GEORGIA

ALREADY HAVING A KNACK FOR COOKING and a desire to enjoy a more organic, simpler life, Jay Grantier looked for ways to learn more about his family's recipes. "I began talking with my mom about the old family recipes, and as I pored over handwritten notes on index cards, napkins, and bits of paper, I discovered a trend among my family—the love for canning." Living in a farming community in upstate New York, the family didn't focus just on canning vegetables, but developed a love for all types of canning, including pickles, jam, jelly, and preserves.

For Jay, each jar is a piece of art, and he wants the taste to be something people will always remember. "I enjoy the overall satisfaction of preparing and presenting items from my garden and local u-pick farms to a whole new generation. There is nothing like taking an old cherished recipe and adding a creative twist or ingredient to give it a new makeover.

"Looking back over the time I spent with my mom and grandmother and trying to recreate the family recipes, I have learned that nothing can really replace that time I spent with them. For me, I get to spend time with them again every time I am canning. I hear their voices helping me cut the fruit, watch the water temperature, and how to ensure that the food on the inside of that jar represents something beautiful."

Jay made his mark on the fair canning competition world in a big way. Competing at state, regional, and county fairs for more than 6 years, he has already taken home over 200 blue ribbons and several Best in Show awards. Jay has also been the overall Blue Ribbon Sweepstakes winner at the Georgia National Fair for the last 5 years. "Each time I win a ribbon or sweepstakes award, I know that I haven't just simply won for doing something that I love. I've also spent time in the kitchen cherishing the memory of loved ones and sharing their wonderful recipe with others."

7. Process 4-ounce, 8-ounce, and pint jars in a water bath canner for 10 minutes (see p. 34 for instructions). Remove from the water bath canner and let cool for 12 to 24 hours. Check the seals and remove the screw bands. Store jars in a cool, dry, dark place for up to 1 year.

Apricot Pineapple Preserves

CONTRIBUTOR: LINDA J. AMENDT, CALIFORNIA

MAKES ABOUT SIX
8-OUNCE JARS

1 can (20 ounces) juice-packed pineapple tidbits, drained

4½ cups granulated sugar

3¾ cups peeled, pitted, and quartered apricots (about 2½ pounds apricots)

½ cup freshly squeezed lemon juice

½ teaspoon unsalted butter (optional)

1 pouch (3 ounces) liquid pectin

The combination of apricot and pineapple is one of Linda's favorites. She loves apricot pineapple jam, but wanted a spread with larger pieces, so she set off into the kitchen and combined her apricot preserves recipe with her pineapple preserves recipe to create this blue ribbon winner.

1. Place the pineapple tidbits in an 8-quart stainless steel stockpot. Sprinkle 2 cups of the sugar over the pineapple, then cover and let stand for 1 hour.

2. Uncover the pot and stir in the remaining 2½ cups sugar, then cook over medium-high heat, stirring constantly, until the sugar is completely dissolved. Add the apricots, lemon juice, and butter, if using. Bring the mixture to a boil, stirring frequently, reduce the heat, and boil gently for 5 minutes.

3. Increase the heat to medium high and bring the mixture to a full rolling boil, stirring constantly. Stir in the pectin. Return the mixture to a full rolling boil, stirring constantly. Boil for 1 minute, stirring constantly.

4. Remove the pot from the heat and skim off any foam. Let the preserves cool in the pot for 5 minutes, stirring occasionally.

5. Ladle the preserves into hot jars, leaving ¼-inch headspace. Remove any air bubbles. Wipe the jar rims and threads with a clean, damp paper towel. Apply hot lids and screw bands.

6. Process 4-ounce, 8-ounce, and pint jars in a water bath canner for 10 minutes (see p. 34 for instructions). Remove from the water bath canner and let cool for 12 to 24 hours. Check the seals and remove the screw bands. Store jars in a cool, dry, dark place for up to 1 year.

Watermelon Preserves

CONTRIBUTOR: VICTORIA THOMPSON, ALASKA

**MAKES ABOUT FOUR
8-OUNCE JARS**

1 medium watermelon

2 cups granulated sugar

¼ cup freshly squeezed
lemon juice

1 teaspoon ground
cinnamon

1 teaspoon ground cloves

Victoria's mother made these preserves for her when she was a child, about 70 years ago. She cooked on a wood stove and had been canning for so long that she instinctively knew how much of each ingredient to put in and when the preserves were done. The lemon juice is Victoria's addition—she likes the way it brightens the flavor of the preserves.

1. Prepare the watermelon rind: Using a soft scrub brush, thoroughly scrub the watermelon, then rinse well and dry. Using a sharp knife, cut the melon into slices and trim off as much of the red flesh as possible from the white rind. Cut the outer green peel from the white rind and dice the rind. Discard the green peel (and eat the red flesh!) Measure out 4 cups of diced watermelon rind.

2. Place the watermelon rind in a large glass bowl. Pour the sugar over the watermelon, making sure it completely covers the rind. Cover and refrigerate overnight.

3. Transfer the watermelon mixture to a 4-quart stainless steel stockpot. Stir in the lemon juice, cinnamon, and cloves. Bring the mixture to a boil over medium heat, stirring constantly. Reduce the heat to low, then cover the pot and simmer, stirring frequently, until the syrup thickens to the consistency of honey. This may take up to 3 hours. Watch carefully so the preserves do not scorch. Remove the pot from the heat and skim off any foam.

4. Ladle the preserves into hot jars, leaving ¼-inch headspace. Remove any air bubbles. Wipe the jar rims and threads with a clean, damp paper towel. Apply hot lids and screw bands.

5. Process 8-ounce and pint jars in a water bath canner for 10 minutes (see p. 34 for instructions). Remove from the water bath canner and let cool for 12 to 24 hours. Check the seals and remove the screw bands. Store jars in a cool, dry, dark place for up to 1 year.

Georgia Peach and Basil Preserves

CONTRIBUTOR: JAY GRANTIER, GEORGIA

MAKES ABOUT EIGHT 8-OUNCE JARS

5 pounds peaches, peeled, pitted, and cut into slices

3½ cups granulated sugar

¼ cup water

¼ cup freshly squeezed lemon juice

2 whole stems fresh basil leaves, plus 8 small basil leaves (optional)

July is Jay's favorite time of the year in Georgia—it's peach season! Nothing tastes better than a savory peach preserve, so he crafted one with his favorite combination—peaches and basil. Let the flavors mellow for at least 7 days before serving the preserves. It's yummy on a biscuit, vanilla bean ice cream, or a grilled pork chop.

1. In an 8-quart stainless steel stockpot, layer the peaches and sugar. Cover, set aside, and let the mixture macerate at room temperature for 24 hours.

2. Add the water and lemon juice to the peach mixture. Bring the peach mixture to a boil over medium-high heat, stirring frequently. Reduce the heat and boil, stirring frequently, for 5 minutes. Remove the pot from the heat; cool, cover, and let rest for 24 hours at room temperature.

3. Add the basil stems to the pot, then bring the peach mixture to a boil over medium-high heat, stirring frequently. Reduce the heat and simmer, stirring frequently, for 25 minutes, or until the preserves reach the desired consistency.

4. Remove the pot from the heat and skim off any foam. Remove and discard the basil stems. Let the preserves cool in the pot for 5 minutes, stirring occasionally.

5. Place 1 small basil leaf for decoration along the inside of each hot jar, if desired. Carefully ladle the preserves into the jars, leaving ¼-inch headspace. Remove any air bubbles. Wipe the jar rims and threads with a clean, damp paper towel. Apply hot lids and screw bands.

6. Process 4-ounce, 8-ounce, and pint jars in a water bath canner for 10 minutes (see p. 34 for instructions). Remove from the water bath canner and let cool for 12 to 24 hours. Check the seals and remove the screw bands. Store jars in a cool, dry, dark place for up to 1 year.

Island Kiwi and Pineapple Preserves

CONTRIBUTOR: JAY GRANTIER, GEORGIA

MAKES SIX TO SEVEN 8-OUNCE JARS

4 cups peeled, sliced, and halved kiwi (16 to 20 medium kiwi)

1 medium pineapple, peeled, cored, and cut into ½-inch cubes (about 4 cups)

3 cups granulated sugar

3 to 4 tablespoons rum

Finely grated zest of 1 lime

Kiwi vines grow in areas with a mild winter, and Jay has one in his yard that yields a huge crop every year, so he created this recipe to use the fruit bounty. These preserves won the North Georgia Agriculture Best in Show award. Jay includes a jar of this preserve in the welcome baskets for guests at his beach condo in Gulf Shores, Alabama. It makes a great topping for morning biscuits before heading out for a day at the beach.

1. In an 8-quart stainless steel stockpot, combine the kiwi and pineapple. Pour the sugar over the fruit, then cover, set aside, and let rest for 24 hours at room temperature.

2. The next day, use a potato masher to lightly crush the fruit to release any trapped air, but do not mash.

3. Slowly bring the fruit mixture to a boil over medium heat, stirring frequently. Reduce the heat and boil, stirring frequently, for 5 minutes. Remove the pot from the heat, cool, cover, and let rest for 24 hours at room temperature.

4. Stir in the rum. Bring the fruit mixture to a boil over medium-high heat, stirring frequently. Reduce the heat and simmer, stirring frequently, for 25 minutes, or until the preserves reach the desired consistency. Stir in the lime zest.

5. Remove the pot from the heat and skim off any foam. Let the preserves cool in the pot for 5 minutes, stirring occasionally.

6. Ladle the preserves into hot jars, leaving ¼-inch headspace. Remove any air bubbles. Wipe the jar rims and threads with a clean, damp paper towel. Apply hot lids and screw bands.

7. Process 4-ounce, 8-ounce, and pint jars in a water bath canner for 10 minutes (see p. 34 for instructions). Remove from the water bath canner and let cool for 12 to 24 hours. Check the seals and remove the screw bands. Store jars in a cool, dry, dark place for up to 1 year.

Piña Colada Preserves

CONTRIBUTOR: LINDA J. AMENDT, CALIFORNIA

MAKES ABOUT EIGHT
8-OUNCE JARS

3 cans (20 ounces each) juice-packed pineapple tidbits

½ cup freshly squeezed lemon juice

5 cups granulated sugar

1¼ cups sweetened flaked coconut

2 pouches (3 ounces each) liquid pectin

½ cup rum

TIP

You can substitute 4 cups peeled, cored, and chopped fresh pineapple and ¾ cup pineapple juice for the pineapple tidbits.

Pineapple, coconut, and rum come together to create jars of fragrant, sunny preserves. Open a jar in the middle of winter and you'll be carried away with relaxing thoughts of gentle island trade winds and warm sandy beaches.

1. Drain the pineapple tidbits, reserving ¾ cup pineapple juice.

2. In an 8-quart stainless steel stockpot, combine the pineapple, reserved pineapple juice, and lemon juice. Sprinkle 3 cups of the sugar over the pineapple. Cover and let stand for 2 hours.

3. Uncover the pot and stir in the remaining 2 cups sugar, then bring the mixture to a boil over medium-high heat, stirring constantly. Reduce the heat and boil gently until the pineapple starts to turn translucent, about 7 minutes. Stir in the coconut.

4. Increase the heat to medium high and bring the mixture to a full rolling boil, stirring constantly. Stir in both pouches of pectin. Return the mixture to a full rolling boil, stirring constantly. Boil for 1 minute, stirring constantly.

5. Remove the pot from the heat and skim off any foam. Stir in the rum. Let the preserves cool in the pot for 5 minutes, stirring occasionally.

6. Ladle the preserves into hot jars, leaving ¼-inch headspace. Remove any air bubbles. Wipe the jar rims and threads with a clean, damp paper towel. Apply hot lids and screw bands.

7. Process 4-ounce, 8-ounce, and pint jars in a water bath canner for 10 minutes (see p. 34 for instructions). Remove from the water bath canner and let cool for 12 to 24 hours. Check the seals and remove the screw bands. Store jars in a cool, dry, dark place for up to 1 year.

* Fruits & Vegetables *

Canning fruits and vegetables is a wonderful way to preserve an abundant orchard or garden harvest so you can enjoy a taste of summer sunshine all year long. An assortment of canned fruits and vegetables on the pantry shelf helps make meal preparation faster and easier, too.

Canning Fruit

You can enjoy home-canned fruit on its own; as an alternative to syrup on pancakes, waffles, and French toast; as a topping for ice cream; or in baking recipes. For the best color, flavor, and texture, use beautiful, unblemished fruit at the peak of ripeness.

✳ PREPARING FRUIT ✳

Rinse the fruit under cool running water and drain well on paper towels. To prevent fruit deterioration, only rinse and prepare enough for one canning batch at a time. Most fruit should be peeled before canning, including peaches, pears, apples, and pineapple. Apricots are usually canned with the peels on because it helps the fruit maintain its shape during processing. Delicate fruits that should not be peeled include cherries, grapes, and berries.

Depending on the type of fruit you are canning, it can be packed whole, halved, sliced, or cut into spears or chunks. For the best result, select fruit that is about the same size and cut into pieces that are uniform in shape and appearance. To prevent light-colored fruits from turning brown after peeling, soak the fruit in an anti-oxidant solution before canning. You can find antioxidant crystals, or fruit preservatives, in grocery stores alongside the canning supplies. Follow the manufacturer's instructions for use and length of soaking time.

✳ PACKING JARS ✳

The most common way to pack fruit into the jars is using the hot pack method—boil a mix of sugar and water to create a syrup, then add the fruit and cook briefly before packing it into the jars. This allows the fruit to absorb some of the sugar and also to become more pliable so it can be packed snugly into the jars. A tighter pack means the fruit is less likely to float in the jars after canning. After being packed into the jars, the fruit is covered with the hot syrup. Fruit may also be packed into the jars raw and covered with a boiling syrup. This is known as a raw pack and is the best method for canning delicate fruits, such as grapes, cherries, and berries.

Fruit can be canned in sugar syrup, fruit juice, or even water. I prefer to use a light to medium sugar syrup for canning fruit. The sugar will help the fruit maintain its shape and texture, and also preserve and enhance the flavor. Fruit packed in heavy syrup is more likely to float in the jar because the higher sugar concentration makes the syrup heavier than the fruit.

Canning Vegetables

For the best results, can vegetables as soon as possible after picking or purchase from your local farmers' market. Fresh, crisp, young, tender vegetables yield the best canned products. Large or fully matured vegetables contain more water, have larger seeds, and are more likely to turn soft and break down when canned. Depending on the type or variety, overripe vegetables can either be mushy or starting to dry out. Bruised or damaged vegetables may contain bacteria or excessive enzymes, which can lead to spoilage.

❋ PACKING JARS ❋

As with fruit, there are two methods used to pack vegetables into jars for canning—the hot pack method and the raw pack method.

In the hot pack method, the vegetables are cooked in simmering water for a few minutes to partially cook and also to allow air trapped inside the vegetable pieces to escape and be replaced with liquid. Without the air, the vegetables are more pliable and heavier, permitting more vegetables to be packed into the jars and reducing the chances of them floating in the jars after processing. The raw pack method is just what it sounds like. Raw vegetables are packed snugly into the jars and then covered with boiling water.

For both packing methods, salt may be added to each jar of vegetables for seasoning, but it is not required for safe food preservation. You can add up to $\frac{1}{2}$ teaspoon salt per pint jar or 1 teaspoon salt per quart jar. Canning or pickling salt is recommended to prevent the liquid in the jar from turning cloudy.

No matter which packing method you use, the headspace for all vegetable packs is 1 inch. This allows room for the vegetables to expand and the liquid to boil during pressure canner processing. If there is too little headspace in the jar, some of the liquid will be forced out of the jar as the contents heat. If there is too much headspace, not enough air will be vented from the jar and the jar and lid may not form a tight vacuum seal.

❋ PROCESSING VEGETABLES ❋

Vegetables are low-acid foods and must be processed in a pressure canner. During pressure canning, the internal temperature of the jars will reach 240°F, which can only be reached in a pressure canner. (Jars processed in a water bath canner will only reach an internal temperature of 212°F, which is too low to safely process low-acid foods.) Except for tomatoes canned with bottled lemon juice or vinegar, pressure canning is the only safe method for canning vegetables and vegetable products.

Apricot Nectar

CONTRIBUTOR: LINDA J. AMENDT, CALIFORNIA

MAKES ABOUT 4 PINT JARS OR TWO 1-QUART JARS

4 cups pitted, peeled, and sliced ripe apricots (about 3 pounds apricots)

4 cups water

2 cups granulated sugar

2 tablespoons freshly squeezed lemon juice

Flavorful with a gorgeous color, this juice won several Best of Division and other special awards. Linda makes it in early summer when local apricots are at the peak of ripeness. Linda likes the sweetness of this nectar, and so did the judges, but you can reduce the sugar if you prefer a tangier juice.

1. In an 8-quart stainless steel stockpot, combine the apricots and water. Bring the mixture to a boil over medium heat, stirring occasionally. Reduce the heat, cover, and simmer for 10 to 15 minutes, or until the fruit is tender. Remove the pot from the heat and skim off any foam.

2. Press the apricots and liquid through a food mill or fine-mesh sieve. Discard the stringy pulp.

3. Rinse the pot and return the apricot juice to it. Stir in the sugar and cook over medium heat, stirring constantly, until the sugar is completely dissolved. If the juice is too thick, add more water to thin it to the desired consistency. Stir in the lemon juice. Remove the pot from the heat.

4. Ladle the juice into hot jars, leaving ½-inch headspace. Wipe the jar rims and threads with a clean, damp paper towel. Apply hot lids and screw bands.

5. Process pint and quart jars in a water bath canner for 15 minutes (see p. 34 for instructions). Remove from the water bath canner and let cool for 12 to 24 hours. Check the seals and remove the screw bands. Store jars in a cool, dry, dark place for up to 1 year.

Tipsy Pineapple

CONTRIBUTOR: PHYLLIS BUSTILLOS, TEXAS

MAKES ABOUT 6 PINT JARS
OR THREE 1-QUART JARS

2 whole pineapples

1 large orange

3½ cups water

3 cups granulated sugar

1 tablespoon freshly
squeezed lemon juice

1 cup coconut rum

SERVING SUGGESTION

The pineapple can be
eaten right out of the jar
or added to cakes, sweet
breads, or fruit compotes.
The juice is fantastic used
as a sweetener in iced
tea, cocktails, and fruit
smoothies. The possibilities are endless.

This pineapple and its juice are a wonderful treat with many uses. To allow the flavor to fully develop, store the sealed jars in a dark, cool, dry place for at least 2 weeks before opening.

1. Peel the pineapples and remove the core. Cut the pineapple into ½- to 1-inch chunks. Set aside.

2. Using a soft scrub brush, thoroughly scrub the orange, then rinse well and dry. Using a paring knife or vegetable peeler, remove only the outer colored portion of the peel in thin strips. Slice the peel into thin slivers, about 2 to 3 inches long.

3. In an 8-quart stainless steel stockpot, combine the water, 1½ cups of the sugar, and the orange peel. Cook over medium-low heat, stirring constantly, until the sugar is completely dissolved. Increase the heat to medium, bring the mixture to a boil, and boil gently for 5 minutes.

4. Add the pineapple pieces and lemon juice to the syrup and return to a boil. Reduce the heat and simmer gently for 10 minutes. Using a slotted spoon, remove the pineapple and orange peel from the pan. Cover and set aside.

5. Add the remaining 1½ cups sugar to the syrup and heat, stirring until completely dissolved. Bring the syrup to a boil and then boil for 10 minutes. Remove from the heat and let cool slightly. Stir in the coconut rum.

6. Using a slotted spoon, pack the pineapple into hot jars, leaving ½-inch headspace. Ladle the hot syrup into the jars, covering the pineapple and maintaining the ½-inch headspace. Remove any air bubbles. Wipe the jar rims and threads with a clean damp paper towel. Apply hot lids and screw bands.

7. Process pint jars in a water bath canner for 15 minutes; quart jars for 20 minutes (see p. 34 for instructions). Remove from the water bath canner and let cool for 12 to 24 hours. Check the seals and remove the screw bands. Store jars in a cool, dry, dark place for up to 1 year.

PHYLLIS BUSTILLOS

ALVARADO, TEXAS

PHYLLIS BUSTILLOS' earliest memories of canning are as a young girl when her mother took Phyllis, her twin sister, and four brothers to the large farming fields outside Brownwood, Texas. After the crops were harvested by tractors, the farmers would allow the public to pick the remaining produce. The family would pick and can many bushels of peas, corn, beans, and fruit of all sorts. "While picking, I thought the baskets would never fill. Then, while processing the produce, I thought the baskets would never empty!"

"The finished products look like little pieces of artwork in a jar."

After many years of visiting the State Fair of Texas with her mother to look at the beautiful award-winning canned goods, Phyllis told her mother, "We really need to enter our canning." In 2003, Phyllis finally accomplished this goal. "Upon winning my first ribbons, I excitedly took them to show my mother, who at the time was in a nursing facility. As many of my State Fair friends would say, 'I was hooked,' and my daughters and I have entered the canning competitions at the Fair every year since." The family "BBQ Team," which includes the men in

the family, has also won many competition trophies and ribbons. Phyllis' youngest daughter, Brenda, asked her mother and sister to enter the canning competition at the 2013 North Texas State Fair. "Going along for the ride," Phyllis entered four items and brought home three blue ribbons and a Reserve Champion ribbon. "Not bad for my first entries in that competition! "

What Phyllis enjoys most about canning is the finished product. "They look like little pieces of artwork in a jar. I also love that my teenage grandson loves my jams so much he began hiding the jars I give to his family so that he can have them for himself." Her granddaughters have already become involved in the gardening process, and Phyllis looks forward to teaching them how to can the harvest.

Sweet Cherries

CONTRIBUTORS: ROMERO FAMILY, COLORADO

MAKES FOUR 1-QUART JARS

5¼ cups water

2¼ cups granulated sugar

10 pounds sweet cherries, stemmed and pitted

When canning fair entry jars, the Romeros leave the cherries whole—the pits help prevent them from bursting and shrinking. They also discard the syrup the cherries have been heated in and make a fresh batch of syrup to fill the jars so that the syrup is crystal clear to show off the cherries and earn that blue ribbon. For home use, they remove the pits and then measure the pitted cherries and also can the cherries with the syrup used to heat the cherries.

1. In an 8-quart stainless steel stockpot, combine the water and sugar. Bring the mixture to a boil over medium-high heat, stirring constantly, until the sugar is completely dissolved. Reduce the heat to low and add the cherries to the syrup. Slowly heat the mixture over low until the cherries are hot, about 2 minutes.

2. Using a slotted spoon, pack the cherries into hot jars, leaving ½-inch headspace. Ladle the hot syrup into the jars, covering the cherries and maintaining the ½-inch headspace. Remove any air bubbles. If necessary, add more syrup to maintain the headspace. Wipe the jar rims and threads with a clean, damp paper towel. Apply hot lids and screw bands.

3. Process pint jars in a water bath canner for 15 minutes; quart jars for 20 minutes (see p. 34 for instructions). Remove from the water bath canner and let cool for 12 to 24 hours. Check the seals and remove the screw bands. Store jars in a cool, dry, dark place for up to 1 year.

DID YOU KNOW? The Colorado State Fair is the largest single event in the state of Colorado. The Fair also hosts the largest parade in the state.

Grapes

CONTRIBUTOR: LINDA J. AMENDT, CALIFORNIA

MAKES ABOUT 4 PINT JARS

4 cups water

1½ cups granulated sugar

8½ cups stemmed firm ripe grapes

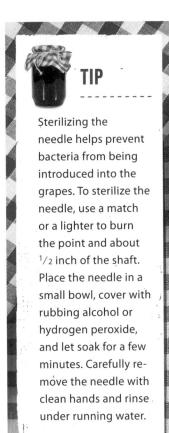

TIP

Sterilizing the needle helps prevent bacteria from being introduced into the grapes. To sterilize the needle, use a match or a lighter to burn the point and about ¹/₂ inch of the shaft. Place the needle in a small bowl, cover with rubbing alcohol or hydrogen peroxide, and let soak for a few minutes. Carefully remove the needle with clean hands and rinse under running water.

Red flame grapes are Linda's favorite variety for canning, but other varieties of red, black, and Thompson seedless grapes all make good canned grapes. Just be sure to start with firm, crisp fruit; otherwise, they will turn very soft during processing.

1. In a 4-quart stainless steel stockpot, combine the water and sugar. Bring the mixture to a boil over medium-high heat, stirring constantly, until the sugar is completely dissolved. Boil for 5 minutes, then reduce the heat to low, cover, and keep hot until needed.

2. Prick the ends of each grape two or three times with a large sterilized needle to help keep the skins from splitting during processing.

3. Pack the grapes into hot jars, leaving ½-inch headspace. Gently shake the jars during packing to attain a snug pack. Ladle the hot syrup into the jars, covering the grapes and maintaining the ½-inch headspace. Remove any air bubbles. If necessary, add more syrup to maintain the headspace. Wipe the jar rims and threads with a clean, damp paper towel. Apply hot lids and screw bands.

4. Process pint jars in a water bath canner for 15 minutes; quart jars for 20 minutes (see p. 34 for instructions). Remove from the water bath canner and let cool for 12 to 24 hours. Check the seals and remove the screw bands. Store jars in a cool, dry, dark place for up to 1 year.

*Grapes and Amaretto pears
(recipe on p. 146)*

Canned Pears

CONTRIBUTOR: ARIANNA EDWARDS, UTAH

MAKES ABOUT 7 TO 8 PINT JARS

10 cups water

3½ cups granulated sugar

2 teaspoons freshly squeezed lemon juice

1 teaspoon ascorbic acid crystals or fruit preservative

About 10 pounds pears

This recipe is extremely easy and the pears, packed in a light syrup, taste wonderful! They are terrific served on a brunch buffet, accompanying roasted winter vegetables, or with vanilla ice cream for dessert.

1. In an 8-quart stainless steel stockpot, combine the water and sugar. Cook over medium-low heat, stirring constantly, until the sugar is completely dissolved. Reduce the heat to low, cover, and keep the syrup hot until needed.

2. Fill a large bowl with water and add the lemon juice and ascorbic acid crystals. Stir until dissolved.

3. Peel the pears, cut them in halves or quarters, and core. Place them in the lemon water for a few minutes to prevent browning. Using a slotted spoon, remove the pears from the water and drain well.

4. Pack the pears into hot jars, leaving ½-inch headspace. Ladle the hot syrup into the jars, covering the pears and maintaining the ½-inch headspace. Remove any air bubbles. If necessary, add more syrup to maintain the headspace. Wipe the jar rims and threads with a clean, damp paper towel. Apply hot lids and screw bands.

5. Process pint jars in a water bath canner for 20 minutes; quart jars for 25 minutes (see p. 34 for instructions). Remove from the water bath canner and let cool for 12 to 24 hours. Check the seals and remove the screw bands. Store jars in a cool, dry, dark place for up to 1 year.

ARIANNA EDWARDS

HOLLADAY, UTAH

WHEN ARIANNA EDWARDS was 5 years old, her sister started taking piano lessons. Every week, her family would just sit and wait for her to finish. "One day, an elderly man, Mr. Capson, told us that it was ridiculous to just wait around for my sister and he invited my family to his home. From that day on, we visited him every week, and every time he would feed us some of his wonderful homemade canned food or some fresh produce from his garden. Within a month he began teaching me and the rest of my family how to can and how to make our garden better." At first, Arianna was shy and didn't want to participate in the canning. But Mr. Capson encouraged her and helped Arianna come out of her shell. "He became my canning mentor," she says.

Arianna quickly fell in love with canning. "The entire canning process is fun and relaxing. I especially like preparing the fruit or vegetables I'm going to use. I love to can whenever I get the chance, and it truly is one of my most enjoyable activities."

She has been canning for about 10 years and started entering fair competitions about 5 years ago. "When my mom first encouraged me to enter my canned food in the Utah State Fair, I insisted they weren't good enough and that they would never win anything. Thankfully, that wasn't true. Because of my amazing mom, I now enter my canned food in the fair every year." Her mother did know best—Arianna has brought home many blue ribbons and also earned the Champion Youth Canner award at the Utah State Fair.

DID YOU KNOW? Home-canned foods were once a necessity for pioneer survival. Canning the abundant harvest from summer gardens allowed people to preserve produce to feed their families throughout the cold winter months when fresh crops were not available and food was scarce.

Amaretto Pears

CONTRIBUTOR: LINDA J. AMENDT, CALIFORNIA

MAKES ABOUT 6 PINT JARS OR THREE 1-QUART JARS

5 cups room-temperature water

2 cups granulated sugar

8 cups cold water

2 tablespoons ascorbic acid crystals or fruit preservative

7½ to 8 pounds small, unblemished, firm Bartlett pears

½ cup amaretto, or 1 tablespoon pure almond extract

Amaretto, an almond-flavored liqueur, gives these pears a special flavor that was a big hit with the judges and led to a Best of Show award. You can use pure almond extract instead of amaretto to create non-alcoholic pears. Amaretto Pears make scrumptious pear tarts.

1. In an 8-quart stainless stockpot, combine the 5 cups room-temperature water and the sugar. Bring to a boil over medium-high heat, stirring constantly, until the sugar is completely dissolved. Boil for 5 minutes, then reduce the heat to low, cover, and keep the syrup hot until needed.

2. In a large bowl, combine the 8 cups cold water and the ascorbic acid crystals, stirring until completely dissolved.

3. Using a sharp paring knife, peel the pears one at a time and cut into quarters lengthwise. Using a small spoon or melon baller, remove the center core and stem from each pear piece. Immediately drop the pieces into the ascorbic acid solution for a few minutes to prevent browning.

4. Using a slotted spoon, remove the pears from the solution, rinse under cool water, and drain well. Add the drained pears to the hot syrup. Gently heat the pears over medium-low heat, stirring occasionally, for 2 to 3 minutes. Remove the pot from the heat and stir in the amaretto.

5. Ladle ¼ cup of the syrup into each hot jar. Using a slotted spoon, pack the pears into the jars, leaving ½-inch headspace.

6. Line a fine-mesh sieve with 3 layers of damp fine-mesh cheese-cloth and strain the syrup through the sieve. Ladle the hot syrup into the jars, covering the pears and maintaining the ½-inch headspace. Remove any air bubbles. If necessary, add more syrup to maintain the headspace. Wipe the jar rims and threads with a clean, damp paper towel. Apply hot lids and screw bands.

7. Process pint jars in a water bath canner for 20 minutes; quart jars for 25 minutes (see p. 34 for instructions). Remove from the water bath canner and let cool for 12 to 24 hours. Check the seals and remove the screw bands. Store jars in a cool, dry, dark place for up to 1 year.

VARIATION: AMARETTO PEACHES

Make amaretto peaches by following the same instructions for the pears. Use small, firm freestone peaches in place of the pears. Use a spoon or melon baller to remove the red fibers from the center of the peaches before dropping the fruit into the ascorbic acid solution.

THE REESE FAMILY

BARBARA REESE, NOKESVILLE, VIRGINIA;
MELINDA REESE, RICHMOND, VIRGINIA;
JACOB SNYDER & JULIA SNYDER, ROANOKE, VIRGINIA

WHEN BARBARA REESE and her husband moved to Nokesville in northern Virginia in 1979, she had never gardened, canned, or even attended a county fair. But the next year, her husband decided to plant a huge garden. When the green beans were ready to pick, her neighbor asked what she was going to do with them. When Barbara said she was going to freeze the beans, her neighbor insisted that she needed to can them instead and walked her through the process. When fair time came around, Barbara decided to enter her green beans.

The day after the judging, Barbara and her family went to see how their items did. "When we got to the green beans, I had a blue ribbon hanging on my jar! I was stunned. There were 66 quarts of green beans entered in the competition and I won! How awesome!"

The next generation of canners is now making their mark, with Barbara's grandchildren, Julia and Jacob Snyder, learning to can and entering fair competitions.

· The next year, she bought a canner and she and her daughters were off and running. Melinda helped her can that first year. As Vicki and Jenny grew older, they would sometimes help can as well, especially when it was time to prepare fair entries, but Melinda was the one who always helped, sometimes giving up time with her friends so she could can for the fair.

In 1984, Barbara was asked to help in the Junior Food Preservation department at the fair. "It was a great experience being able to listen to what the judges said about the canned goods." One of Barbara's favorite memories is the year that the judges, in trying to decide which entry should be awarded Best of Show, narrowed it down to Melinda's carrots and peaches. Barbara knew they were both Melinda's entries, but the judges didn't. They debated back and forth and finally gave the award to the carrots because the peaches were so perfect they figured the mother must have helped with them. "They were perfect and Melinda did them all by herself. After the judging, I was able to share this with the judges."

Barbara and her daughters have all judged entries over the years and Barbara now coordinates the judges for the Prince William County Fair. The next generation of canners is now making their mark, with Barbara's grandchildren, Julia and Jacob Snyder, learning to can and entering fair competitions. "Both have already won blue ribbons and Best of Show awards for their efforts, and they enjoy competing against each other as much as my girls did."

Peach Halves

CONTRIBUTOR: MELINDA REESE, VIRGINIA

**MAKES ABOUT SIX
1-QUART JARS**

2 quarts water

2 cups granulated sugar

10 to 12 pounds round
unblemished peaches

Perfect peaches are a challenge to can because if you pack them too tight, they'll break, and if you don't pack them tight enough, they'll float. Melinda has just the right touch—she's won lots of blue ribbons for her peaches.

1. In a 4-quart stainless steel stockpot, combine the water and sugar. Bring the mixture to a boil over medium-high heat, stirring constantly until the sugar is completely dissolved. Boil the syrup for 1 minute, then reduce the heat to low and keep hot until needed.

2. Fill an 8-quart stainless steel stockpot with water and bring to a boil. Cut a small X on the bottom of the peaches, then dip them into the boiling water for 30 seconds to 1 minute to loosen the skins. Transfer to a bowl of ice water for 2 minutes to cool and stop the cooking. Drain well.

3. Cut the peaches into even halves. Remove the pits and peels, then rinse and drain well.

4. Pack the peaches, cavity side down, into hot jars, leaving ½-inch headspace. Overlap the peaches from side to side to create a pretty appearance and snug pack.

5. Ladle the hot syrup into the jars, covering the peaches and maintaining the ½-inch headspace. Remove any air bubbles. If necessary, add more syrup to maintain the headspace. Wipe the jar rims and threads with a clean, damp paper towel. Apply hot lids and screw bands.

6. Process pint jars in a water bath canner for 25 minutes; quart jars for 30 minutes (see p. 34 for instructions). Remove from the water bath canner and let cool for 12 to 24 hours. Check the seals and remove the screw bands. Store jars in a cool, dry, dark place for up to 1 year.

Maraschino Cherries

CONTRIBUTOR: LINDA J. AMENDT, CALIFORNIA

**MAKES ABOUT FIVE
8-OUNCE JARS**

8 cups cold water

2 tablespoons ascorbic
acid crystals or fruit
preservative

2½ pounds sour cherries
or Royal Anne cherries,
stemmed and pitted

3 cups granulated sugar

1½ cups water

2 tablespoons red food
coloring

1 tablespoon pure
almond extract

These are so much better than the store-bought kind. Be sure
to use ripe but firm cherries. If the cherries are too soft, they
won't hold their shape well. Allow the flavor to develop for
4 weeks before opening the jars.

1. In a large bowl, combine the 8 cups cold water and ascorbic acid
   crystals, stirring until completely dissolved. Add the pitted cherries and let soak for 15 minutes. Drain the cherries, rinse, and
   drain well.

2. In a 4-quart stainless steel stockpot, combine the sugar and
   1½ cups water. Bring the mixture to a boil over medium-high
   heat, stirring constantly, until the sugar is completely dissolved.
   Stir in the food coloring, then add the drained cherries to the
   syrup. Reduce the heat and simmer for 3 minutes. Remove the
   pot from the heat and let cool completely. Cover and let stand at
   room temperature for 24 hours.

3. Uncover the pot and bring the cherry mixture to a boil over
   medium heat. Immediately remove the pot from the heat and
   stir in the almond extract.

4. Using a slotted spoon, pack the cherries into hot jars, leaving
   ½-inch headspace. Ladle the hot syrup into the jars, covering the
   cherries and maintaining the ½-inch headspace. Remove any air
   bubbles. If necessary, add more syrup to maintain the headspace.
   Wipe the jar rims and threads with a clean, damp paper towel.
   Apply hot lids and screw bands.

5. Process 8-ounce jars in a water bath canner for 10 minutes; pint
   jars for 15 minutes (see p. 34 for instructions). Remove from the
   water bath canner and let cool for 12 to 24 hours. Check the seals
   and remove the screw bands. Store jars in a cool, dry, dark place
   for up to 1 year.

Yellow Wax Beans

CONTRIBUTOR: BARBARA REESE, VIRGINIA

MAKES ABOUT 8 PINT JARS OR FOUR 1-QUART JARS

6 pounds yellow wax beans

4 teaspoons table salt

Boiling water

Yellow wax beans have a pretty pale color and slightly sweet flavor. They can be hard to come by in stores, so the Reese family grows them in their garden. If you live in an area where they are popular, you may be able to find fresh beans at a local farmers' market. These beans were a blue ribbon winner for Barbara at the State Fair of Virginia, but when she and her daughters entered these beans in the Prince William County Fair, there was no youth category so they were competing against one another. Although they all took home their share of blue ribbons for this recipe, the girls loved it when they beat Barbara!

1. Rinse the beans thoroughly and drain well. Trim the ends and remove any strings, then snap the beans into 1-inch pieces.

2. Pack the beans into hot jars, leaving 1-inch headspace. Add ½ teaspoon salt to each pint jar or 1 teaspoon salt to each quart jar.

3. Ladle the boiling water into the jars, covering the beans and maintaining the 1-inch headspace. Remove any air bubbles. If necessary, add more liquid to maintain the headspace. Wipe the jar rims and threads with a clean, damp paper towel. Apply hot lids and screw bands.

4. Process pint jars for 20 minutes and quart jars for 25 minutes at 11 pounds of pressure in a dial-gauge pressure canner or at 10 pounds of pressure in a weighted-gauge pressure canner (see p. 36 for instructions).

5. After the processing time is complete, remove the canner from the heat. Let the pressure return to zero before removing the jars from the canner. Let cool for 12 to 24 hours. Check the seals and remove the screw bands. Store jars in a cool, dry, dark place for up to 1 year.

Basketweave Carrot Coins

CONTRIBUTOR: MILDRED RINGHAUSEN, ILLINOIS

MAKES ABOUT 4 PINT JARS

5 pounds whole carrots, 1 to 1¼ inches in diameter

2 teaspoons canning or pickling salt

Boiling water

TIP

Use carrots of uniform diameter and cut to the same thickness to create the best appearance. Place carrot slices of the same size in the outer rows around the inside of the jar, and use the remaining carrots to tightly pack the centers of each row to keep the carrots from moving.

The basketweave placement of the carrots makes a stunning product, thoroughly impressing the judges and deserving of a permanent placement in Mildred's century-old kitchen. While stunning looking, the carrot coins are also delicious in stews and mixed vegetable dishes, as well as in salads or served as a side dish.

1. Trim off the carrot tops and the taproot. Thoroughly scrub the carrots to remove any dirt; rinse and dry well. Peel the carrots and cut into ¼-inch slices.

2. Pack the carrots into hot pint jars. Place the first three or four outer rows of carrots in the jar in a basketweave, or brick, pattern, staggering the rows so the carrots in the row above cover the joint line of the carrots in the row below. Carefully fill in the center of the rows, packing the pieces very tightly in each row so the carrots do not move. Use a skewer or a chopstick to help position the carrots.

3. Continue tightly packing the rows of carrots into the jars, leaving 1-inch headspace. Add ½ teaspoon salt to each pint jar of carrots.

4. Ladle the boiling water into the jars, covering the carrots and maintaining the 1-inch headspace. Remove any air bubbles. If necessary, add more liquid to maintain the headspace. Wipe the jar rims and threads with a clean, damp paper towel. Apply hot lids and screw bands.

5. Process pint jars for 25 minutes at 11 pounds of pressure in a dial-gauge pressure canner or at 10 pounds of pressure in a weighted-gauge pressure canner (see p. 36 for instructions).

6. After the processing time is complete, remove the canner from the heat. Let the pressure return to zero before removing the jars from the canner. Let cool for 12 to 24 hours. Check the seals and remove the screw bands. Store jars in a cool, dry, dark place for up to 1 year.

Crinkle-Cut Carrots

CONTRIBUTOR: BETH WALLACE, ARKANSAS

MAKES ABOUT 7 PINT JARS
OR THREE TO FOUR
1-QUART JARS

8½ pounds whole
carrots, each about
1 inch diameter

3½ teaspoons pickling
or canning salt

Boiling water

TIP

If you don't have a
crinkle-cut slicer,
you can cut the
carrots into slices
with a sharp knife.

The crinkle cut gives these carrots a fancy appearance, making them very pretty when served for dinner. For competition, pack the jars with carrot slices that are the same size and color. Nearly every time Beth enters these carrots, they win first place and frequently take Best of Show as well.

1. Thoroughly scrub the carrots to remove any dirt; rinse and drain well. Peel the carrots and rinse again. Using a crinkle-cut slicer, cut the carrots into slices of uniform size, about ¼ inch thick.

2. Pack the carrots into hot jars, leaving 1-inch headspace. Add ½ teaspoon salt to each pint jar or 1 teaspoon salt to each quart jar.

3. Ladle the boiling water into the jars, covering the carrots and maintaining the 1-inch headspace. Remove any air bubbles. If necessary, add more liquid to maintain the headspace. Wipe the jar rims and threads with a clean, damp paper towel. Apply hot lids and screw bands.

4. Process pint jars for 25 minutes and quart jars for 30 minutes at 11 pounds of pressure in a dial-gauge pressure canner or at 10 pounds of pressure in a weighted-gauge pressure canner (see p. 36 for instructions).

5. After the processing time is complete, remove the canner from the heat. Let the pressure return to zero before removing the jars from the canner. Let cool for 12 to 24 hours. Check the seals and remove the screw bands. Store jars in a cool, dry, dark place for up to 1 year.

Black-Eyed Peas

CONTRIBUTOR: BARBARA REESE, VIRGINIA

MAKES ABOUT 6 PINT JARS OR THREE 1-QUART JARS

6 pounds fresh black-eyed peas

1 tablespoon table salt

Boiling water

Barbara's children hated harvesting black-eyed pea pods because the plants always had ants. But the whole family loves the peas, and these jars always took home a blue ribbon at the fair.

1. Shell the peas, rinse, and drain well.

2. Pack the peas into hot jars, leaving 1-inch headspace. Add ½ teaspoon salt to each pint jar or 1 teaspoon salt to each quart jar.

3. Ladle the boiling water into the jars, covering the peas and maintaining the 1-inch headspace. Remove any air bubbles. If necessary, add more liquid to maintain the headspace. Wipe the jar rims and threads with a clean, damp paper towel. Apply hot lids and screw bands.

4. Process pint jars for 40 minutes and quart jars for 50 minutes at 11 pounds of pressure in a dial-gauge pressure canner or at 10 pounds of pressure in a weighted-gauge pressure canner (see p. 36 for instructions).

5. After the processing time is complete, remove the canner from the heat. Let the pressure return to zero before removing the jars from the canner. Let cool for 12 to 24 hours. Check the seals and remove the screw bands. Store jars in a cool, dry, dark place for up to 1 year.

DID YOU KNOW? The Shoot the Star carnival game—where you use a BB gun to shoot every bit of a star off the target with just 100 BBs—is one of the most difficult games at state fairs. In the 1980s, the FBI even ran a study on the chances a player has of winning the game. They determined that the odds are best when the star is an inch or less in diameter.

Black Beans

CONTRIBUTOR: CAROLYN DEMARCO, OREGON

MAKES ABOUT 10 PINT JARS

4 quarts cold water

4⅔ tablespoons canning or pickling salt

1 pound dried black beans

SERVING SUGGESTION

These beans are great for taco or burrito fillings, either used on their own or added to ground meat. They can also be puréed and seasoned for a healthy bean dip or thinned with vegetable stock for black bean soup.

Dried black beans are an inexpensive and filling alternative or addition to meat, especially for Mexican dishes, but they require enough preparation that they are tough to use for a midweek meal. Although you can buy black beans in a can, Carolyn prefers the creamier texture and more flavorful taste of black beans when she has taken the time to prepare dried beans. By canning them herself, she can have black bean burritos any night of the week without sacrificing taste or texture.

1. In a large bowl or other container, combine the cold water and 3 tablespoons of the salt, stirring until completely dissolved. Add the beans, cover, and let soak overnight at room temperature.

2. Rinse the beans well and drain. Place in an 8-quart stainless steel stockpot and add enough fresh water to cover the beans. Over medium-high heat, bring the mixture to a boil, then reduce the heat and boil for 30 minutes.

3. Add ½ teaspoon salt to each hot pint jar or 1 teaspoon salt to each hot quart jar.

4. Ladle the beans and cooking liquid into the jars, leaving 1-inch headspace. Remove any air bubbles. Wipe the jar rims and threads with a clean, damp paper towel. Apply hot lids and screw bands.

5. Process pint jars for 75 minutes and quart jars for 90 minutes at 11 pounds of pressure in a dial-gauge pressure canner or at 10 pounds of pressure in a weighted-gauge pressure canner (see p. 36 for instructions).

6. After the processing time is complete, remove the canner from the heat. Let the pressure return to zero before removing the jars from the canner. Let cool for 12 to 24 hours. Check the seals and remove the screw bands. Store jars in a cool, dry, dark place for up to 1 year.

CAROLYN DEMARCO

EUGENE, OREGON

CAROLYN DEMARCO'S first experience with canning was when she was a kid. Along with her parents and two brothers, she would spend hours picking green beans at a u-pick farm. The family would then spend many more hours snapping the beans into bite-sized pieces. "My mom would then spend days processing all the beans in quart jars. I could hear the rocking hiss of the pressure canner as I fell asleep at night, which is probably why I find the sound of a pressure canner downright soothing."

"It's very satisfying to turn fresh produce into a cupboard full of neatly arranged canned goods."

Many years later, after getting married, Carolyn started canning her own preserves. When she and her husband moved into a new house, Carolyn put in a garden and wanted to be able to preserve what she grew. She sought out the local extension service offered by Oregon State University and began taking canning classes. "I gradually outfitted myself with the necessary tools and just dove in, canning jams and tomatoes, and then discovered the tastiness of pickles. Not just dills, but pickled pineapple,

watermelon rind, and green beans!"

In the extension service classes, she heard about entering canned goods at the county fair. The next year, she decided to enter some of her jams and other goodies into the competition. "If nothing else, I could get a free fair ticket if I submitted at least 25 entries. I was blown away when I attended the fair and saw that 23 of my 25 entries won ribbons, and 9 won blue ribbons! I was hooked!"

Carolyn gets satisfaction out of canning food to have a supply of tasty, preservative-free fruits and vegetables. "It's very satisfying to turn fresh produce into a cupboard full of neatly arranged canned goods." She also enjoys the thrill and pride of entering her canned items in the fair. "My proudest achievement was making sauerkraut for the first time—after taking a fermentation class with the extension service—and submitting it to the fair, where it won a blue ribbon!"

Crowder Peas

CONTRIBUTOR: SANDRA BEASLEY, NORTH CAROLINA

MAKES ABOUT 4 PINT JARS OR TWO 1-QUART JARS

4 to 5 pounds crowder pea pods

Boiling water

SERVING SUGGESTION

Boil the peas, uncovered, for 10 minutes. Serve them with rice and green beans, combine with cooked pinto beans and add to soup, blend the peas with cooked pinto beans when making re-fried beans, or use them in place of kidney beans in chili recipes.

Crowder peas, also known as Southern field peas, grow in abundance in North Carolina and are a milder version of black-eyed peas. Because shelling the peas can be a bit tedious, the Beasley family has made it fun—they put on a movie and give everyone some pods, a bowl for the peas, and a large trash can. The peas fly at their home!

1. Rinse the pea pods and drain well. Lay the pods out on towels and let them dry overnight.

2. The next day, shell the peas. Rinse the peas thoroughly and pick out any remaining pods.

3. Place the peas in an 8- to 10-quart stainless steel stockpot and add enough water to cover. Bring to a boil over medium-high heat, then reduce the heat and boil for 3 minutes, stirring occasionally. Remove the pot from the heat.

4. Using a slotted spoon, pack the peas into hot jars, leaving 1-inch headspace. Ladle the boiling water into the jars, covering the peas and maintaining the 1-inch headspace. Remove any air bubbles. If necessary, add more liquid to maintain the headspace. Wipe the jar rims and threads with a clean, damp paper towel. Apply hot lids and screw bands.

5. Process pint jars for 40 minutes and quart jars for 50 minutes at 11 pounds of pressure in a dial-gauge pressure canner or at 10 pounds of pressure in a weighted-gauge pressure canner (see p. 36 for instructions).

6. After the processing time is complete, remove the canner from the heat. Let the pressure return to zero before removing the jars from the canner. Let cool for 12 to 24 hours. Check the seals and remove the screw bands. Store jars in a cool, dry, dark place for up to 1 year.

Whole Green Beans

CONTRIBUTOR: BARBARA REESE, VIRGINIA

MAKES ABOUT 8 PINT JARS
OR FOUR 1-QUART JARS

8 pounds fresh whole
green beans

4 teaspoons table salt

Boiling water

When tightly packed in jars, these raw-packed beans are a beautiful sight to see. These have consistently been blue ribbon winners. Whole green beans look best when positioned in jars vertically. Choose uniform, straight, unblemished beans that are approximately 8 inches long for quart jars or beans 4 inches long for pint jars.

1. Rinse the beans thoroughly to remove any dirt and drain well. Trim the ends and remove any strings.

2. Pack the beans vertically into hot jars, leaving 1-inch headspace. Add ½ teaspoon salt to each pint jar and 1 teaspoon salt to each quart jar.

3. Ladle the boiling water into the jars, covering the beans and maintaining the 1-inch headspace. Remove any air bubbles. If necessary, add more liquid to maintain the headspace. Wipe the jar rims and threads with a clean, damp paper towel. Apply hot lids and screw bands.

4. Process pint jars for 20 minutes and quart jars for 25 minutes at 11 pounds of pressure in a dial-gauge pressure canner or at 10 pounds of pressure in a weighted-gauge pressure canner (see p. 36 for instructions).

5. After the processing time is complete, remove the canner from the heat. Let the pressure return to zero before removing the jars from the canner. Let cool for 12 to 24 hours. Check the seals and remove the screw bands. Store jars in a cool, dry, dark place for up to 1 year.

Thyme Green Beans

CONTRIBUTOR: LINDA J. AMENDT, CALIFORNIA

MAKES ABOUT 6 PINT JARS
OR THREE 1-QUART JARS

5 to 8 sprigs fresh thyme

6½ pounds unblemished, young, tender green beans

2 tablespoons freshly squeezed lemon juice

1 tablespoon canning or pickling salt

Linda's aunt Jeanie Lee taught her that "it takes thyme to cook green beans." The judges at numerous fairs loved the flavor of the thyme, giving the beans high praise—"Great job. These beans are a pleasure to judge!"—and awarding them Best of Division for the most outstanding vegetable exhibit. Linda cuts the beans into pieces for a family pack, but you can leave the beans whole for a fancy pack, if you prefer. Adding a small amount of fresh lemon juice to the water will help the green beans maintain more of their natural color during blanching.

1. Thoroughly rinse the green beans to remove any dirt and drain well.

2. Fill an 8-quart stainless steel stockpot about half full of water. Tie the thyme sprigs in a piece of cheesecloth, add to the water, and then bring the water to a boil over medium-high heat.

3. Using a sharp knife, trim the stem ends from the beans. Slice the green beans into uniform pieces about 1 inch long.

4. Remove the thyme pouch from the water. Carefully add the green beans to the water, and then stir in the lemon juice. Reduce the heat and simmer for 5 minutes. Remove the pot from the heat.

5. Using a slotted spoon, pack the green beans into hot jars, leaving 1-inch headspace. Add ½ teaspoon salt to each pint jar of beans or 1 teaspoon salt to each quart jar.

6. Line a fine-mesh sieve with 2 to 3 layers of fine-knit cheesecloth. Strain the cooking liquid through the sieve. Ladle the hot liquid into the jars, covering the beans and maintaining the 1-inch headspace. Remove any air bubbles. If necessary, add more liquid to maintain the headspace. Wipe the jar rims and threads with a clean, damp paper towel. Apply hot lids and screw bands.

7. Process pint jars for 20 minutes and quart jars for 25 minutes at 11 pounds of pressure in a dial-gauge pressure canner or at 10 pounds of pressure in a weighted-gauge pressure canner (see p. 36 for instructions).

8. After the processing time is complete, remove the canner from the heat. Let the pressure return to zero before removing the jars from the canner. Let cool for 12 to 24 hours. Check the seals and remove the screw bands. Store jars in a cool, dry, dark place for up to 1 year.

VARIATION:
DILLED GREEN BEANS
- -
To make dilled green beans, substitute fresh dill sprigs for the thyme sprigs.

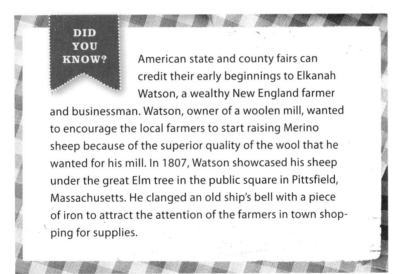

DID YOU KNOW? American state and county fairs can credit their early beginnings to Elkanah Watson, a wealthy New England farmer and businessman. Watson, owner of a woolen mill, wanted to encourage the local farmers to start raising Merino sheep because of the superior quality of the wool that he wanted for his mill. In 1807, Watson showcased his sheep under the great Elm tree in the public square in Pittsfield, Massachusetts. He clanged an old ship's bell with a piece of iron to attract the attention of the farmers in town shopping for supplies.

Roasted Roma Tomatoes

CONTRIBUTOR: NANCY CHARRON, WASHINGTON

MAKES ABOUT 3 PINT JARS

5 pounds ripe Roma tomatoes

6 to 8 large cloves garlic, peeled and slivered (about 1 head garlic)

1 teaspoon canning or pickling salt

1 teaspoon freshly ground black pepper

1 teaspoon citric acid

TIP

Be sure to use only plum or paste tomatoes; other tomato varieties will fall apart during cooking.

When the Charrons have a bountiful tomato supply, this recipe is their favorite way to prepare them for later use. Roasted tomatoes are easy to make and so good. Fully ripe tomatoes with a solid, deep red color will have the best flavor.

To make a smoky-flavored tomato sauce, put the roasted tomatoes and garlic slivers in a blender and process until almost smooth; transfer to the stockpot. Bring the sauce to a boil, stirring frequently to prevent sticking and scorching. Add ¼ teaspoon citric acid to each hot pint jar. Fill the jars with sauce, leaving ½-inch headspace. Process pint jars in a water bath canner for 35 minutes. Makes about 3 pint jars.

1. Position a rack in the center of the oven and heat the oven to 450°F.

2. Cut the tomatoes in half lengthwise and place cut side down on a large rimmed baking sheet, roasting pan, or two 9 x 13-inch baking pans. Sprinkle with the slivers of garlic, salt, and pepper. Roast until the juice from the tomatoes runs clear in the pan and the peels of the tomatoes have visible black stripes or blisters, 30 to 40 minutes. If needed to obtain desired color, broil for a few minutes to char the skins.

3. Transfer the tomatoes to a 6-quart stainless steel stockpot, scraping the pan to get all the juices and garlic. Bring the mixture just to a boil over medium to medium-high heat, stirring only as needed to prevent sticking. Stirring too much or too vigorously will cause the tomatoes to break apart. Remove the pot from the heat.

4. Add ¼ teaspoon citric acid to each hot pint jar. Ladle the tomatoes and juice into the jars, leaving ½-inch headspace. Remove any air bubbles. Wipe the jar rims and threads with a clean, damp paper towel. Apply hot lids and screw bands.

5. Process pint jars in a water bath canner for 40 minutes (see p. 34 for instructions). Remove from the water bath canner and let cool for 12 to 24 hours. Check the seals and remove the screw bands. Store jars in a cool, dry, dark place for up to 1 year.

Sweet Potatoes

CONTRIBUTOR: SANDRA BEASLEY, NORTH CAROLINA

**MAKES ABOUT 4 PINT JARS
OR TWO 1-QUART JARS**

4 to 6 pounds sweet potatoes

Boiling water

TIP

Sweet potatoes have enough natural sweetness that there's no need to add syrup, sugar, or salt to the jars. Leaving these out also makes the sweet potatoes more versatile for use in recipes.

Although raw sweet potatoes keep well for months in a cool, dark place, the Beasleys like to can them so they are cooked and ready for use in recipes like sweet potato waffles, cornbread, or homemade crescent rolls. Sandra's daughter Ruth loves to make rolls on the spur of the moment, so these jars enable her to do just that. The family usually cans sweet potatoes in pint jars, which are just the right size to add to recipes.

1. Using a soft scrub brush, thoroughly scrub the sweet potatoes, then rinse well and dry.

2. Peel the sweet potatoes and cut into ½-inch cubes. You can also cut the potatoes into spears or other desired shapes.

3. Pack the sweet potatoes into hot jars, leaving 1-inch headspace. Ladle the boiling water into the jars, covering the sweet potatoes and maintaining the 1-inch headspace. Remove any air bubbles. If necessary, add more liquid to maintain the headspace. Wipe the jar rims and threads with a clean, damp paper towel. Apply hot lids and screw bands.

4. Process pint jars for 65 minutes and quart jars for 90 minutes at 11 pounds of pressure in a dial-gauge pressure canner or at 10 pounds of pressure in a weighted-gauge pressure canner (see p. 36 for instructions).

5. After the processing time is complete, remove the canner from the heat. Let the pressure return to zero before removing the jars from the canner. Let cool for 12 to 24 hours. Check the seals and remove the screw bands. Store jars in a cool, dry, dark place for up to 1 year.

Asparagus

CONTRIBUTOR: SANDRA BEASLEY, NORTH CAROLINA

MAKES ABOUT 4 PINT JARS OR TWO 1-QUART JARS

7 pounds asparagus

Boiling water

The Beasleys love asparagus. When they can buy it fresh for a good price, they purchase it in bulk and can it for future use, like making eggs Benedict or combined with sautéed onions for a side dish. For a treat for the eyes, look for purple asparagus at the farmers' market.

1. Rinse the asparagus to remove any dirt and drain well on a wire rack or several layers of paper towels. Remove the tough ends and cut into pieces 1 inch shorter than the jar height. Rinse again and drain well.

2. Snugly pack the asparagus, spear end up, into hot jars, leaving 1-inch headspace. Ladle the boiling water into the jars, covering the asparagus and maintaining the 1-inch headspace. Remove any air bubbles. If necessary, add more liquid to maintain the headspace. Wipe the jar rims and threads with a clean, damp paper towel. Apply hot lids and screw bands.

3. Process pint jars for 30 minutes and quart jars for 40 minutes at 11 pounds of pressure in a dial-gauge pressure canner or at 10 pounds of pressure in a weighted-gauge pressure canner (see p. 36 for instructions).

4. After the processing time is complete, remove the canner from the heat. Let the pressure return to zero before removing the jars from the canner. Let cool for 12 to 24 hours. Check the seals and remove the screw bands. Store jars in a cool, dry, dark place for up to 1 year.

Vegetable Soup

CONTRIBUTOR: JANET GAMBLE, IDAHO

MAKES 12 TO 13 QUARTS

4 quarts peeled and quartered tomatoes (7 to 9 pounds)

4 quarts peeled and chopped potatoes (8 to 10 pounds)

6 cups peeled and chopped carrots (10 to 14 carrots)

4 cups cut or snapped green beans (1-inch pieces) (1½ to 2 pounds)

4 onions, chopped

2 cups chopped celery (4 to 6 stalks)

18 cups water

12 beef soup base cubes

1 cup pearl barley

2 tablespoons table salt

1 tablespoon Italian seasoning

1 teaspoon Mrs. Dash® seasoning (optional)

½ teaspoon freshly ground black pepper

Homemade vegetable soup is so much better than soup out of a can from the grocery store. This one is delicious! For vegetable beef, Janet adds some cooked ground beef to the soup when she heats it up.

1. In a 16- to 20-quart stainless steel stockpot, combine all of the ingredients in the order listed and stir to combine. Bring the mixture to a boil over medium-high heat, stirring frequently. Reduce the heat, cover, and simmer for 30 minutes, stirring occasionally. The vegetables should be just tender but not soft. Remove the pot from the heat.

2. Ladle the soup into hot pint jars, leaving 1-inch headspace. Remove any air bubbles. Wipe the jar rims and threads with a clean, damp paper towel. Apply hot lids and screw bands.

3. Process pint jars for 60 minutes and quart jars for 75 minutes at 11 pounds of pressure in a dial-gauge pressure canner or at 10 pounds of pressure in a weighted-gauge pressure canner (see p. 36 for instructions).

4. After the processing time is complete, remove the canner from the heat. Let the pressure return to zero before removing the jars from the canner. Let cool for 12 to 24 hours. Check the seals and remove the screw bands. Store jars in a cool, dry, dark place for up to 1 year.

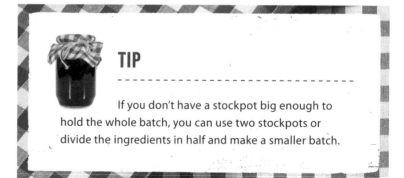

TIP

If you don't have a stockpot big enough to hold the whole batch, you can use two stockpots or divide the ingredients in half and make a smaller batch.

Mushrooms

CONTRIBUTOR: SANDRA BEASLEY, NORTH CAROLINA

MAKES ABOUT 3 PINT JARS

6 pounds small white or brown mushrooms

Boiling water

TIP

Never can wild mushrooms because they might contain harmful bacteria.

Canned mushrooms are a staple for the Beasley family, and these freshly canned ones are a treat. They are great in omelets, pasta sauce, or when combined with the Beasleys' canned asparagus.

1. Carefully clean each mushroom with a soft brush or damp paper towel to remove all dirt. Rinse under cold water and drain well.

2. Cut off the stems and discard. Leave small mushrooms whole and cut large mushrooms in half.

3. Place the mushrooms in a 6-quart stainless steel stockpot and add enough water to cover. Bring to a boil over medium-high heat, then reduce the heat and boil for 5 minutes. Remove the pot from the heat.

4. Using a slotted spoon, pack the mushrooms into hot jars, leaving 1-inch headspace. Ladle the boiling water into the jars, covering the mushrooms and maintaining the 1-inch headspace. Remove any air bubbles. If necessary, add more liquid to maintain the headspace. Wipe the jar rims and threads with a clean, damp paper towel. Apply hot lids and screw bands.

5. Process pint jars for 45 minutes at 11 pounds of pressure in a dial-gauge pressure canner or at 10 pounds of pressure in a weighted-gauge pressure canner (see p. 36 for instructions).

6. After the processing time is complete, remove the canner from the heat. Let the pressure return to zero before removing the jars from the canner. Let cool for 12 to 24 hours. Check the seals and remove the screw bands. Store jars in a cool, dry, dark place for up to 1 year.

* Pickles *

Crispy, crunchy cucumber pickles and tangy vegetable pickles are canning staples. But blue ribbon pickles don't happen by accident. Paying attention to the details, selecting quality produce and other ingredients, and careful processing will yield high-quality results.

Selecting Produce

Produce starts to deteriorate quickly, so it is important to pickle fruits and vegetables as soon after harvest as possible. Pickling cucumbers and squash, like zucchini, can develop hollow centers if too many days pass between harvest and canning. If these vegetables are left whole, the hollow centers can trap air pockets that may cause the pickles to float in the jars and also harbor bacteria that may not be killed during processing.

Select firm, fresh, unblemished produce of uniform size and shape. Use pickling varieties of cucumbers for making most pickles. Regular slicing cucumbers and English cucumbers have large seeds and contain a lot of moisture, which will not make good pickled products.

Preparing Vegetables

Rinse vegetables under cool running water and scrub gently with a soft brush to remove all dirt and sand. Be careful not to scrub too hard and damage the produce. Cut a thin slice off the blossom end of cucumbers and squash to remove the blossom scar. The blossom end can contain bacteria and enzymes that can contaminate the pickles or cause scum to form in the jars. For root vegetables, such as carrots or beets, cut off the root and stem ends. These can also harbor bacteria and should always be removed.

Depending on the type of pickles you are making, the produce can be left whole or cut into wedges, spears, slices, or even chunks. The key is to make all of the pieces the same shape, size, and thickness. This will not only make pretty pickles, but also allow the pieces to evenly absorb the pickling liquid and have a uniform flavor and texture.

Vinegar

White vinegar and cider vinegar are the traditional choices for canning pickles, but you can also make wonderful pickles using wine, herb, and fruit vinegars. The important factor for safe pickling is that the vinegar must have an acidity level of at least 5%. Vinegars with a lower acidity level may allow the growth of harmful bacteria in the pickle jars after processing. Never reduce the ratio or amount of vinegar in a pickle recipe, which can make the pickles unsafe to can. If you prefer pickles that are less tart, increase the amount of sugar in the syrup.

Salt

Salt is an important ingredient in making pickles, particularly cucumber and squash pickles. Not only does it add flavor, but it also helps to draw liquid out of the vegetables so the vegetables can absorb more syrup, which produces better-tasting pickles. It also makes the pickles heavier so they are less likely to float in the jars after processing. While pickles may be safely prepared with a reduced amount of salt, or even no salt, the quality of cucumber, squash, and some other pickles will definitely suffer.

I recommend using canning or pickling salt to make pickles. In some cases, kosher salt may be substituted for canning salt. With iodized or non-iodized table salt, the non-caking additives in table salts may make the brine or syrup cloudy, through the pickles will still be safe to eat. Reduced-sodium salts may be used in pickle recipes, but they will produce similar results to using table salt. The pickles will also have a different taste than normally expected.

Low-Temperature Pasteurization for Pickles

Processing cucumber pickles at a lower temperature for a longer amount of time produces pickles with a crisper texture than those processed in a boiling water bath. But the processing temperature must be carefully managed to avoid possible spoilage. Low-temperature pasteurization is only recommended for processing cucumber pickles.

To process whole, spear, or sliced cucumber pickles using the low-temperature pasteurization method, place filled jars in a water bath canner filled halfway with water heated to about 140°F. Add enough additional hot water to cover the jars by 1 to 2 inches. Heat the water until the temperature reaches between 180° and 185°F before starting the timer. I recommend an instant-read thermometer to check the water temperature. Process the jars for 30 minutes, maintaining a 180° to 185°F water temperature for the entire processing time. Check the temperature periodically with the thermometer to be certain that the water temperature is at least 180°F during the entire 30 minutes. Temperatures higher than 185°F may cause the pickles to soften.

Sweet Lime Pickles

CONTRIBUTOR: LAURA MILOSAVICH, COLORADO

MAKES ABOUT SEVEN TO
NINE 1-QUART JARS

2 gallons water

2 cups pickling lime

7 pounds pickling
cucumbers, rinsed and
sliced ¼ inch thick

9 cups granulated sugar

8 cups white vinegar

1 tablespoon canning or
pickling salt

2 teaspoons pickling
spice

1 teaspoon celery seeds

TIP - - - - - - - -

Do not use containers or pans made of aluminum for preparing pickles, as the metal can react with the lime or vinegar.

These are the best sweet lime pickle slices. They take a little more time to make than most other sliced pickles, but are worth it. These pickles are great in ham salad, on sandwiches, or eaten right out of the jar!

1. In a large mixing bowl, enamel or glass pickling jar, or plastic food-safe bucket, combine the water and lime, and stir until the lime is completely dissolved. Add the cucumber slices and let them soak at room temperature for 12 hours or overnight.

2. Using a slotted spoon, carefully remove the cucumbers from the lime water; discard the lime water. Rinse the cucumber slices three times in cold water, changing the water after each rinsing.

3. Fill the large mixing bowl with cold water. Add the rinsed cucumber slices and top with crushed or cubed ice. Let the cucumber slices soak for 3 hours in the ice water. Drain well.

4. In an 8- to 10-quart stainless steel stockpot, combine the sugar, vinegar, salt, pickling spice, and celery seeds. Bring the mixture to a gentle boil over medium heat, stirring constantly until the sugar dissolves. Remove the pot from the heat and add the drained cucumber slices. Cover and let the slices soak in the syrup at room temperature for 5 to 6 hours, or overnight.

5. Bring the cucumber mixture to a boil over medium-high heat. Reduce the heat and boil gently for 35 minutes. Remove the pot from the heat.

6. Using a slotted spoon, pack the pickle slices into hot jars, leaving ½-inch headspace. Ladle the hot syrup into the jars, covering the pickles and maintaining the ½-inch headspace. Remove any air bubbles. Wipe the jar rims and threads with a clean, damp paper towel. Apply hot lids and screw bands.

7. Process pint and quart jars in a water bath canner for 15 minutes (see p. 34 for instructions). Remove from the water bath canner and let cool for 12 to 24 hours. Check the seals and remove the screw bands. Store jars in a cool, dry, dark place for up to 1 year.

Hot Dill Pickles

CONTRIBUTOR: LILLIE BETIK CROWLEY, TEXAS

MAKES ONE 1-QUART JAR

5 to 7 pickling
cucumbers, depending
on size

½ cup 10% acidity white
vinegar (for less tart
pickles, use 5% vinegar)

1 or 2 cloves garlic,
peeled

1 jalapeño or cayenne
pepper (optional)

A few fresh dill leaves or
flower heads, or 1 scant
teaspoon dill seed

1 tablespoon canning or
pickling salt

1 teaspoon crab boil
seasoning (for spicier
pickles; optional)

1 teaspoon granulated
sugar

Boiling water

This recipe also works for carrot sticks, green beans, or a medley of vegetables. Red and green pepper pickles look wonderful on a relish tray at Christmastime. If you don't like dill, you can use pickling spice instead. You can multiply this recipe to make as many quart jars of pickles as you want.

1. Using a soft scrub brush, gently scrub the cucumbers, then rinse well and dry. If the cucumbers are large, cut them into spears or sticks.

2. Pack the cucumbers into a hot quart jar, leaving ½-inch headspace. Add the vinegar, garlic, jalapeño or cayenne pepper, dill leaves, salt, crab boil seasoning, and sugar to the jar.

3. Ladle the boiling water into the jar, covering the cucumbers and maintaining the ½-inch headspace. Remove any air bubbles. Wipe the jar rims and threads with a clean, damp paper towel. Apply hot lids and screw bands.

4. Process quart jars in a water bath canner for 20 minutes (see p. 34 for instructions). Remove from the water bath canner and let cool for 12 to 24 hours. Check the seals and remove the screw bands. Store jars in a cool, dry, dark place for up to 1 year.

Recipe adapted from *Country Cooking with Lillie Crowley*—God's Blessings.

LILLIE BETIK CROWLEY

ENNIS, TEXAS

LILLIE BETIK CROWLEY (1926–2014) was the oldest of ten children born to immigrant Czech-American parents in Ennis, Texas. Raised in the Czech culture and as the eldest daughter, she learned to cook and became responsible for meal preparation for the family. She spoke Czech until she was taught English in grade school. Lillie started canning at a very early age. Growing up on a farm, Lillie learned to cook with seasonal foods from the garden and how to preserve the harvest for later use. She was taught to spare nothing and never let any food go to waste.

Lillie enjoyed cooking and canning with the blessings from her garden.

In 1947, she married Lee Crowley and her cooking skills became extremely helpful as she raised her own family of 14 children. Lillie Crowley enjoyed cooking with the produce from her own garden and using simple and organic ingredients. Lillie would can over 1,000 jars of vegetables and fruits a year with the bounty from her prolific garden or by picking fresh produce from a nearby farm or growing wild along the road and fence lines of country roads. She always felt that canning and cooking were her blessings, her joy, a way to express her creativity, and her escape in life.

Lillie first entered the State Fair of Texas in 1958 and continued to compete for 20 years. After a while, she so dominated the competition that fewer and fewer people would enter their exhibits. Lillie was asked to retire from the competition in 1978 and become a fair judge and canning coordinator instead. In recognition of her skill and accomplishments, the Fair offered Lillie the opportunity to develop a daily cooking show to demonstrate her winning recipes at the Fair. For 30 years, she presented *Country Cooking with Lillie Crowley* every day of the Fair season, frequently delivering three 1-hour shows a day to capacity crowds. After retiring from the show in 2008, she enjoyed visiting the Fair as a celebrity chef.

Shortly before passing away in January 2014, Lillie realized her dream and completed work on her cookbook, *Country Cooking with Lillie Crowley—God's Blessings*.

BARBARA SCHALLER

BURNSVILLE, MINNESOTA

BARBARA SCHALLER, the youngest of 13 children, was reared on a small subsistence farm. Her mom canned tons of stuff to feed her large family, and Barbara helped with skinning the peaches and tomatoes. Canning since her early years of marriage, 48 years ago, Barbara enjoys pretty much everything about canning except the timing. "Mom always said 'You have to can when the fruit is ready, Barbie, not when you are ready.' True words, those, as summers and kitchens can be hot here in July and August." She also likes the sense of satisfaction she gets from canning, especially tomatoes. "Most canned tomatoes contain calcium chloride to keep them firm. In my opinion, canned tomatoes should not be firm when they are cooked."

> ## "Mom always said, 'You have to can when the fruit is ready, not when you are ready.' True words."

A couple of years after Barbara and her husband moved into their home 45 years ago, her mom gave them a small plum tree, which they planted in the backyard. But Barbara did nothing with the plums, just letting them fall to the ground and rot. Her competitive canning began a number of years later after her husband became tired of slipping on the fallen plums while mowing the lawn and said she needed to do something with the plums or he would be forced to prune the tree to ground level. Her neighbor recommended making plum jelly. "She told me to buy a package of Sure-Jell pectin and

follow the directions. I did. A few years later, my brother-in-law's aunt, who was a sewing judge at the Minnesota State Fair, told me I should enter the canning contests. I entered four jars—two pickles, plum jelly, and corn relish. The pickles placed fourth and fifth and the jelly and relish both won blue ribbons. There's nothing like success to encourage a person. I have never looked back."

"My husband loves my bread-and-butter pickles and when I give away a jar, he says, 'Quit giving away my pickles!' I told him they would be his pickles when he helped make them. So I now have a willing cucumber scrubber at my beck and call."

Entering fair competitions since 1981, Barbara has earned over 100 blue ribbons and a number of special awards, including awards from the M. A. Gedney® Company, Ball, and Sure-Jell. The award that means the most to her is being named the Minnesota State Fair's Prestigious Processor of the Pantry five times. Canners are allowed to enter up to 20 classes and the award is based on a point system for entries earning first- through fifth-place finishes in the Canned and Preserved Foods division. The canner with the most cumulative points is declared the winner of the award.

Barb's Bread-and-Butter Pickles

CONTRIBUTOR: BARBARA SCHALLER, MINNESOTA

MAKES 7 TO 8 PINTS

4 quarts thinly sliced medium pickling cucumbers (about 25 cucumbers)

3 cups sliced onions (about 4 medium onions)

2 green bell peppers (or 1 red and 1 green pepper), chopped

3 cloves garlic, sliced

⅓ cup canning or pickling salt

5 cups granulated sugar

3 cups cider vinegar

2 tablespoons mustard seeds

1½ teaspoons celery seeds

1½ teaspoons ground turmeric

This recipe was adapted from one Barbara found in an old *Better Homes & Gardens* cookbook. These pickles have been awarded nine blue ribbons in the 15 times she's entered them in competition. In 2001, they received a prize from the M. A. Gedney Company for the Best Pickle at the Minnesota State Fair. These are her husband's favorite pickles.

1. In a large container, combine the cucumbers, onions, bell peppers, and garlic. Add the salt. Cover with cracked ice and mix thoroughly. Let stand for 3 hours. Drain well.

2. In an 8-quart stainless steel stockpot, combine the sugar, cider vinegar, mustard seeds, celery seeds, and turmeric. Cook over medium-high heat, stirring constantly, until the sugar is completely dissolved. Add the drained cucumber mixture and heat just until the mixture comes to a boil. Remove the pot from the heat.

3. Using a slotted spoon, pack the pickles into hot jars, leaving ½-inch headspace. Ladle the hot syrup into the jars, covering the pickles and maintaining the ½-inch headspace. Remove any air bubbles. Wipe the jar rims and threads with a clean, damp paper towel. Apply hot lids and screw bands.

4. Process pint jars in a water bath canner for 10 minutes (see p. 34 for instructions). Remove from the water bath canner and let cool for 12 to 24 hours. Check the seals and remove the screw bands. Store jars in a cool, dry, dark place for up to 1 year.

Baby Beet Pickles

CONTRIBUTOR: LINDA J. AMENDT, CALIFORNIA

**MAKES ABOUT 6 PINT JARS
OR THREE 1-QUART JARS**

6 pounds 1- to 1½-inch-
diameter baby beets
(80 to 90 small beets)

3 cups raspberry vinegar
or red-wine vinegar
(5% acidity)

1½ cups white vinegar

2 cups granulated sugar

⅔ cup water

2 teaspoons whole
allspice

1½ teaspoons canning or
pickling salt

½ cinnamon stick

SERVING SUGGESTION

Beet pickles make a won-
derful addition to a green
salad or relish tray or
served with roast pork.

These tasty beet pickles have a sweet, spicy flavor enhanced by raspberry vinegar. Small beets make the best pickles and they can be canned whole. Larger beets should be quartered before canning.

1. Cut off the beet greens, leaving 1 inch of the stem. Using a soft scrub brush, thoroughly scrub the beets in cold water, then rinse well and dry. Trim the taproot to ½ inch long.

2. Fill an 8-quart stainless steel stockpot half full of water and bring to a boil over medium-high heat. In four batches, cook the beets just until tender, 8 to 10 minutes depending on the size of the beets. Remove the beets from the water with a slotted spoon and immediately transfer to a bowl of ice water for 1 minute to stop the cooking and loosen the skins. Drain well. Peel the beets, trimming off the stems and taproots.

3. In an 8-quart stainless steel stockpot, combine the raspberry vinegar, white vinegar, sugar, water, allspice, salt, and cinnamon stick. Bring to a boil over medium-high heat, stirring constantly, until the sugar is completely dissolved. Add the peeled beets and simmer for 5 minutes. Remove the pot from the heat.

4. Using a slotted spoon, pack the beets into hot jars, leaving ½-inch headspace.

5. Line a fine-mesh sieve with 2 to 3 layers of damp fine-knit cheesecloth. Strain the pickling syrup through the sieve. Ladle the hot syrup into the jars, covering the beets and maintaining the ½-inch headspace. Remove any air bubbles. If necessary, add more syrup to maintain the headspace. Wipe the jar rims and threads with a clean, damp paper towel. Apply hot lids and screw bands.

6. Process both pint and quart jars in a water bath canner for 30 minutes (see p. 34 for instructions). Remove from the water bath canner and let cool for 12 to 24 hours. Check the seals and remove the screw bands. Store jars in a cool, dry, dark place for up to 1 year.

Reese Family Bread-and-Butter Pickles

CONTRIBUTOR: JULIA SNYDER, VIRGINIA

MAKES 5 TO 6 PINT JARS

16 to 20 medium cucumbers, thinly sliced

10 small onions, thinly sliced

⅓ cup canning or pickling salt

3 cups cider vinegar

2 cups granulated sugar

2 tablespoons mustard seeds

2 teaspoons celery seeds

2 teaspoons ground turmeric

1 teaspoon ground ginger

1 teaspoon whole peppercorns

These pickles are a Reese family favorite—and the only type that everyone in the family eats. They use whatever cucumbers are growing in the garden that year, often slicing or salad varieties; slender cucumbers make the best pickles. In 2014, granddaughter Julia took home the Grand Champion of Pickles award in the youth division at the Salem Fair with these pickles.

1. In a large bowl, layer the cucumber and onions slices, sprinkling salt on top of each layer. Cover with ice cubes. Let stand for 1½ hours. Drain, rinse thoroughly, and then drain well.

2. In an 8-quart stainless steel stockpot, combine the vinegar, sugar, mustard seeds, celery seeds, turmeric, ginger, and peppercorns. Cook the mixture over medium-high heat, stirring constantly, until the sugar is completely dissolved. Add the drained cucumber mixture and bring to a boil. Remove the pot from the heat.

3. Using a slotted spoon, pack the pickles into hot jars, leaving ½-inch headspace. Ladle the hot syrup into the jars, covering the pickles and maintaining the ½-inch headspace. Remove any air bubbles. Wipe the jar rims and threads with a clean, damp paper towel. Apply hot lids and screw bands.

4. Process pint jars in a water bath canner for 10 minutes (see p. 34 for instructions). Remove from the water bath canner and let cool for 12 to 24 hours. Check the seals and remove the screw bands. Store jars in a cool, dry, dark place for up to 1 year.

> **DID YOU KNOW?**
>
> According to legend, bread-and-butter pickles got their name during the Great Depression. Cucumber slices were sandwiched between bread and butter as a cheap meal. Today these pickles are more likely used to top burgers.

Dilled Asparagus Pickles

CONTRIBUTOR: GEORGE YATES, TEXAS

MAKES 6 PINT JARS

4 pounds fresh
asparagus

2½ cups white-wine
vinegar

2½ cups water

2 teaspoons celery seeds

2 teaspoons mustard
seeds

2 teaspoons dill seeds

2 teaspoons crushed
red pepper flakes

6 cloves garlic

6 sprigs fresh dill

6 small jalapeño,
serrano, or cayenne
peppers

Asparagus makes wonderful pickles. You can adjust the amount of dill and spices to suit your personal taste. For moderate heat, use a small jalapeño pepper in each jar. For hot pickles, use a small serrano or cayenne pepper.

1. Rinse the asparagus and trim to about 4 inches in length.

2. In a large saucepan, combine the vinegar and water and bring to a boil over medium heat. Reduce the heat to low, cover, and keep hot.

3. Evenly divide the celery seeds, mustard seeds, dill seeds, and red pepper flakes between 6 pint jars. Add one garlic clove, a fresh dill sprig, and a hot pepper to each jar.

4. Pack the asparagus spears into the jars, placing the tips up and leaving ½-inch headspace.

5. Ladle the hot vinegar mixture into the jars, covering the asparagus and leaving ½-inch headspace. Remove any air bubbles. Wipe the jar rims and threads with a clean, damp paper towel. Apply hot lids and screw bands.

6. Process pint jars in a water bath canner for 10 minutes (see p. 34 for instructions). Remove from the water bath canner and let cool for 12 to 24 hours. Check the seals and remove the screw bands. Store jars in a cool, dry, dark place for up to 1 year.

Pickled Cauliflower

CONTRIBUTOR: ROBIN TARBELL-THOMAS, IOWA

MAKES ABOUT 6 PINT JARS

6 teaspoons canning or pickling salt

12 cups cauliflower florets (about 9 pounds cauliflower)

4 cups white vinegar

4 cups distilled water

4 cups granulated sugar

2 cups thinly sliced onions

1 cup chopped red bell peppers (¼-inch pieces)

2 tablespoons mustard seeds

1 tablespoon celery seeds

1 teaspoon ground turmeric

1 teaspoon crushed red pepper flakes

Cauliflower is a wonderful vegetable to turn into pickles that make a perfect addition to any meal. They are worth every bite.

1. Fill a 12-quart stockpot half full of water. Stir in the salt. Over medium-high heat, bring the water to a boil. Add the cauliflower and boil for 3 minutes. Drain the cauliflower well and set aside to cool.

2. In an 8-quart stainless steel stockpot, combine the vinegar, distilled water, and sugar. Over medium-high heat, stirring constantly, heat until the sugar is completely dissolved. Add the onions, red bell peppers, mustard seeds, celery seeds, turmeric, and red pepper flakes. Bring the mixture to a boil. Reduce the heat and simmer for 5 minutes. Reduce the heat to low and keep hot.

3. Pack the cauliflower into hot jars, leaving ½-inch headspace. Ladle the hot syrup mixture into the jars, covering the cauliflower and maintaining the ½-inch headspace. Remove any air bubbles. Wipe the jar rims and threads with a clean, damp paper towel. Apply hot lids and screw bands.

4. Process pint jars in a water bath canner for 15 minutes (see p. 34 for instructions). Remove from the water bath canner and let cool for 12 to 24 hours. Check the seals and remove the screw bands. Store jars in a cool, dry, dark place for up to 1 year.

Sweet Pickle Spears

CONTRIBUTOR: SANDRA BEASLEY, NORTH CAROLINA

MAKES ABOUT 7 PINT JARS

4 pounds small pickling cucumbers

Boiling water

4 cups granulated sugar

3¾ cups white vinegar

3 tablespoons canning or pickling salt

4 teaspoons celery seeds

4 teaspoons ground turmeric

1½ teaspoons mustard seeds

This recipe has been handed down for at least four generations in the Beasley family. Sandra's great-great grandma, Mary Agnes Abernathy Robb, is who she believes created the recipe. The family often makes batches of 53 pint jars from 30 pounds of cucumbers! These pickles are a family favorite at Memorial Day dinners.

1. Using a soft scrub brush, gently scrub the cucumbers, then rinse well and dry. Trim off the blossom and stem ends of each cucumber. Cut each cucumber lengthwise into quarters, creating spears.

2. Place the cucumber spears in large metal bowl. Add enough boiling water to cover, then let stand for 2 hours.

3. In an 8-quart stainless steel stockpot, combine the sugar, vinegar, salt, celery seeds, turmeric, and mustard seeds. Bring the mixture to a boil over medium-high heat, stirring constantly until the sugar is completely dissolved, then reduce the heat to low and keep hot until needed.

4. Drain the cucumbers well. Pack the drained cucumber spears into hot jars, leaving ½-inch headspace. Ladle the hot syrup into the jars, covering the tops of the cucumbers and maintaining the ½-inch headspace. Remove any air bubbles. Wipe the jar rims and threads with a clean, damp paper towel. Apply hot lids and screw bands.

5. Process pint jars in a water bath canner for 10 minutes (see p. 34 for instructions). Remove from the water bath canner and let cool for 12 to 24 hours. Check the seals and remove the screw bands. Store jars in a cool, dry, dark place for up to 1 year.

Dill Pickle Spears

CONTRIBUTOR: ARIANNA EDWARDS, UTAH

**MAKES ABOUT FOUR
1-QUART JARS**

30 to 36 pickling
cucumbers (3 to 4 inches
long)

3 cups white vinegar

3 cups water

6 tablespoons canning or
pickling salt

1 bunch fresh dill sprigs

4 cloves garlic, peeled

2 tablespoons mustard
seeds

These pickles taste best when you use cucumbers straight from your garden. You can also cut the cucumbers into $1/4$-inch slices to make dill pickle slices instead of spears, if you prefer. Arianna uses wide-mouth jars to make packing the pickles easier.

1. Using a soft scrub brush, gently scrub the cucumbers, then rinse well and dry. Cut a $1/8$-inch slice from the blossom end of each cucumber, then cut each cucumber lengthwise into 4 to 6 wedge-shaped spears. The number of spears per cucumber depends on the width of the cucumber and how big you want the spears. Set aside.

2. In a 3- to 4-quart stainless steel stockpot, combine the vinegar, water, and salt and bring the mixture to a boil over medium-high heat, stirring constantly until the salt is dissolved. Reduce the heat, cover, and keep hot.

3. Place a generous layer of dill, 1 garlic clove, and 1½ teaspoons mustard seeds in the bottom of each quart jar.

4. Pack the cucumber spears into the bottom of the jars. After you have finished packing the first layer of spears, add another layer of dill and finish packing the jars with another layer of cucumbers, leaving ½-inch headspace.

5. Ladle the hot pickling liquid into the jars, covering the cucumbers and maintaining the ½-inch headspace. Remove any air bubbles. Wipe the jar rims and threads with a clean, damp paper towel. Apply hot lids and screw bands.

6. Process pint and quart jars in a water bath canner for 10 minutes (see p. 34 for instructions). Remove from the water bath canner and let cool for 12 to 24 hours. Check the seals and remove the screw bands. Store jars in a cool, dry, dark place for up to 1 year.

Dilly Beans

CONTRIBUTOR: CATHIE MERRIHEW, VERMONT

MAKES ABOUT 8 PINT JARS

4 pounds young green beans

8 teaspoons crushed red pepper flakes

8 teaspoons mustard seeds

8 cloves garlic, peeled

8 heads fresh dill

5 cups white vinegar

5 cups water

½ cup canning or pickling salt

TIP

For the best appearance and ease of packing the jars, choose straight beans. For a colorful alternative, add a quartered carrot stick to four sides of the jars while packing the beans.

Cathie's husband told her that his mom made the best dilly beans and asked her to try to duplicate them. Using the recipe written on a scrap of paper, Cathie makes these beans as a special treat at family functions. Her grandsons would even walk around teething on them when they were babies. These beans have won several blue ribbons at the Champlain Valley Fair.

1. Trim the green beans to 4 inches in length. Set aside.

2. Place 1 teaspoon red pepper flakes, 1 teaspoon mustard seeds, and 1 garlic clove in each pint jar. Fill each jar half-full of beans, standing them up straight and leaving ½-inch headspace. Add 1 whole dill head to the center of each jar. Continue to add beans until the jars are full.

3. In a 6-quart stainless steel stockpot, combine the vinegar, water, and salt and bring to a boil over medium-high heat, stirring constantly until the salt is dissolved.

4. Ladle the hot vinegar mixture into the jars, covering the beans and leaving ½-inch headspace. Remove any air bubbles. Wipe the jar rims and threads with a clean, damp paper towel. Apply hot lids and screw bands.

5. Process pint jars in a water bath canner for 10 minutes (see p. 34 for instructions). Remove from the water bath canner and let cool for 12 to 24 hours. Check the seals and remove the screw bands. Store jars in a cool, dry, dark place for up to 1 year.

Best Dill Pickles

CONTRIBUTOR: LAURA MILOSAVICH, COLORADO

MAKES SEVEN 1-QUART JARS

Enough pickling cucumbers to fill 7 quart jars (fifty-five to sixty-five 3- to 4-inch cucumbers)

9 cups water

6 cups white vinegar

½ cup canning or pickling salt

3 tablespoons mustard seeds

7 heads fresh dill

7 medium to large cloves garlic, peeled

7 small red chile peppers (optional)

7 freshly picked grape leaves (optional)

SERVING SUGGESTION

These pickles are wonderful chopped and added to potato salad.

These pickles are crisp and spicy. Laura says her secret is to place a clean dry grape leaf in each jar, which helps keep the pickles crisp. For the best flavor and texture, store the jars in a cool, dark, dry location for 3 to 6 months before opening.

1. Using a soft scrub brush, gently scrub the cucumbers, then rinse well and dry. Cut a ⅛-inch slice from the blossom end of each cucumber. Set aside.

2. In an 8-quart stainless steel stockpot, combine the water, vinegar, salt, and mustard seeds. Bring the mixture to a boil over medium-high heat, stirring constantly until the salt is dissolved, then reduce the heat, cover, and keep hot.

3. Pack the cucumbers into hot quart jars, leaving ½-inch headspace. To each jar, add 1 large head of dill, 1 garlic clove, 1 chile pepper, if using, and 1 grape leaf, if using.

4. Ladle the hot pickling liquid into the jars, covering the tops of the cucumbers and maintaining the ½-inch headspace. Remove any air bubbles. Wipe the jar rims and threads with a clean, damp paper towel. Apply hot lids and screw bands.

5. Process pint and quart jars in a water bath canner for 20 minutes (see p. 34 for instructions). Remove from the water bath canner and let cool for 12 to 24 hours. Check the seals and remove the screw bands. Store jars in a cool, dry, dark place for up to 1 year.

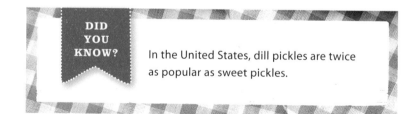

DID YOU KNOW? In the United States, dill pickles are twice as popular as sweet pickles.

Golden Glow Sweet Pickles

CONTRIBUTOR: CATHIE MERRIHEW, VERMONT

- -

MAKES ABOUT 7 PINT JARS

3 quarts peeled and seeded bite-sized chunks very ripe cucumbers

6 medium onions, sliced

2 red bell peppers, seeded and cut into 1-inch squares

¼ cup canning or pickling salt

3 cups white vinegar

3½ cups granulated sugar

15 whole cloves

2 tablespoons mustard seeds

1 teaspoon celery seeds

1 teaspoon ground turmeric

Some of the best recipes are old. This recipe was given to Cathie by a friend, Theresa Steady, who has been canning and preserving for most of her 80-plus years. It's a great way to use up overripe, oversized slicing cucumbers that got missed while harvesting the garden and are still firm but have taken on a lighter green or golden color. Cathie added the red pepper for a splash of color and took home the blue ribbon.

1. In a large bowl or container, combine the cucumbers, onions, bell peppers, and salt. Add enough water to cover the vegetables, then cover the container and let soak at room temperature overnight. Drain and rinse the cucumber mixture. Drain well.

2. In an 8-quart stainless steel stockpot, combine the vinegar, sugar, cloves, mustard seeds, celery seeds, and turmeric. Bring the mixture to a boil over medium-high heat. Add the drained cucumber mixture to the syrup, return to a boil, then reduce the heat and cook, stirring frequently, until the vegetables are tender, 5 to 10 minutes. Remove the pot from the heat.

3. Using a slotted spoon, pack the pickles into hot jars, leaving ½-inch headspace. Ladle the hot syrup into the jars, covering the pickles and maintaining the ½-inch headspace. Remove any air bubbles. Wipe the jar rims and threads with a clean, damp paper towel. Apply hot lids and screw bands.

4. Process pint jars in a water bath canner for 10 minutes (see p. 34 for instructions). Remove from the water bath canner and let cool for 12 to 24 hours. Check the seals and remove the screw bands. Store jars in a cool, dry, dark place for up to 1 year.

Squash Pickles

CONTRIBUTOR: ALAN GRAVENOR, MARYLAND

MAKES ABOUT 4 PINT JARS

8 cups ⅛-inch-thick slices squash (3 to 4 pounds)

2 cups sliced onions (2 to 3 medium)

2 tablespoon canning or pickling salt

2 cups white vinegar

2 cups granulated sugar

2 cups ⅛-inch-thick slices green bell peppers (3 to 4 medium)

1 teaspoon mustard seeds

1 teaspoon celery seeds

SERVING SUGGESTION

These tasty pickles are great in the summertime on a grilled hamburger or year-round as an accompaniment to any dinner.

These squash pickles are the cousin to the cucumber bread-and-butter pickles. They can be made from yellow summer squash or green zucchini squash or a mixture of both, whichever you prefer. Slice the squash and onions the same thickness for a uniform texture.

1. In a large mixing bowl, combine the squash, onions, and salt. Let stand for 1 hour. Drain the squash and onions and rinse several times to remove the salt.

2. In an 8-quart stainless steel stockpot, combine the vinegar, sugar, bell peppers, mustard seeds, and celery seeds. Bring the mixture to a boil over medium heat, then reduce the heat to low and simmer for 3 minutes.

3. Add the drained squash and onions to the pepper mixture and bring to a full boil over medium-high heat. Reduce the heat and boil for 5 minutes. Remove the pot from the heat.

4. Using a slotted spoon, pack the pickles into hot jars, leaving ½-inch headspace. Ladle the hot syrup into the jars, covering the pickles and maintaining the ½-inch headspace. Remove any air bubbles. Wipe the jar rims and threads with a clean, damp paper towel. Apply hot lids and screw bands.

5. Process pint jars in a water bath canner for 15 minutes (see p. 34 for instructions). Remove from the water bath canner and let cool for 12 to 24 hours. Check the seals and remove the screw bands. Store jars in a cool, dry, dark place for up to 1 year.

Cinnamon Pickled Watermelon Rind

CONTRIBUTOR: ANNA MAYERHOFER, NEW YORK

MAKES SIX TO SEVEN 8-OUNCE JARS

1 medium watermelon

Canning or pickling salt

1 lemon, lightly scrubbed and rinsed, then thinly sliced and seeded

2 cups white vinegar

2 cups water

2 pounds granulated sugar (about 4¾ cups)

Four 3-inch cinnamon sticks, plus more for packing the jars

2 teaspoons whole cloves

1 teaspoon ground allspice

SERVING SUGGESTION

Use pickled watermelon rind as a relish for a chicken salad sandwich, grilled fish, or hamburgers, or as a cocktail garnish.

This recipe enhances summer cookouts as well as the Thanksgiving table. You can use any variety of watermelon to make these pickles. For a pretty appearance, use a small cookie cutter to cut the watermelon rind into shapes.

1. Cut the red watermelon flesh from the rind, leaving a very small amount of pink flesh on the rind. With a vegetable peeler or a paring knife, remove the outer green skin from the rind. Cut the watermelon rind into cubes 1 inch or smaller. Measure out 2 pounds (3½ to 4 cups) of rind.

2. Place the prepared watermelon rind in a 2-gallon stoneware crock or a large ceramic or glass container. Measure and add enough water to completely cover the rind. Add ¼ cup of salt for each quart of water used to cover the rind. Cover the container and let soak at room temperature overnight.

3. Drain the watermelon rind well and transfer to an 8-quart stainless steel stockpot. Add enough fresh water to cover the rind. Bring the mixture to a gentle boil over medium heat and cook until the rind is tender but not soft, 12 to 14 minutes. Drain well and return the rind to the stockpot. Set aside.

4. In a 2-quart saucepan, combine the lemon slices and enough water to cover. Cook the lemon over medium heat until tender and nearly all the water boils away, 10 to 12 minutes. Watch carefully so the lemon does not scorch.

5. Add the cooked lemon, vinegar, the water, sugar, cinnamon sticks, cloves, and allspice to the cooked watermelon rind. Cook the watermelon mixture over medium heat, stirring frequently, until the rind is translucent, 25 to 30 minutes.

ANNA MAYERHOFER

CAMILLUS, NEW YORK

AS A SMALL CHILD, Anna Mayerhofer learned how to can from her mother. Her parents had a number of fruit trees and a large garden at their home in western New York State. Anna would help her mother can the abundant produce harvests. From childhood into adulthood, picking cherries, peaches, apples, Concord grapes, strawberries, blueberries, currants, and tomatoes has been an enjoyable activity for family and friends getting together for a day. To this day, picking fruits and berries is still a fun outing for Anna's family.

One of Anna's specialties is watermelon rind pickles, which she cuts into a variety of pretty shapes to suit the holiday or event where they will be served. Anna sees canning as a lifelong adventure and especially likes to make relishes and jellies.

"I like the process of picking, cleaning, cooking, and canning the fruits or vegetables. When I inherited my mother's steamer for making jellies, I was thrilled! With this old machine, making jelly is so easy—no cheesecloth needed to strain the juice!" Now when Anna makes jelly using the steamer, she recalls fond memories of canning with her mother.

6. Using a slotted spoon, pack the watermelon rind into hot jars, leaving ½-inch headspace. You can add an extra piece of cinnamon stick to each jar, if desired. Ladle the hot syrup into the jars, covering the rind and maintaining the ½-inch headspace. Remove any air bubbles. If necessary, add more syrup to maintain the headspace. Wipe the jar rims and threads with a clean, damp paper towel. Apply hot lids and screw bands.

7. Process 8-ounce and pint jars in a water bath canner for 10 minutes (see p. 34 for instructions). Remove from the water bath canner and let cool for 12 to 24 hours. Check the seals and remove the screw bands. Store jars in a cool, dry, dark place for up to 1 year.

Sweet Beet Pickle Slices

CONTRIBUTOR: VICTORIA THOMPSON, ALASKA

MAKES ABOUT 4 PINT JARS

12 to 18 medium beets

3 cups cider vinegar

1 cup granulated sugar

2 teaspoons pickling spices

TIP

If you are using large beets, cut the slices into quarters.

Beet pickles are very easy to make and one of Victoria's favorites. She has received many compliments on them. When she makes these pickles during her canning workshops before the fair, people are always asking to take home the jars.

1. Using a soft scrub brush, thoroughly scrub the beets, then rinse well and dry. Trim off the leaves, leaving 3 inches of the stems and roots on the beets.

2. Place the beets in an 8-quart stainless steel stockpot, cover with water, cover the pot, and bring to a boil over medium-high heat. Reduce the heat and cook until the skins start to loosen and will slip off the beets, 5 to 10 minutes. Remove the pot from the heat. Drain the beets and let cool, then cut off the stems and roots and slip the skins from the beets. Cut the beets into ¼-inch-thick slices. Measure out 8 cups sliced beets.

3. In an 8-quart stainless steel stockpot, combine the vinegar, sugar, and pickling spices and stir until the sugar is dissolved. Add the beet slices and bring the mixture to a boil over medium-high heat. Reduce the heat and boil, stirring occasionally, for 15 minutes. Remove the pot from the heat.

4. Using a slotted spoon, snugly pack the beet slices into hot jars, arranging them as neatly as possible and leaving ½-inch headspace. Ladle the hot syrup into the jars, covering the beets and maintaining the ½-inch headspace. Remove any air bubbles. If necessary, add more syrup to maintain the headspace. Wipe the jar rims and threads with a clean, damp paper towel. Apply hot lids and screw bands.

5. Process pint jars in a water bath canner for 30 minutes (see p. 34 for instructions). Remove from the water bath canner and let cool for 12 to 24 hours. Check the seals and remove the screw bands. Store jars in a cool, dry, dark place for up to 1 year.

VICTORIA THOMPSON

NORTH POLE, ALASKA

VICTORIA THOMPSON grew up on a farm where her dad grew truck crops, including watermelons, peas, and tomatoes. Both of her parents lived through the Great Depression, so they never wasted anything. Crops that didn't sell were canned for future use. When they had a particularly bountiful harvest, the extra produce went straight into jars. "At times, my mother would can 300 quart jars of tomatoes and dozens more of other vegetables." From about the age of 10, Victoria would help pick the vegetables early in the morning and then peel or shell them to get them ready for canning. "I would help my mother fill the jars, but she always did the work around the hot stove."

Having been canning for over 50 years, the best part about it for Victoria is seeing the happy looks on the faces of friends and family when they enjoy her canned products. It provides her with a great feeling of satisfaction. Victoria also likes entering her canned goods and baked foods in fair competitions, which she has been doing for 20 years. Bringing home blue ribbons for her entries is always a rewarding experience.

DID YOU KNOW? Because Alaska has very long summer days, giant vegetables are common. The Alaska State Fair has a giant cabbage contest, a tradition started in 1941, when the manager of the Alaska Railroad offered $25 for the largest cabbage. At that time, the prize winner grew a 23-pound cabbage. Since then, the record-winning cabbage weighed in at 94 pounds!

Old Timey Pickles

CONTRIBUTOR: DOROTHY HALTIWANGER, SOUTH CAROLINA

MAKES 3 TO 4 PINT JARS

2 cups cider vinegar

1 cup granulated sugar

1 tablespoon whole cloves

1 tablespoon whole allspice

1 teaspoon canning or pickling salt

2 quarts sliced pickling cucumbers (about 12 to 15 cucumbers)

These pickles have a similar sweetness to bread-and-butter pickles. Dorothy likes to chop them up and use them in slaw, potato salad, chicken salad, and tuna salad.

1. In an 8-quart stainless steel stockpot, combine the vinegar, sugar, cloves, allspice, and salt. Bring to a boil over medium heat, then reduce the heat to low and simmer for 5 minutes.

2. Add the cucumber slices and bring the mixture to a full boil over medium-high heat. Reduce the heat and simmer until the cucumbers lighten in color, 3 to 5 minutes. Remove the pot from the heat.

3. Using a slotted spoon, pack the cucumbers into hot jars, leaving ½-inch headspace. Ladle the hot syrup into the jars, covering the pickles and maintaining the ½-inch headspace. Remove any air bubbles. Wipe the jar rims and threads with a clean, damp paper towel. Apply hot lids and screw bands.

4. Process pint jars in a water bath canner for 15 minutes (see p. 34 for instructions). Remove from the water bath canner and let cool for 12 to 24 hours. Check the seals and remove the screw bands. Store jars in a cool, dry, dark place for up to 1 year.

DOROTHY HALTIWANGER

WEST COLUMBIA, SOUTH CAROLINA

DOROTHY HALTIWANGER has been canning for many years. She grew up on a farm and the family grew most of what they ate. At a young age, she started helping her mother with the canning to preserve the produce for year-round use. When Dorothy got married, she and her husband had a big backyard, so she planted a vegetable garden and has been canning every year since. "I still live in the same house and still have my big backyard garden."

The first blue ribbons Dorothy won at the South Carolina State Fair were for a delicately crocheted baby set. She was so thrilled with the awards that she has been entering home, craft, flower, and agriculture exhibits at the fair ever since. Those entries have earned hundreds of ribbons, including 14 Sweepstakes awards, of which 7 of those were for earning the most blue ribbons in canning. She also won first place for her farm display, an extensive collection of canned and dried foods. Dorothy's display included over 130 jars of different canned jams, jellies, fruits, vegetables, and meats. What does Dorothy like most about competing? "I enter fair competitions for the fun of it."

* Relishes *

Tangy, sweet, and savory, relishes are traditional side dishes. Many people feel a meal isn't complete without one on the table. Relishes can be prepared from a variety of vegetables and can range in flavor from sweet to very hot, depending on your preference and the tastes of your family.

Selecting Produce

Select firm, fresh, unblemished produce for making relishes. The fresher the produce, the better the flavor of the finished relish. While most cucumber pickles are best made with pickling cucumbers, relishes are more forgiving, and many can be made with standard slicing cucumbers. Just be sure to remove any large seeds before chopping or grinding the cucumbers.

Preparing Vegetables

Rinse vegetables under cool running water and scrub gently with a soft brush to remove all dirt and sand. Be careful not to scrub too hard and damage the produce. Cut a thin slice off the blossom end of cucumbers and squash to remove the blossom scar. This end can contain bacteria and enzymes that can contaminate the relish.

When a relish recipe calls for ground vegetables, you can use a meat grinder or a stand mixer with the grinder attachment to prepare the produce. Instead of grinding, you can also use a food processor to very finely chop the vegetables.

Vinegar

As with pickles, to can relishes safely it is important to use a commercially made vinegar with an acidity level of at least 5%. Homemade vinegars, or vinegars with a lower acidity level, are not considered safe for canning. While cider vinegar is commonly used for relishes, white vinegar can add a nice tang. Never reduce the ratio or amount of vinegar in a relish recipe, as this will make the recipe unsafe for canning. If you prefer relishes that are less tart, increase the amount of sugar in the recipe.

Corn Relish

CONTRIBUTOR: ALAN GRAVENOR, MARYLAND

MAKES 5 PINT JARS

9 cups fresh corn kernels (12 to 15 large ears corn), or canned or frozen

2 cups chopped onions (2 to 3 medium onions)

1 cup chopped green bell peppers

½ cup chopped red bell peppers

1 cup granulated sugar

2 tablespoons table salt

1½ tablespoons celery seeds

1½ tablespoons mustard seeds

3 cups cider vinegar

This is an easy, tasty relish that improves during storage. It's a great way to use summer corn and other fresh garden vegetables and is a nice accompaniment to a variety of meals, especially meat and potatoes. Chop the onions and peppers the same size as the corn kernels to create a blue ribbon relish with a uniform texture.

1. In an 8-quart stainless steel stockpot, combine the corn, onions, bell peppers, sugar, salt, celery seeds, mustard seeds, and vinegar. Bring to a boil over high heat, stirring frequently.

2. Cover, reduce the heat to medium low, and simmer for 15 minutes, stirring occasionally to prevent scorching. Remove the pot from the heat.

3. Ladle the relish into hot jars, leaving ½-inch headspace. Remove any air bubbles. Wipe the jar rims and threads with a clean, damp paper towel. Apply hot lids and screw bands.

4. Process pint jars in a water bath canner for 15 minutes (see p. 34 for instructions). Remove from the water bath canner and let cool for 12 to 24 hours. Check the seals and remove the screw bands. Store jars in a cool, dry, dark place for up to 1 year.

Zucchini Relish

CONTRIBUTOR: SHEILA BUSTILLOS, TEXAS

MAKES ABOUT SEVEN 8-OUNCE JARS OR 3 TO 4 PINT JARS

4 medium zucchini, stem and blossom ends removed, finely chopped

2 medium onions, finely chopped

½ medium red bell pepper, seeds and membranes removed, finely chopped

½ medium green bell pepper, seeds and membranes removed, finely chopped

3 tablespoons pickling salt

1 cup granulated sugar

¾ cup cider vinegar

1 teaspoon dry mustard

1 teaspoon celery seeds

½ teaspoon crushed red pepper flakes

1 tablespoon water

2 teaspoons cornstarch

SERVING SUGGESTION

This relish is great in deviled eggs, on hot dogs, or on top of grilled chicken.

You will be a big hit at a summer barbecue with this zucchini relish! This relish is sweet, but you can make it spicier by adding more red pepper flakes. Sheila grows her own zucchini, so this relish is a staple in her house.

1. In a large bowl, combine the zucchini, onions, and bell peppers and toss until evenly blended. Sprinkle with the salt and stir well. Let stand for 1 hour, stirring occasionally.

2. Drain the vegetables in a colander lined with a single layer of cheesecloth or in a large fine-mesh sieve. Rinse well and drain again, pressing out the excess liquid. Use a paper towel to extract extra water, if necessary.

3. In an 8-quart stainless steel or enamel stockpot, combine the drained vegetables, sugar, vinegar, mustard, celery seeds, and red pepper flakes. Bring the mixture to a boil over high heat, then reduce the heat and boil gently, uncovered, stirring frequently, for 15 minutes, or until the vegetables are tender.

4. In a small bowl, blend the water and cornstarch until smooth. Stir the cornstarch mixture into the vegetables. Cook, stirring frequently, until the liquid turns translucent and thickens, about 5 minutes. Remove the pot from the heat.

5. Ladle the relish into hot jars, leaving ½-inch headspace. Remove any air bubbles. Wipe the jar rims and threads with a clean, damp paper towel. Apply hot lids and screw bands.

6. Process 8-ounce jars in a water bath canner for 10 minutes; pint jars for 15 minutes (see p. 34 for instructions). Remove from the water bath canner and let cool for 12 to 24 hours. Check the seals and remove the screw bands. Store jars in a cool, dry, dark place for up to 1 year.

Sweet and Tangy Tomato Relish

CONTRIBUTOR: BRENDA BUSTILLOS, TEXAS

MAKES ABOUT FIVE 8-OUNCE JARS OR 2 PINT JARS

4 medium plum tomatoes, quartered

2 medium green bell peppers, seeds and membranes removed, quartered

1 cup coarsely chopped sweet onions (about 1 large onion)

1 cup coarsely chopped green cabbage

4 teaspoons kosher salt

1 cup granulated sugar

1 cup white vinegar

½ cup water

1 teaspoon mustard seeds

1 teaspoon celery seeds

1 teaspoon ground turmeric

SERVING SUGGESTION

Use this delightful relish to season flaked tuna fish and cold summer salads or use as a backyard barbecue condiment for brats and dogs.

Brenda cannot imagine a game-day bratwurst or cold summer salad without this perfectly pleasing relish. Chow-chow fans beware—this may become your next go-to relish recipe!

1. Put the tomatoes, bell peppers, onions, and cabbage in a food processor and process until finely chopped. Drain.

2. Transfer the chopped vegetables to a medium bowl and sprinkle with the salt. Refrigerate, covered, for 4 to 12 hours.

3. Rinse the vegetables with cold water and drain well in a colander lined with a single layer of cheesecloth or in a large fine-mesh sieve.

4. In a 6-quart stainless steel stockpot, combine the sugar, vinegar, water, mustard seeds, celery seeds, and turmeric. Add the drained vegetables to the syrup. Bring the mixture to a boil over medium-high heat, stirring frequently. Reduce the heat and simmer, uncovered, for 10 to 15 minutes, or until thickened to the consistency you prefer. Remove the pot from the heat.

5. Ladle the relish into hot jars, leaving ½-inch headspace. Remove any air bubbles. Wipe the jar rims and threads with a clean, damp paper towel. Apply hot lids and screw bands.

6. Process 8-ounce jars in a water bath canner for 10 minutes; pint jars for 15 minutes (see p. 34 for instructions). Remove from the water bath canner and let cool for 12 to 24 hours. Check the seals and remove the screw bands. Store jars in a cool, dry, dark place for up to 1 year.

Jacob's Zucchini Relish

CONTRIBUTOR: JACOB SNYDER, VIRGINIA

**MAKES ABOUT TWELVE
8-OUNCE JARS OR
6 PINT JARS**

4 to 5 pounds medium zucchini, stem and blossom ends removed, coarsely chopped

6 to 8 large onions, peeled and quartered

⅓ cup canning salt

2½ cups cider vinegar

4 cups granulated sugar

1 tablespoon ground nutmeg

1 tablespoon dry mustard

2 teaspoons celery salt or seasoned salt

1 teaspoon ground turmeric

1 red bell pepper, seeds and membranes removed, finely chopped

1 green bell pepper, seeds and membranes removed, finely chopped

One year, Jacob decided that he wanted to can zucchini relish instead of regular cucumber relish. No one in his family or had ever made zucchini relish. Although the relish turned out great, Jacob's dad was the only one in the family to eat it so he gave away several jars. Everyone who tried it loved it, so much that Jacob continues to make the relish each year for the fair and to give as gifts. In 2014, this relish earned the Reserve Grand Champion of Pickles in the youth division at the Salem Fair.

1. Put the zucchini and onions in a food processor and process until very finely chopped.

2. In a large bowl, combine the zucchini, onions, and salt and mix well. Cover and let stand at room temperature overnight.

3. Drain the zucchini mixture in a colander lined with a single layer of cheesecloth or in a large fine-mesh sieve. Rinse with cold water and drain again, pressing out the excess liquid. Set aside.

4. In an 8-quart stainless steel stockpot, combine the vinegar, sugar, nutmeg, mustard, celery salt, turmeric, and red and green bell peppers, stirring until well blended. Bring the mixture to a boil over medium-high heat, stirring frequently.

5. Add the drained zucchini mixture to the syrup and return to a boil, stirring frequently. Reduce the heat and simmer for 30 minutes, stirring occasionally. Remove the pot from the heat.

6. Ladle the relish into hot pint jars, leaving ½-inch headspace. Remove any air bubbles. Wipe the jar rims and threads with a clean, damp paper towel. Apply hot lids and screw bands.

7. Process 8-ounce and pint jars in a water bath canner for 10 minutes (see p. 34 for instructions). Remove from the water bath canner and let cool for 12 to 24 hours. Check the seals and remove the screw bands. Store jars in a cool, dry, dark place for up to 1 year.

Chow-Chow

CONTRIBUTOR: ROBIN TARBELL-THOMAS, IOWA

MAKES ABOUT 12 PINT JARS

4 quarts chopped cabbage (about 2 large heads)

12 onions, chopped

12 green bell peppers, seeds and membranes removed, chopped

6 red bell peppers, seeds and membranes removed, chopped

2 quarts cored and chopped green tomatoes (3 to 4 pounds)

½ cup kosher salt

4 quarts cider vinegar

5 cups granulated sugar

4 tablespoons dry mustard

4 tablespoons mustard seeds

3 tablespoons celery seeds

3 tablespoons prepared mild yellow mustard

2 tablespoons whole mixed pickling spices

1 tablespoon ground turmeric

1 tablespoon ground ginger

Every picnic or barbecue should feature a jar or two of chow-chow. It is the perfect topping for grilled hot dogs or anything else you are serving. Chow-chow looks so pretty and tastes so sweet and spicy that you may want to make a double batch.

1. In an 8-quart stainless steel stockpot or other large container, combine the cabbage, onions, bell peppers, green tomatoes, and salt. Cover and let stand at room temperature overnight.

2. Drain the vegetables in a colander. Rinse well and drain again. Set aside.

3. In a 12-quart stainless steel stockpot, combine the vinegar, sugar, dry mustard, mustard seeds, celery seeds, yellow mustard, pickling spices, turmeric, and ginger. Bring the mixture to a boil over medium-high heat, stirring constantly, until the sugar is completely dissolved. Reduce the heat and simmer for 20 minutes.

4. Add the drained vegetables to the syrup and simmer for 10 minutes. Increase the heat and bring the mixture to a boil. Remove the pot from the heat.

5. Ladle the chow-chow into hot jars, leaving ½-inch headspace. Remove any air bubbles. Wipe the jar rims and threads with a clean, damp paper towel. Apply hot lids and screw bands.

6. Process pint jars in a water bath canner for 15 minutes (see p. 34 for instructions). Remove from the water bath canner and let cool for 12 to 24 hours. Check the seals and remove the screw bands. Store jars in a cool, dry, dark place for up to 1 year.

Sweet Cucumber Relish

CONTRIBUTOR: LINDA J. AMENDT, CALIFORNIA

MAKES ABOUT EIGHT 8-OUNCE JARS OR 4 PINT JARS

6 cups finely chopped medium pickling cucumbers (about 4 pounds cucumbers)

2 cups finely chopped onions (2 to 3 medium onions)

3 tablespoons pickling or kosher salt

2 to 3 quarts ice-cold water

3 cups granulated sugar

2 cups cider vinegar

1½ teaspoons mustard seeds

1½ teaspoons celery seeds

Linda started making this relish when she learned she was allergic to peppers and couldn't eat store-bought relish any longer. When she opened the first jar, she was in relish heaven! It turned out the judges were fond of her relish, too, so she continued entering it into fair competitions and bringing home blue ribbons.

1. In a large bowl, layer the cucumbers, onions, and salt. Add enough of the cold water to completely cover the vegetables. Cover and let stand for 2 hours.

2. Drain the vegetables in a colander lined with a single layer of cheesecloth or in a large fine-mesh sieve. Rinse well and drain again, pressing out the excess liquid. Set aside.

3. In a 6- to 8-quart stainless steel stockpot, combine the sugar, vinegar, mustard seeds, and celery seeds. Bring the mixture to a boil over medium-high heat, stirring constantly until the sugar is completely dissolved. Add the drained vegetables to the syrup and return to a boil. Reduce the heat and simmer for 10 minutes, stirring frequently. Remove the pot from the heat.

4. Ladle the relish into hot pint jars, leaving ½-inch headspace. Remove any air bubbles. Wipe the jar rims and threads with a clean, damp paper towel. Apply hot lids and screw bands.

5. Process 8-ounce jars in a water bath canner for 10 minutes; pint jars for 15 minutes (see p. 34 for instructions). Remove from the water bath canner and let cool for 12 to 24 hours. Check the seals and remove the screw bands. Store jars in a cool, dry, dark place for up to 1 year.

Hamburger and Hot Dog Relish

CONTRIBUTOR: LOUISE PIPER, IOWA

**MAKES ABOUT SIX
8-OUNCE JARS**

7 cups peeled, seeded,
and ground pickling
cucumbers (5 to
6 pounds cucumbers)

3 cups peeled and
ground carrots (1 to
1½ pounds carrots)

3 red bell peppers, seeded
and ground

4 medium white onions,
ground

¼ cup canning or kosher
salt

5 cups granulated sugar

3 cups cider vinegar

1 tablespoon celery seeds

1 tablespoon mustard
seeds

When Louise makes pickles and relishes, she uses cucumbers harvested from her garden; her goal is "24 hours from vine to brine." The freshness is apparent in this relish, a family favorite of Louise's three adult children and eight grandchildren. It won the Best Overall Relish at the Iowa State Fair.

1. In a large glass bowl or crock, combine the ground vegetables, then sprinkle the salt over the top. Cover the bowl with waxed paper or a clean dishtowel and let stand at room temperature for 3 hours. Drain well in a large fine-mesh strainer.

2. In a 6- to 8-quart stainless steel stockpot, combine the sugar, cider vinegar, celery seeds, and mustard seeds. Bring the mixture to a boil over medium-high heat, stirring constantly, until the sugar is completely dissolved.

3. Add the drained vegetables to the syrup and bring the mixture to a boil, stirring frequently. Reduce the heat and simmer, stirring occasionally, until the vegetables are tender, about 20 minutes. Remove the pot from the heat.

4. Ladle the relish into hot jars, leaving ½-inch headspace. Remove any air bubbles. Wipe the jar rims and threads with a clean, damp paper towel. Apply hot lids and screw bands.

5. Process 8-ounce jars in a water bath canner for 10 minutes; pint jars for 15 minutes (see p. 34 for instructions). Remove from the water bath canner and let cool for 12 to 24 hours. Check the seals and remove the screw bands. Store jars in a cool, dry, dark place for up to 1 year.

LOUISE PIPER

GARNER, IOWA

LOUISE PIPER grew up on a farm in central Iowa. Her mother had a large garden and did a lot of canning and freezing to preserve the bountiful food she grew to help feed the family throughout the winter. Louise helped her mother with the canning duties. When Louise became a wife, homemaker, and mother, she just thought that canning was the thing to do.

Louise's favorite part about canning is making something special to share with family, friends, and neighbors.

"When my three children were growing up, I always had a garden of my own. However, I did not really enjoy working in the garden that much. I still grow rhubarb, but for many years now, I go to local berry patches and orchards for much of my fruit." She loves going to the farmers' market for fresh produce and also barters with people who have extra fruit. "Many times I've traded loaves of homemade yeast bread for asparagus, Concord grapes, plums, and any other crops I could find."

She gives her home-canned items to her family and good friends year-round, as well as for birthday, wedding, and anniversary presents, "get well" gifts, and Christmas gifts. Her favorite part about canning is making something special to share with family, friends, and neighbors. "I have always enjoyed making jams, jellies, butters, homemade relishes and pickles, and tomato juice." Louise likes experimenting and combining different type of fruits in her jams and jellies, creating her own unique flavor blends.

The judges enjoy Louise's canning as well and have awarded her entries hundreds of blue ribbons at the Clay County Fair and the Iowa State Fair. Louise is honored to have also earned many Sweepstakes awards, overall Best of Division awards, and Best of Show awards, often beating out over a thousand other entries to take home the top honors.

Red Pickle Relish

CONTRIBUTOR: NANCY CHARRON, WASHINGTON

MAKES ABOUT 8 PINT JARS

8 cups finely chopped pickling cucumbers (5½ to 6½ pounds cucumbers)

4 medium yellow onions, finely chopped

5 medium red or yellow bell peppers, seeds and membranes removed, finely chopped

3 medium green bell peppers, seeds and membranes removed, finely chopped

¼ cup pickling salt or ½ cup kosher salt

2 teaspoons celery seeds

2 teaspoons ground turmeric

8 cups cold water

4 cinnamon sticks

1 tablespoon whole cloves or ½ teaspoon ground cloves

1 teaspoon whole allspice

8 cups cider vinegar

This is a rich, savory, red tomato pickle relish. It takes 2 days to complete, but it's so worth it! On the first day, you prepare the separate pickle and tomato mixtures, and then cook and can the relish on the second day. To allow the flavor to develop, wait for at least 3 weeks before opening the jars.

1. In a 12-quart stainless steel stockpot or large bowl, combine the cucumbers, onions, bell peppers, salt, celery seeds, turmeric, and cold water, stirring to mix well. Cover and let stand at room temperature for 8 to 12 hours.

2. Combine the cinnamon sticks, cloves, and allspice in a spice bag or a few layers of cheesecloth and tie closed.

3. In an 8- to 10-quart stainless steel stockpot, combine the spice bag and cider vinegar and bring to a boil over medium heat. Reduce the heat and simmer, uncovered, for 20 minutes.

4. Add the chopped tomatoes to the vinegar mixture and bring to a boil, then reduce the heat and simmer until the tomato-vinegar mixture forms a thickened purée, about 45 minutes. Add the sugar and both mustard seeds and stir until the sugar is completely dissolved. Remove the pot from the heat, cover, and let stand at room temperature overnight.

5. Drain the cucumber mixture in a colander lined with a single layer of cheesecloth or in a large fine-mesh sieve, then add to the tomato purée. Bring the mixture to a boil over medium-high heat. Reduce the heat and simmer, uncovered, until most of the liquid has evaporated, 30 to 45 minutes. Remove the pot from the heat and remove the spice bag.

6. Ladle the relish into hot jars, leaving ½-inch headspace. Remove any air bubbles. Wipe the jar rims and threads with a clean, damp paper towel. Apply hot lids and screw bands.

7. Process pint jars in a water bath canner for 15 minutes (see p. 34 for instructions). Remove from the water bath canner and let cool for 12 to 24 hours. Check the seals and remove the screw bands. Store jars in a cool, dry, dark place for up to 1 year.

8 cups peeled, seeded, and chopped Roma tomatoes (5 to 7 pounds tomatoes)

4 cups granulated sugar

¼ cup yellow mustard seeds

¼ cup spicy brown mustard seeds

SERVING SUGGESTION

Nancy's favorite way to use this relish—other than the obvious, with her husband's awesome grilled hamburgers—is to generously slather it on a cold roast pork or turkey sandwich.

Sweet Jalapeño Relish

CONTRIBUTOR: PHYLLIS BUSTILLOS, TEXAS

**MAKES ABOUT FIVE
8-OUNCE JARS**

¾ pound jalapeño peppers

1 large red bell pepper

4 medium carrots, peeled

1 medium onion

3 cups granulated sugar

2 cups cider vinegar

1 tablespoon mustard seeds

1 tablespoon dill seeds

This sweet, colorful relish is a favorite of the Bustillos family, especially with the men. It is wonderful served with barbecue, Mexican food, meats, salads, and as an appetizer over cream cheese. You can use all green jalapeño peppers or a mixture of green, red, yellow, or orange jalapeños for even more color.

1. Cut the jalapeño peppers and bell pepper in half. Remove the seeds and membranes, and cut into julienne strips about 2 inches long. Set aside.

2. Cut the carrots and onion into julienne strips about ⅛ inch thick and 2 inches long. Set aside.

3. In an 8-quart stainless steel stockpot, combine the sugar and cider vinegar and cook over medium heat, stirring constantly, until the sugar completely dissolves. Add the julienned vegetables and bring the mixture to a boil. Reduce the heat and simmer until the relish starts to thicken, 20 to 25 minutes.

4. Add the mustard seeds and dill seeds to the vegetable mixture. Simmer, stirring frequently, until the relish is thick, 30 to 40 minutes. Remove the pot from the heat.

5. Ladle the relish into hot jars, leaving ½-inch headspace. Remove any air bubbles. Wipe the jar rims and threads with a clean, damp paper towel. Apply hot lids and screw bands.

6. Process 8-ounce and pint jars in a water bath canner for 15 minutes (see p. 34 for instructions). Remove from the water bath canner and let cool for 12 to 24 hours. Check the seals and remove the screw bands. Store jars in a cool, dry, dark place for up to 1 year.

Eggplant Caponata

CONTRIBUTOR: ROXANNE M. PETRUNTI, MASSACHUSETTS

MAKES SIX 8-OUNCE JARS

3 medium tomatoes, peeled, cored, and chopped (or one 15-ounce can chopped tomatoes)

⅓ cup pitted black olives, coarsely chopped

⅓ cup pitted green olives, coarsely chopped

1½ tablespoons capers

1 large eggplant (about 1½ pounds), skin left on, chopped into ¾-inch pieces,

1 cup diced celery (about 2 stalks)

1 large yellow onion, chopped into ¼-inch pieces

1 cup red-wine vinegar

2 tablespoons granulated sugar

1 tablespoon freshly squeezed lemon juice

Table salt

Freshly ground black pepper

As far back as she can remember, Roxanne's grandmother made eggplant caponata for all the holidays. She always made it in a big black cast iron skillet that she purchased in 1954 for $2. She passed the recipe and skillet down to Roxanne's mother, and now Roxanne's mom, twin sister Cherylanne, and Roxanne can the eggplant caponata to enjoy at every holiday.

1. In a medium bowl, combine the tomatoes, black olives, green olives, and capers. Set aside.

2. Position a rack in the center of the oven and heat the oven to 400°F. Line a large baking sheet with parchment paper. Spread the chopped eggplant on the parchment in a single layer. Bake until browned on all sides, about 15 minutes, stirring partway through baking. Transfer the eggplant to a large bowl.

3. In a large cast iron or nonstick skillet, over medium heat, cook the celery with a small amount of water until slightly golden and soft, 10 to 12 minutes. Transfer the celery to the bowl with the eggplant. Add the onions to the pan and cook over medium heat until they are soft and golden.

4. Add the cooked eggplant and celery, the tomato-olive mixture, the wine vinegar, sugar, lemon juice, and salt and pepper to taste to the skillet. Stir until well mixed and cook over low heat, stirring frequently, for about 20 minutes. Remove the pan from the heat.

5. Ladle the caponata into hot jars, leaving ½-inch headspace. Remove any air bubbles. Wipe the jar rims and threads with a clean, damp paper towel. Apply hot lids and screw bands.

6. Process 8-ounce jars in a water bath canner for 15 minutes; pint jars for 20 minutes (see p. 34 for instructions). Remove from the water bath canner and let cool for 12 to 24 hours. Check the seals and remove the screw bands. Store jars in a cool, dry, dark place for up to 1 year.

Yellow Zucchini Relish

CONTRIBUTOR: JANET GAMBLE, IDAHO

MAKES 4 TO 5 PINT JARS

10 cups finely chopped or shredded unpeeled yellow zucchini (5 to 7 pounds zucchini)

4 cups chopped onions (about 5 medium onions)

1 large red bell pepper, seeds and membranes removed, chopped

5 tablespoons pickling or canning salt

3½ cups granulated sugar

3 cups white vinegar

1 can (4 ounces) chopped green chiles

4 teaspoons celery seeds

1 tablespoon ground turmeric

1 teaspoon freshly ground black pepper

½ teaspoon ground nutmeg

This is the Gamble family's favorite zucchini relish because it has green chiles to add a little kick without being hot. Janet prefers using yellow zucchini rather than green in this recipe because it looks very pretty in the jars and makes the relish special. She finely chops the squash, but chops the other vegetables a little larger so the colors stand out in the relish.

1. In a large glass, ceramic, or stainless steel container, combine the zucchini, onions, and bell peppers. Sprinkle with the salt and stir well, then cover and refrigerate overnight.

2. Drain the zucchini mixture in a colander lined with a single layer of cheesecloth or in a large fine-mesh sieve, then rinse and drain again.

3. In an 8-quart stainless steel stockpot, combine the sugar, vinegar, chiles, celery seeds, turmeric, black pepper, and nutmeg. Bring the mixture to a boil over medium-high heat, stirring constantly, until the sugar is dissolved. Reduce the heat and simmer for 10 minutes, stirring frequently. Remove the pot from the heat.

4. Ladle the relish into hot jars, leaving ½-inch headspace. Remove any air bubbles. Wipe the jar rims and threads with a clean, damp paper towel. Apply hot lids and screw bands.

5. Process 8-ounce jars in a water bath canner for 10 minutes; pint jars for 15 minutes (see p. 34 for instructions). Remove from the water bath canner and let cool for 12 to 24 hours. Check the seals and remove the screw bands. Store jars in a cool, dry, dark place for up to 1 year.

Hot Zucchini Relish

CONTRIBUTOR: BETH WALLACE, ARKANSAS

MAKES 5 TO 6 PINT JARS

10 cups peeled and ground zucchini (6 to 8 pounds zucchini)

4 cups ground onions (about 5 medium onions)

5 tablespoons pickling salt

2½ cups cider vinegar

4 cups granulated sugar

1 jar or can (28 ounces) diced pimientos, drained

2 large jalapeño peppers with seeds, finely chopped

2 teaspoons celery seeds

1 teaspoon dry mustard

1 teaspoon ground turmeric

1 teaspoon ground nutmeg

1 teaspoon cornstarch

½ teaspoon freshly ground black pepper

This relish is a great substitute for pickles and is very good served alongside sautéed vegetables. It also is a wonderful hot dog topping. You can adjust the amount of pimientos depending on your personal taste.

1. In an 8-quart stainless steel stockpot, combine the zucchini, onions, and salt and stir well. Cover and let stand at room temperature overnight.

2. Drain the zucchini mixture in a colander lined with a single layer of cheesecloth or in a large fine-mesh sieve. Rinse twice and drain again. Return the zucchini mixture to the pot.

3. Add the vinegar, sugar, pimientos, jalapeños, celery seeds, mustard, turmeric, nutmeg, cornstarch, and black pepper to the zucchini mixture. Bring the mixture to a simmer over medium heat, then reduce the heat and simmer for 30 minutes. Remove the pot from the heat.

4. Ladle the relish into hot jars, leaving ½-inch headspace. Remove any air bubbles. Wipe the jar rims and threads with a clean, damp paper towel. Apply hot lids and screw bands.

5. Process 8-ounce and pint jars in a water bath canner for 10 minutes (see p. 34 for instructions). Remove from the water bath canner and let cool for 12 to 24 hours. Check the seals and remove the screw bands. Store jars in a cool, dry, dark place for up to 1 year.

TIP

To reduce the heat of this relish, remove and discard the jalapeño seeds and membranes before finely chopping.

Mémère Bergeron's Hamburger Relish

CONTRIBUTOR: STELLA DOYON, MAINE

MAKES 6 TO 8 PINT JARS

12 cucumbers, roughly chopped

3 red bell peppers, seeds and membranes removed, roughly chopped

2 pounds onions, roughly chopped

⅓ cup pickling salt

2 quarts white vinegar

4 cups granulated sugar

2 teaspoons whole cloves

2 teaspoons whole allspice

1 teaspoon celery seeds

¼ cup dry mustard

1 teaspoon ground turmeric

½ cup cornstarch

½ cup cold water

SERVING SUGGESTION

Not only is the relish great with hot dogs and hamburgers, but Stella's Mémère would use this to make her own tartar sauce. Mix equal parts mayonnaise and relish, adding some relish liquid to thin the sauce to the consistency you prefer.

Mémère (Grandmother) Bergeron's hamburger relish is a family favorite passed down through the generations. You can use either pickling or slicing cucumbers in this recipe. The finished relish yield varies depending on the size of the vegetables.

1. In a large bowl, combine the chopped cucumbers, bell peppers, and onions. Sprinkle the salt over the vegetables, cover, and let stand at room temperature overnight.

2. Rinse the vegetables with cold water and drain well in a fine-mesh sieve. Using a food processor, meat grinder, or knife, finely chop the vegetables, then drain again in a fine-mesh sieve.

3. In an 8-quart stainless steel stockpot, combine the chopped vegetables, vinegar, and sugar.

4. Place the cloves, allspice, and celery seeds in a spice bag or several layers of cheesecloth and tie closed. Add the spice bag to the vegetable mixture and bring the mixture to a boil over medium-high heat. Reduce the heat and simmer for 20 minutes.

5. Add the dry mustard and turmeric to the relish and stir until thoroughly combined. Return the mixture to a boil.

6. In a small bowl, whisk together the cornstarch and cold water until well blended. Add the cornstarch mixture to the relish and boil for 5 minutes. Remove the pot from the heat and remove the spice bag.

7. Ladle the relish into hot jars, leaving ½-inch headspace. Remove any air bubbles. Wipe the jar rims and threads with a clean, damp paper towel. Apply hot lids and screw bands.

8. Process 8-ounce jars in a water bath canner for 10 minutes; pint jars for 15 minutes (see p. 34 for instructions). Remove from the water bath canner and let cool for 12 to 24 hours. Check the seals and remove the screw bands. Store jars in a cool, dry, dark place for up to 1 year.

STELLA DOYON

AUBURN, MAINE

STELLA DOYON'S canning experiences started when she was about 15 years old, working beside her mother, Germaine, who guided her through the process. "At the time, canning wasn't something I wanted to do, but had to do. It was explained very simply to me, 'Do you want to eat this winter? Then, I need your help'. That was 42 years ago, and now, for me, canning is more a labor of love. Canning has become therapeutic, allowing me to calm myself following a stressful day. It also allows me to challenge myself with either some new recipe or technique that I want to try out."

> ## "Canning is a labor of love. It has become therapeutic, allowing me to calm myself following a stressful day."

When Stella was young and attended fairs with her family, she "was in awe of all the wonderful vegetables, canned goods, afghans, and sweaters that were on display in the exhibitor hall." At the age of 19, Stella took the plunge and started entering canning, baking, needlework, crocheting, and knitting competitions at her local fairs. Since then, she has brought home over 400 blue ribbons and many special awards for her high-quality entries.

Stella started doing craft demonstrations, but had to retire early because of a back issue. Looking for another type of activity where she could give back to the community, she thought about how to share her canning experience. Because many more people in her area were planting gardens and also wanting to preserve what they grew, Stella took a course from an extension educator with the University of Maine. She is now a Master Food Preserver with the University of Maine Cooperative Extension Service with the skills to teach; answer questions about canning, freezing, and drying; and also judge canned goods. In 2013, Stella received an unexpected surprise when she was named the Outstanding Master Food Preserver Volunteer of the Year for her contributions and dedicated service to the program.

* Sauces & Salsas *

When you have a variety of homemade sauces and salsas on the shelf, a delicious meal is never far away.

Ingredients

- -

❈ TOMATOES ❈

Tomatoes have been a staple canning ingredient for generations and are one of the most popular ingredients in a number of canned products. Roma tomatoes or other plum tomatoes are an excellent choice for making sauces and other preserves because they are significantly less juicy and have a firmer flesh than salad or slicing tomatoes. Plum tomatoes will yield a sauce with a strong flavor and smooth, thick texture. If a recipe calls for Roma or plum tomatoes, substituting other types may result in a thinner sauce, requiring additional cooking time, or softer tomato pieces in salsas. Beefsteak tomatoes also work well for some salsas and other preserves; however, salad or slicing tomatoes and many heirloom tomatoes break down when canned.

When choosing tomatoes, look for those that are fully ripe, firm to the touch with a slight give when pressed, and have a deep red color. Underripe tomatoes will lack flavor, while overripe or soft tomatoes can fall apart when canned and also contain a lot of juice, resulting in thin sauces or salsas. Tomatoes with dark-colored flesh will produce preserves with an intense flavor and a lovely red color.

Tomatoes have a low acidity level. To raise the acidity level for safe water bath canning, you'll need to add lemon juice, lime juice, or vinegar to the recipe. Be sure to use the specific type of acid called for in the ingredients. Never reduce the amount of acid in a tomato recipe, as this may encourage bacteria growth.

❈ CHILE PEPPERS ❈

You can adjust the amount and type of chile peppers called for in a recipe to suit your personal taste. If you like a lot of heat, increase the amount of peppers. For milder sauces or salsas, reduce it. I strongly recommend wearing gloves when handling and chopping chile peppers because the oils in hot peppers can cause chemical burns. Never touch your face, eyes, or mouth when working with chile peppers.

❈ ACID ❈

Never reduce the amount of acid in a sauce or salsa recipe. The vinegar, lemon juice, or lime juice is required for safe canning. If the recipe indicates bottled lemon juice or lime juice, do not substitute freshly squeezed juice for the bottled juice. Bottled juice has a consistent acidity level, which is required to raise the acidity level of the product high enough to make it safe for water bath processing.

BBQ Sauce

CONTRIBUTOR: VALERIE J. FONG, CALIFORNIA

MAKES 4 OR 5 PINT JARS

4 to 6 quarts Roma or other plum tomatoes, peeled, cored, and chopped

3 bell peppers (1 red, 1 orange, and 1 yellow), seeded and chopped

1 white onion, chopped

1 red onion, chopped

½ bunch fresh thyme leaves, stems removed

1 cup fresh basil leaves

10 to 12 cloves garlic, chopped

1 tablespoon olive oil

2 cups firmly packed brown sugar

1 can (12 ounces) tomato paste

1 cup dry red wine

½ cup Worcestershire sauce

¼ cup balsamic vinegar

2 tablespoons granulated sugar

1 tablespoon Tabasco

1 tablespoon freshly ground black pepper

2 teaspoons garlic powder

1 teaspoon table salt

This rich barbecue sauce is flavorful and zesty, with a nice Cabernet Sauvignon wine adding depth of flavor. The spices can be adjusted to fit any palate.

1. In a large skillet over medium-high heat, sauté the tomatoes, bell peppers, white and red onions, thyme, basil, and garlic in the olive oil until tender, 5 to 8 minutes. Transfer the mixture to an 8-quart stainless steel stockpot. Over medium heat, simmer the vegetables until soft, stirring occasionally, about 2 hours.

2. Using a blender, purée the vegetables in small amounts until smooth (hold a towel over the blender lid to ensure hot vegetables don't splash up). Return the puréed mixture to the stockpot. Stir in the brown sugar, tomato paste, wine, Worcestershire, vinegar, granulated sugar, Tabasco, black pepper, garlic powder, and salt.

3. Cook the sauce over medium-low heat, stirring frequently, until the volume is reduced by at least one-third and the sauce is thick when dropped by the spoonful onto a plate. This can take several hours. Or you can cook the mixture in a slow cooker on low heat, with the lid offset on the rim of the pot, stirring occasionally, until the sauce is thick, about 2 hours. Remove the pot from the heat.

4. Ladle the sauce into hot jars, leaving ½-inch headspace. Remove any air bubbles. Wipe the jar rims and threads with a clean, damp paper towel. Apply hot lids and screw bands.

5. Process pint jars in a water bath canner for 20 minutes (see p. 34 for instructions). Remove from the water bath canner and let cool for 12 to 24 hours. Check the seals and remove the screw bands. Store jars in a cool, dry, dark place for up to 1 year.

SERVING SUGGESTION

This sauce makes a delicious marinade for chicken, steaks, ribs, and beef as a marinade. Brush on additional fresh sauce (not the sauce used as the marinade) before serving.

VALERIE J. FONG

SACRAMENTO, CALIFORNIA

VALERIE FONG first became interested in canning around the age of 4, in the mid-1950s, because she had seen a blue ribbon draped over a winning jar of jewel-like jelly beautifully displayed at the old state fairgrounds. After asking her father if she could take one of the ribbons home, he patiently explained that the ribbons were only given to those who had winning entries. Years later, this early visit to the California State Fair was still a clear memory and so Valerie's life-long journey of taking home a blue ribbon began.

> "I like thinking of ways to blend flavors together to produce something that turns out to be surprisingly good, that could possibly be a blue ribbon winner, and has that 'wow factor' when it reaches your palate."

Her early childhood memories of home canning were out of necessity during the hot summers in Sacramento, when a family friend left a box of peaches on the front porch or a neighbor offered a couple of burlap bags filled with sweet corn. After eating some of it fresh, there was that moment when her mother would think of ways to preserve these items and avoid wasting these wonderful gifts. Her family did not own a freezer, but instead borrowed two shelves from a neighbor's garage freezer. In the winter months, being asked to get two bags of corn out of the freezer for dinner meant putting on your jacket and walking six houses down the street and back again with the goods in hand.

Following Valerie's first jam entries at the California State Fair, she attended the annual open judging and took pages of notes. Valerie became a certified Master Food Preserver through a program offered by the University of California Cooperative Extension. She currently is an active member of this program, with over 25 years of service. Having this advanced training has helped Valerie to understand the essential principles and science of safe food preservation, enabling her to create new and exciting entries for competition.

Valerie enjoys the creative aspect of canning. "I like thinking of ways to blend flavors together to produce something that turns out to be surprisingly good, that could possibly be a blue ribbon winner, and has that 'wow factor' when it reaches your palate…and you just know it is a keeper." In 2013, Valerie won the Best of Show award for the Jam and Jelly Show at the California State Fair. She had been hoping for this top honor following several Best of Show wins for the State Fair's other two preserved shows—the Soft Spreads and Fruit Show, and the Pickle, Relish, Sauce, and Salsa Show. Valerie calls this latest Best of Show win her "Triple Crown" of preserved foods.

Valerie has earned hundreds of blue ribbons, dozens of special awards, and eight Best of Show awards. She also is a Lifetime Member of the Inaugural Class of the Sure-Jell Hall of Fame.

Tomato Sauce

CONTRIBUTOR: CAROLYN DEMARCO, OREGON

MAKES ABOUT 6 PINTS

10 pounds plum
tomatoes, cored and
quartered

6 tablespoons bottled
lemon juice

1 tablespoon canning or
pickling salt (optional)

Canning your own tomato sauce is a great way to minimize salt in your cooking and an economical way to always have a pantry staple on hand. Homemade tomato sauce is an essential base for making spaghetti sauce, barbecue sauce, soups, and stews.

1. In a large stockpot, over medium heat, bring the tomatoes to a boil. Reduce the heat and simmer, stirring frequently, until the tomatoes are mostly broken down. Remove the pot from the heat.

2. Strain the tomatoes through a colander set over a large bowl, reserving both the tomato chunks and the liquid. Rinse the stockpot.

3. Purée the reserved tomato chunks in a food processor or with a hand-held immersion blender and then press through a food mill or fine-mesh sieve. Return the tomato purée to the stockpot. Strain the reserved liquid through a fine-mesh sieve to remove the seeds, then add the strained liquid to the stockpot. Discard the seeds.

4. Bring the tomato mixture to a boil over medium-high heat. Reduce the heat to medium low and boil, stirring frequently, until the sauce is reduced approximately by half, 60 to 90 minutes. Remove the pot from the heat.

5. Add 1 tablespoon bottled lemon juice to each hot pint jar. Add ½ teaspoon salt to each pint jar, if desired. For quart jars, add 2 tablespoons bottled lemon juice and 1 teaspoon salt to each jar.

6. Ladle the sauce into the jars, leaving ½-inch headspace. Remove any air bubbles. Wipe the jar rims and threads with a clean, damp paper towel. Apply hot lids and screw bands.

7. Process pint jars in a water bath canner for 35 minutes; quart jars for 40 minutes (see p. 34 for instructions). Remove from the water bath canner and let cool for 12 to 24 hours. Check the seals and remove the screw bands. Store jars in a cool, dry, dark place for up to 1 year.

Cranberry Ketchup

CONTRIBUTOR: LINDA J. AMENDT, CALIFORNIA

MAKES ABOUT FOUR 8-OUNCE
JARS OR 2 PINT JARS

2 bags (12 ounces each)
fresh or thawed frozen
cranberries

1¼ cups red-wine
vinegar

1¼ cups water

2 cups firmly packed
light brown sugar

¼ teaspoon ground
cinnamon

⅛ teaspoon ground
allspice

⅛ teaspoon ground
nutmeg

Try this unique condiment on your turkey or ham sandwich to turn any day into a holiday. You can increase or omit the spices to suit your family's taste.

1. In a 4-quart stainless steel stockpot, combine the cranberries, vinegar, and water. Bring the mixture to a boil over medium-high heat, then reduce the heat and simmer, stirring frequently, until all the cranberries have softened and popped, about 20 minutes. Remove the pot from the heat and skim off any foam.

2. Press the cranberry mixture through a food mill or fine-mesh sieve. Discard the skins and seeds. Rinse out the stockpot and return the cranberry pulp to the pot.

3. Stir in the brown sugar, cinnamon, allspice, and nutmeg and bring the mixture to a boil over medium heat, stirring constantly. Reduce the heat and simmer, stirring frequently, until the mixture thickens to the consistency you prefer, about 10 minutes. As the ketchup thickens, stir constantly to prevent sticking and scorching. Remove the pot from the heat.

4. Ladle the ketchup into hot jars, leaving ½-inch headspace. Remove any air bubbles. Wipe the jar rims and threads with a clean, damp paper towel. Apply hot lids and screw bands.

5. Process 8-ounce jars in a water bath canner for 10 minutes; pint jars for 15 minutes (see p. 34 for instructions). Remove from the water bath canner and let cool for 12 to 24 hours. Check the seals and remove the screw bands. Store jars in a cool, dry, dark place for up to 1 year.

> **DID YOU KNOW?**
>
> The Oregon State Fair has a time capsule that will be opened in 2065. In August 1965, Governor Mark Hatfield created a time capsule to commemorate the fair's 100th anniversary.

Chili Sauce

CONTRIBUTOR: ARIANNA EDWARDS, UTAH

MAKES 10 TO 12 PINT JARS

1 peck tomatoes (about 13½ pounds)

6 cups chopped onions (7 to 8 medium onions)

6 medium green bell peppers, seeded and chopped

¼ cup ground hot peppers

1¾ cups white vinegar

2 cups firmly packed dark brown sugar

¼ cup table salt

1½ teaspoons freshly ground black pepper

1½ teaspoons ground allspice

1½ teaspoons ground cloves

The fresher the veggies you use, the better this sauce tastes! Arianna likes to use a combination of jalapeño and Hungarian wax peppers to give the sauce some nice heat, but you can use your favorite peppers to create the heat level you desire. She also includes the hot pepper seeds for an extra kick, but you can remove them before making the sauce, if you prefer.

1. Core and peel the tomatoes, then grind in a food grinder, food processor, or blender.

2. In a 12-quart stainless steel stockpot, combine the ground tomatoes, onions, bell peppers, and hot peppers. Stir in the vinegar. Add the brown sugar, salt, black pepper, allspice, and cloves and stir until well combined.

3. Bring the mixture to a boil over medium-high heat, stirring frequently. Reduce the heat to low and simmer, stirring frequently, until most of the liquid is boiled off, about 2 hours. Remove the pot from the heat.

4. Ladle the sauce into hot jars, leaving ½-inch headspace. Remove any air bubbles. Wipe the jar rims and threads with a clean, damp paper towel. Apply hot lids and screw bands.

5. Process pint jars in a water bath canner for 20 minutes (see p. 34 for instructions). Remove from the water bath canner and let cool for 12 to 24 hours. Check the seals and remove the screw bands. Store jars in a cool, dry, dark place for up to 1 year.

DID YOU KNOW? Machine-spun cotton candy was invented in 1897 by William Morrison (a dentist) and John C. Wharton (a confectioner). It was introduced as "fairy floss" at the 1904 World's Fair in St. Louis, Missouri, and was sold for 25 cents a box.

Tomato Ketchup

CONTRIBUTORS: ROMERO FAMILY, COLORADO

MAKES ABOUT 3 PINT JARS

4 quarts plum tomatoes, peeled, cored, and chopped

¾ cup chopped onions

½ cup chopped red bell peppers

1½ cups cider vinegar

1 cup granulated sugar

1 tablespoon table salt

1 tablespoon paprika

1¼ teaspoons celery seeds

1 teaspoon whole allspice

1 teaspoon mustard seeds

1 cinnamon stick

Homemade ketchup takes a while to make, but it is oh so worth it! Slightly tangy, slightly sweet, and lighter than commercial types, this one is a gem. For this recipe, the Romero family likes to use Roma or beefsteak tomatoes, depending on what they have available at the time.

1. In an 8-quart stainless steel stockpot, combine the tomatoes, onions, and bell peppers. Bring the mixture to a simmer over medium heat, stirring frequently, and cook until the tomatoes are tender. Remove the pot from the heat.

2. Using a food mill, purée the tomato mixture. Return the tomato purée to the stockpot and cook over low heat, stirring frequently, until the mixture is thick and reduced by half. Stir in the vinegar, sugar, salt, and paprika.

3. Tie the celery seeds, allspice, mustard seeds, and cinnamon stick in a spice bag or a few layers of cheesecloth. Add the spice bag to the tomato mixture. Simmer the ketchup, stirring frequently to prevent scorching, until it reaches the desired thickness, 15 to 30 minutes. Remove the pot from the heat and remove the spice bag.

4. Ladle the ketchup into hot jars, leaving ½-inch headspace. Remove any air bubbles. Wipe the jar rims and threads with a clean, damp paper towel. Apply hot lids and screw bands.

5. Process pint jars in a water bath canner for 15 minutes (see p. 34 for instructions). Remove from the water bath canner and let cool for 12 to 24 hours. Check the seals and remove the screw bands. Store jars in a cool, dry, dark place for up to 1 year.

Sweet-and-Sour Sauce

CONTRIBUTOR: JANET GAMBLE, IDAHO

MAKES 6 TO 7 PINT JARS

7 cups granulated sugar

1 cup plus 2 tablespoons
ClearJel® powder

4 cups white- or red-wine
vinegar

½ cup soy sauce

2 cans (20 ounces each)
juice-packed pineapple
tidbits, drained and juice
reserved

8 cups peeled and
chopped tomatoes (about
5 pounds tomatoes)

4 cups chopped onions
(about 5 medium onions)

4 cups seeded and
chopped green bell
peppers (6 to 8 medium
peppers)

Janet uses this sauce on top of grilled chicken or beef, cut into thin strips, and served over rice; poured over meatballs; and even as a dip for egg rolls. Her family loves it—and hopes you will, too.

1. In a large bowl, whisk together the sugar and ClearJel until thoroughly blended. Set aside.

2. In an 8-quart stainless steel stockpot, combine the vinegar and soy sauce and bring to a boil over medium-high heat. Stir in the reserved pineapple juice, then add the sugar mixture and stir until completely dissolved. Bring to a boil and cook, stirring constantly, until the mixture is slightly thick, about 5 minutes.

3. Add the tomatoes, onions, bell peppers, and drained pineapple. Return the mixture to a boil, then remove the pot from the heat.

4. Ladle the sauce into hot jars, leaving ½-inch headspace. Remove any air bubbles. Wipe the jar rims and threads with a clean, damp paper towel. Apply hot lids and screw bands.

5. Process pint jars in a water bath canner for 35 minutes (see p. 34 for instructions). Remove from the water bath canner and let cool for 12 to 24 hours. Check the seals and remove the screw bands. Store jars in a cool, dry, dark place for up to 1 year.

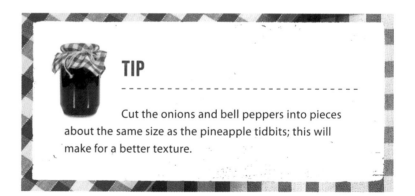

TIP

Cut the onions and bell peppers into pieces about the same size as the pineapple tidbits; this will make for a better texture.

JANET GAMBLE

BLACKFOOT, IDAHO

JANET GAMBLE is the oldest child in her family and has been canning on her own since she was about 14, but she started helping her mother can from the time she was old enough to understand what to do.

"One of my fondest memories of canning was when my grandmother, a couple of aunts, my mother, my sister, and I all helped can peaches. It was like an assembly line. I remember how much fun it was and how we all worked together to get the fruit in the jars. That is probably when I learned to love canning."

> **It gives Janet great satisfaction to see the labors of gardening transformed into beautiful jars of food to serve her family.**

On another occasion, Janet's mother had to go help her father in the field. At age 15, Janet was left to can the peaches that needed to be done right away. "I was so impressed that my mother had that degree of confidence in me to do the job."

Janet has had a large garden most of her life, and it gives her great satisfaction to see the labors of gardening transformed into beautiful jars of food to serve her family. "The thing I enjoy most about canning is the end result—seeing the product in jars and how great it is to see them on the storage shelf."

Even though some people tried to discourage her from entering fair competitions, she took the chance and discovered the rewards of trying her best. Janet has been entering fair competitions on a yearly basis since 2007 and has won about 100 blue ribbons and several special awards in canning and baking competitions.

Tomato Basil Sauce

CONTRIBUTOR: NANCY CHARRON, WASHINGTON

MAKES ABOUT 4 PINT JARS

12 cups peeled and chopped ripe Roma or other plum tomatoes (8 to 9 pounds tomatoes)

10 cloves garlic, minced (about 1 head garlic)

4 cups chopped fresh basil leaves

8 shallots, minced

4 tablespoons red-wine vinegar

6 teaspoons granulated sugar

4 teaspoons freshly squeezed lemon juice

2 teaspoons pickling salt

1 teaspoon freshly ground coarse black pepper

8 scallions (including green tops), thinly sliced

1 can (12 ounces) tomato paste

With the richness of plum tomatoes and fresh basil, this sauce captures the flavors of summer in a jar to enjoy all year long!

1. In an 8-quart stainless steel stockpot, combine the tomatoes, garlic, basil, shallots, vinegar, sugar, lemon juice, salt, and pepper.

2. Bring the mixture to a boil over medium-high heat, stirring frequently. Reduce the heat and boil gently, stirring frequently, for 5 minutes. Stir in the scallions and tomato paste, then return the mixture to a full boil. Remove the pot from the heat.

3. Ladle the sauce into hot jars, leaving ½-inch headspace. Remove any air bubbles. Wipe the jar rims and threads with a clean, damp paper towel. Apply hot lids and screw bands.

4. Process pint jars in a water bath canner for 35 minutes; quart jars for 40 minutes (see p. 34 for instructions). Remove from the water bath canner and let cool for 12 to 24 hours. Check the seals and remove the screw bands. Store jars in a cool, dry, dark place for up to 1 year.

Tomatillo Salsa

CONTRIBUTOR: SHIRLEY ROSENBERG, UTAH

MAKES ABOUT 3 PINT JARS

6 cups chopped husked tomatillos (about 3 pounds)

1 cup chopped onions (1 to 2 medium onions)

1 cup chopped seeded green sweet peppers, such as bell or banana peppers (1 to 2 medium peppers)

1 cup finely chopped seeded green hot peppers, such as a combination of Anaheim and jalapeño peppers (about ¾ pound peppers)

1 cup chopped fresh cilantro

¾ cup white vinegar

¼ cup freshly squeezed lime juice

4 cloves garlic, finely chopped

2 teaspoons ground cumin

½ teaspoon table salt

Some people think a tomatillo is a relative of the tomato, but it's not. This green fruit with papery husks is actually related to the cape gooseberry and is a staple in Mexican food. Shirley loves green sauces made from tomatillos and learned about tomatillos from a Hispanic friend. Now she grows them in her garden (she found seeds online). She added hot peppers to this recipe because her family likes it hot. You can adjust the amount and type of hot peppers to suit your heat preferences.

1. In an 8-quart stainless steel stockpot, combine the tomatillos, onions, sweet peppers, hot peppers, cilantro, vinegar, lime juice, garlic, cumin, and salt. Bring the mixture to a boil over medium-high heat, stirring frequently, then reduce the heat to medium and simmer, stirring frequently, for 10 minutes. Remove the pot from the heat.

2. Ladle the salsa into hot jars, leaving ½-inch headspace. Remove any air bubbles. Wipe the jar rims and threads with a clean, damp paper towel. Apply hot lids and screw bands.

3. Process pint jars in a water bath canner for 25 minutes (see p. 34 for instructions). Remove from the water bath canner and let cool for 12 to 24 hours. Check the seals and remove the screw bands. Store jars in a cool, dry, dark place for up to 1 year.

Roasted Corn and Sweet Pepper Salsa

CONTRIBUTOR: VALERIE J. FONG, CALIFORNIA

**MAKES FIVE OR SIX
8-OUNCE JARS**

6 cups peeled, cored, seeded, and roughly chopped Roma or other plum tomatoes (4 to 5 pounds tomatoes)

6 cloves garlic, roughly chopped

4 cups fresh white corn kernels (about 8 ears corn)

3 bell peppers (1 red, 1 orange, and 1 yellow), seeded and diced

1 red onion, chopped

2 shallots, finely chopped

3 tablespoons olive oil

1 cup red-wine vinegar

¼ cup balsamic vinegar

¼ cup freshly squeezed lemon juice

2 tablespoons granulated sugar

1 tablespoon table salt

1 teaspoon freshly ground black pepper

1 can (6 ounces) tomato paste

¼ cup finely chopped fresh flat-leaf parsley

This blend of roasted fresh corn and sweet peppers creates a savory salsa that is a delightful addition to a summer outdoor meal. By roasting the vegetables first, their natural sugars really come through and complement the rich flavor of the balsamic vinegar.

While the salsa is terrific with chips and guacamole, it is also excellent on a hamburger in place of regular relish.

1. In a blender, purée the tomatoes and garlic. Set aside.

2. In a large skillet over medium-high heat, sauté the corn, bell peppers, onions, and shallots in olive oil until the vegetables are slightly roasted and lightly charred, 3 to 5 minutes.

3. In an 8-quart stainless steel stockpot, combine the tomato purée and roasted corn mixture. Stir until well blended, then add the red-wine vinegar, balsamic vinegar, lemon juice, sugar, salt, black pepper, and tomato paste. Stir until blended.

4. Bring the mixture to a simmer over medium heat and cook for about 10 minutes, stirring occasionally. Add the parsley and cook for another 2 minutes. Remove the pot from the heat.

5. Ladle the salsa into hot jars, leaving ½-inch headspace. Remove any air bubbles. Wipe the jar rims and threads with a clean, damp paper towel. Apply hot lids and screw bands.

6. Process 8-ounce jars in a water bath canner for 10 minutes (see p. 34 for instructions). Remove from the water bath canner and let cool for 12 to 24 hours. Check the seals and remove the screw bands. Store jars in a cool, dry, dark place for up to 1 year.

SHIRLEY ROSENBERG

ENOCH, UTAH

SHIRLEY ROSENBERG'S family has been canning for generations. "I remember my Mom, Grandma, and Great Grandma all in 'The Cookhouse,' canning almost everything you can think of. We little ones would help by snapping beans and shelling peas." For a lot of their canning fruit, her family would go to u-pick orchards every year. "The truck would be parked right under the tree, so the adults could reach the lower limbs, and us kids could climb up with ice cream buckets over our arms to reach the higher limbs." Most of those orchards are gone now, making way for housing subdivisions.

"Blue ribbons rock!"

Her mom kept nagging Shirley to enter her preserves at the fair, but Shirley kept saying "Oh, it's not good enough." She finally listened to her mom and earned blue ribbons on a number of her first fair entries. "Blue ribbons rock!"

This early success inspired her to try even harder, taking the judges' comments to heart and improving her entries even more. It worked. Shirley took home more blue ribbons and then won her first Sweepstakes award. "That's the big, purple, frilly one at our Fair. After that, I had 'The Fever!' I wanted more

of those big ribbons on my wall!" She decided to branch out and see how well she could do at the Utah State Fair and was again rewarded with several blue ribbons on her first entries. "My paternal grandmother and I now have a friendly competition each year to see who earns more money and more of the higher ribbons."

Growing most of her own produce and working in a small kitchen, Shirley's competitive drive has resulted in her taking home around 400 blue ribbons and numerous special awards. Following her own success, Shirley nagged her sister into entering her canning into the fair and she, too, won blue ribbons her first time. Shirley now encourages her young nephew and niece to enter their homegrown crops at the fair. "My nephew really likes those blue ribbons as well. Looks like the next generation is getting 'The Fever' too!"

Salsa

CONTRIBUTOR: SHIRLEY ROSENBERG, UTAH

MAKES ABOUT 7 PINT JARS

10 cups cored and chopped tomatoes, preferably beefsteak (6 to 7 pounds tomatoes)

5 cups chopped onions (6 to 7 medium onions)

5 cups seeded and chopped sweet peppers, such as bell or banana peppers (7 to 8 medium peppers)

3 cups seeded and finely chopped hot peppers, such as a combination of Anaheim and jalapeño peppers (about 2 pounds peppers)

3 cups chopped fresh cilantro

1½ cups cider vinegar

1 whole head of garlic, finely chopped

4½ teaspoons table salt

A staple condiment in their house, Shirley earned her first Sweepstakes award at the Iron County Fair for this salsa. She loves using a combination of colorful sweet peppers, such as bell peppers, pimientos, and gypsy peppers, for more variety in flavor and appearance. And Shirley's family likes it hot, so she adds a few unseeded serrano and cayenne peppers to the hot pepper mix and increases the proportion of Anaheim peppers so the heat doesn't become nuclear.

1. In an 8-quart stainless steel stockpot, combine the tomatoes, onions, sweet peppers, hot peppers, cilantro, vinegar, garlic, and salt. Bring the mixture to a boil over medium-high heat, stirring frequently, then reduce the heat to medium and simmer, stirring frequently, for 10 minutes. Remove the pot from the heat.

2. Ladle the salsa into hot jars, leaving ½-inch headspace. Remove any air bubbles. Wipe the jar rims and threads with a clean, damp paper towel. Apply hot lids and screw bands.

3. Process pint jars in a water bath canner for 25 minutes (see p. 34 for instructions). Remove from the water bath canner and let cool for 12 to 24 hours. Check the seals and remove the screw bands. Store jars in a cool, dry, dark place for up to 1 year.

Roma Tomato Salsa

CONTRIBUTOR: NANCY CHARRON, WASHINGTON

MAKES ABOUT 18 PINT JARS

28 cups cored and chopped ripe Roma or other plum tomatoes (18 to 21 pounds tomatoes)

5 cups chopped yellow onions (6 to 7 medium onions)

1 cup cored, seeded, and finely chopped Anaheim peppers (about ¾ pound peppers)

2½ cups cored, seeded, and finely chopped Hungarian wax peppers (1½ to 2 pounds peppers)

1 cup finely chopped green jalapeño peppers, with seeds (about ¾ pound peppers)

6 large cloves garlic, finely chopped

2 cups bottled lemon juice

5 teaspoons freshly ground black pepper

3 tablespoons crushed dried Mexican oregano

2 tablespoons pickling salt

Warning: This recipe can cause serious salsa addiction! The Charron family has been enjoying this recipe for over 20 years. The summer flavor of fully ripe plum tomatoes, the heat from the green and yellow chiles, along with the savory notes of black pepper, onion, and oregano make for a party in a jar.

1. In a 12-quart stainless steel stockpot, combine the tomatoes, onions, peppers, and garlic. Stir in the lemon juice, black pepper, oregano, and salt until well combined.

2. Bring to a boil over medium-high heat, stirring frequently. Reduce the heat and simmer, uncovered, stirring occasionally, for 20 minutes. Remove the pot from the heat.

3. Ladle the salsa into hot jars, leaving ½-inch headspace. Remove any air bubbles. Wipe the jar rims and threads with a clean, damp paper towel. Apply hot lids and screw bands.

4. Process pint jars in a water bath canner for 15 minutes (see p. 34 for instructions). Remove from the water bath canner and let cool for 12 to 24 hours. Check the seals and remove the screw bands. Store jars in a cool, dry, dark place for up to 1 year.

TIPS

» It's easy to finely chop the hot peppers in a food processor. However, be sure to clean the blade and bowl of the food processor well since the peppers are hot.

» This salsa has medium heat. You can vary the heat by adjusting the type and amount of the chili peppers.

» Finely chopped fresh cilantro can be added to the salsa just before serving.

Mango Salsa

CONTRIBUTORS: ROMERO FAMILY, COLORADO

MAKES ABOUT 2 PINT JARS

2 large firm ripe mangos, peeled and chopped (about 2½ cups fresh or frozen)

1 small red onion, chopped

½ cup finely chopped fresh cilantro

1 serrano pepper, seeded and minced

3 tablespoons bottled lime juice

2 tablespoons finely chopped candied ginger

1½ tablespoons firmly packed dark brown sugar

½ teaspoon table salt

All of the Romero kids love mangos. Unfortunately, it's not always easy to find perfectly ripe fruit for recipes so they've turned to frozen mangos, which means they can make this salsa year-round. Simply thaw the fruit and you are good to go.

1. In a large saucepan, combine the mangos, red onions, cilantro, serrano peppers, lime juice, candied ginger, brown sugar, and salt. Cook over medium-low heat, stirring frequently, until the mixture is hot all the way through, 5 to 10 minutes. Do not boil. Remove the pot from the heat.

2. Ladle the salsa into hot jars, leaving ½-inch headspace. Remove any air bubbles. Wipe the jar rims and threads with a clean, damp paper towel. Apply hot lids and screw bands.

3. Process pint jars in a water bath canner for 10 minutes (see p. 34 for instructions). Remove from the water bath canner and let cool for 12 to 24 hours. Check the seals and remove the screw bands. Store jars in a cool, dry, dark place for up to 1 year.

* Specialty Preserves *

Everything from conserves, butters, and pie fillings to syrups, ice cream toppings, and flavored vinegars make wonderful additions to the canning pantry. Fun and flavorful, these preserves can turn everyday meals and desserts into special treats.

The techniques used to prepare specialty preserves are the same as those used to make other types of canned foods—follow the recipes carefully and use quality ingredients to create these delectable recipes.

Many fairs have divisions and classes for specialty canned products.

Conserves

Conserves are a specialty type of soft spread with a texture similar to that of a jam and made in the same basic manner. Like jams, conserves should mound up in a spoon, hold their shape, and spread easily. There should be no separation of the fruit and nuts from the juice in the spread, and the conserve should not be runny.

What sets conserves apart from jams is that they traditionally contain two or more fruits and nuts. Conserves may be made with fresh or dried fruits or a combination of both. Nuts give conserves a unique texture and a rich flavor. Stale nuts will ruin the flavor of your conserve, so taste the nuts you are using to be sure they are fresh. To bring out the nutty flavor, toast nuts before using them (see the sidebar on p. 9).

Fruit Butters

Fruit butters are classic, old-fashioned spreads made by slowly cooking puréed fruit or fruit pulp with sugar until enough of the juice evaporates to create a thick, spreadable consistency. This slow cooking concentrates the fruit flavor and produces a smooth texture similar to country-style butter. It is this texture that gives the spread its name.

The flavor and texture of a butter is more rustic than a jam or a jelly—it will mound up and hold its shape, with no separation of liquid, but should not be too firm or cut like a jelly. Butters are made by cooking chopped fruit with a small amount of liquid until the fruit is soft and tender. The cooked fruit is pressed through a fine-mesh sieve or food mill to purée it and remove any fibrous pieces. The puréed fruit is then returned to the pan, sugar is added, and the mixture is cooked slowly over low heat until it is very thick. If the heat is too high or the butter is not stirred often enough, the fruit mixture can scorch and develop an unpleasant burned flavor. An overcooked butter will have a sticky, rubbery texture when cooled.

Spices, such as cinnamon, nutmeg, and ginger, may be added to the butter, or the butter may be left plain to let the flavor of the fruit shine through. Spices added to butters should enhance the flavor of the fruit rather than overpower it. Be mindful: the flavor of the spices will intensify during storage. One spice to be particularly careful about is cloves, as it can be very intense and easily overwhelm the other flavors in a butter. If you use cloves in your butter, use it sparingly.

Apricot Orange Conserve

CONTRIBUTOR: ALAN GRAVENOR, MARYLAND

MAKES ABOUT FIVE
8-OUNCE JARS

3½ cups apricot halves,
chopped and drained
(from two 20-ounce cans)

1½ cups freshly
squeezed orange juice

Grated zest of ½ large
orange

2 tablespoons freshly
squeezed lemon juice

3¼ cups granulated
sugar

½ cup chopped walnuts
or pecans

SERVING SUGGESTION

This conserve is scrump-
tious served over a baked
chicken breast on a bed of
rice or on a baked or fried
ham steak.

This tangy conserve is for the person who loves a fruity, citrusy
flavor. Add some plumped dried blueberries, cherries, or cranberries along with the nuts for an additional fruit taste. This
conserve is made with canned apricots; when fresh apricots are
at the peak of ripeness and flavor, you can substitute them for
the canned apricots with similar results.

1. In a medium stainless steel stockpot, combine the apricots,
   orange juice, orange zest, and lemon juice. Stir in the sugar.
   Cook the mixture over medium heat, stirring constantly, until
   it thickens and reaches the jelly stage (220°F at sea level), about
   20 minutes.

2. Add the nuts and stir well. Remove the pan from the heat and
   skim off any foam.

3. Ladle the conserve into hot jars, leaving ¼-inch headspace.
   Remove any air bubbles. Wipe the jar rims and threads with a
   clean, damp paper towel. Apply hot lids and screw bands.

4. Process 4-ounce, 8-ounce, and pint jars in a water bath canner for
   10 minutes (see p. 34 for instructions). Remove from the water
   bath canner and let cool for 12 to 24 hours. Check the seals and
   remove the screw bands. Store jars in a cool, dry, dark place for
   up to 1 year.

Apple Pie Conserve

CONTRIBUTOR: LINDA J. AMENDT, CALIFORNIA

MAKES ABOUT SEVEN
8-OUNCE JARS

5 cups cored, peeled,
and finely chopped
apples (about 2½ pounds
apples)

1¼ cups unsweetened
apple juice

½ cup golden raisins

1 tablespoon freshly
squeezed lemon juice

4 cups granulated sugar

1 cup firmly packed dark
brown sugar

1½ teaspoons ground
cinnamon

½ teaspoon ground
nutmeg

½ teaspoon unsalted
butter (optional)

½ cup chopped walnuts
or pecans

1 pouch (3 ounces) liquid
pectin

Mmmm, apple pie in a jar! Linda likes to use Granny Smith apples in this conserve, but any good cooking apple, such as Jonathon, Rome, or Northern Spy, will work fine. You can adjust the spices to suit your personal taste and even add a pinch of ground ginger if you like.

1. In an 8-quart stainless steel stockpot, combine the apples, apple juice, raisins, and lemon juice. Bring the mixture to a boil over medium-high heat, then reduce the heat, cover, and simmer for 5 minutes, stirring occasionally.

2. Uncover the pot and stir in the granulated sugar, brown sugar, cinnamon, nutmeg, and butter, if using. Cook over medium-high heat, stirring constantly, until the sugar is completely dissolved. Stir in the walnuts. Increase the heat to medium high and bring to a full rolling boil, stirring constantly.

3. Stir in the pectin. Return the mixture to a full rolling boil, stirring constantly. Boil for 1 minute, stirring constantly. Remove the pot from the heat and skim off any foam.

4. Ladle the conserve into hot jars, leaving ¼-inch headspace. Remove any air bubbles. Wipe the jar rims and threads with a clean, damp paper towel. Apply hot lids and screw bands.

5. Process 4-ounce, 8-ounce, and pint jars in a water bath canner for 10 minutes (see p. 34 for instructions). Remove from the water bath canner and let cool for 12 to 24 hours. Check the seals and remove the screw bands. Store jars in a cool, dry, dark place for up to 1 year.

DID YOU KNOW? At the 1906 Iowa State Fair, the St. Paul Growers Association built a model of the state capitol building out of onions.

Nectarine Conserve

CONTRIBUTOR: LINDA J. AMENDT, CALIFORNIA

MAKES ABOUT EIGHT 8-OUNCE JARS

⅔ cup freshly squeezed orange juice

⅔ cup golden raisins

3 cups pitted, peeled, and crushed nectarines (about 3 pounds nectarines)

½ cup freshly squeezed lemon juice

1 tablespoon finely grated orange zest

6 cups granulated sugar

½ teaspoon unsalted butter (optional)

¾ cup sliced or slivered almonds

2 pouches (3 ounces each) liquid pectin

⅓ cup Grand Marnier, brandy, or rum (optional)

TIP

If the raisins are large, cut them in half after measuring.

This conserve has a beautiful color and tastes like summer sunshine in a jar. For a pretty appearance and uniform texture, remove the red fibers from the center of the nectarines before chopping and crushing the fruit. Little tricks like this make the difference between a good spread and a superior one that wins blue ribbons.

1. Warm the orange juice in a small saucepan over low heat. Do not let it simmer. Remove the pan from the heat and add the raisins; cover and let stand for 1 hour.

2. In an 8-quart stainless steel stockpot, combine the nectarines, lemon juice, and orange zest. Add the raisin mixture, then stir in the sugar and add the butter, if using. Cook the mixture over medium-low heat, stirring constantly, until the sugar is completely dissolved. Stir in the almonds. Increase the heat to medium high and bring to a full rolling boil, stirring constantly.

3. Stir in the pectin. Return the mixture to a full rolling boil, stirring constantly. Boil for 1 minute, stirring constantly.

4. Remove the pot from the heat and skim off any foam. Stir in the Grand Marnier, brandy, or rum, if using. Let the conserve cool in the pot for 5 minutes, stirring occasionally.

5. Ladle the conserve into hot jars, leaving ¼-inch headspace. Remove any air bubbles. Wipe the jar rims and threads with a clean, damp paper towel. Apply hot lids and screw bands.

6. Process 4-ounce, 8-ounce, and pint jars in a water bath canner for 10 minutes (see p. 34 for instructions). Remove from the water bath canner and let cool for 12 to 24 hours. Check the seals and remove the screw bands. Store jars in a cool, dry, dark place for up to 1 year.

Gooseberry Conserve

CONTRIBUTOR: ROBIN TARBELL-THOMAS, IOWA

**MAKES ABOUT FIVE
8-OUNCE JARS**

6 cups whole
gooseberries, stems and
blossom ends removed

1 cup finely chopped
fresh pineapple

1 unpeeled orange, finely
diced and any seeds
removed

1 cup coarsely chopped
golden raisins

4 cups granulated sugar

¾ cup chopped walnuts

Robin says gooseberries remind her of her grandmother picking the berries to make gooseberry pies and gooseberry conserve, and every time she makes this conserve she thinks of her.

1. In an 8-quart stainless steel stockpot, combine the gooseberries, pineapple, oranges, and raisins. Stir in the sugar. Cook over low heat, stirring constantly, until the sugar is completely dissolved.

2. Increase the heat to medium high and bring the mixture to a rapid boil, stirring constantly. Add the walnuts. Boil and stir the mixture until it reaches the jelly stage (220°F at sea level). Remove the pan from the heat.

3. Ladle the conserve into hot jars, leaving ¼-inch headspace. Remove any air bubbles. Wipe the jar rims and threads with a clean, damp paper towel. Apply hot lids and screw bands.

4. Process 4-ounce, 8-ounce, and pint jars in a water bath canner for 10 minutes (see p. 34 for instructions). Remove from the water bath canner and let cool for 12 to 24 hours. Check the seals and remove the screw bands. Store jars in a cool, dry, dark place for up to 1 year.

DID YOU KNOW? By the late 1800s, most of the country's largest fairs were already in full swing. From the New York State Fair in Syracuse, New York, to the San Diego County Fair in Del Mar, California, to the state fairs in Minnesota and Texas, agricultural fairs had become major annual events, attracting exhibitors and visitors from far and wide.

ROBIN TARBELL-THOMAS

CENTERVILLE, IOWA

FOR ROBIN TARBELL-THOMAS, competing at fairs is in her blood. Her family represents four generations of entering and winning ribbons at the Iowa State Fair. Her grandmother, Mildred Phillips, exhibited at county fairs, local festivals, and the Iowa State Fair. Throughout her lifetime, Mildred won over 5,000 ribbons. Robin's mother, Olive Jean Tarbell, has won over 2,000 ribbons and still exhibits at the Iowa State Fair. Entering both baking and canning competitions, Robin has brought home over 3,000 ribbons in her 38 years of entering fairs. Robin's daughter, Molly Thomas, started entering at the Iowa State Fair at the age of four and has carried on the family tradition by winning hundreds of ribbons of her own.

Robin's family represents four generations of entering and winning ribbons at the Iowa State Fair.

Her grandmother and grandfather always had a big, beautiful garden, and they took great pride in its appearance and the bountiful harvest it produced each year. "Getting ready for the state fair was always a busy time. I remember my grandmother sitting on the front porch in the hot Iowa summer working on her entries for the state fair. She would go through the shelled peas, one at a time, so they would all be the same size and color. She was definitely a perfectionist, and all of her canned goods represented her attention to detail. Grandmother had a canning room in her basement that was picture perfect."

One of the highlights from the Iowa State Fair canning competition was when Robin's pickles won the blue ribbon in the division sponsored by Gedney Pickles. As the winner, Robin's pickles were sold by the company. Because the recipe was one that had been passed down from her grandmother, they called the pickles "Gramma's Mellow Dills." Robin, and winners from other fairs, were treated like royalty and went on a media "pickle tour," appearing on television and radio, and making personal appearances in grocery stores. "I never would have received this once-in-a-lifetime experience if my grandmother had not taken the time to teach me the art of canning and if I had never exhibited at the Iowa State Fair. I feel so fortunate and blessed to be a part of my family's canning tradition."

Carrot Cake Conserve

CONTRIBUTOR: SHIRLEY ROSENBERG, UTAH

MAKES FIVE TO SIX
8-OUNCE JARS

1½ cups finely shredded, peeled carrots (about 5 medium carrots)

1¾ cups juice-packed crushed pineapple (about one 20-ounce can) or finely chopped fresh pineapple and juice

1½ cups peeled, cored, and finely chopped pears (about 1½ pounds pears)

½ cup finely chopped raisins or dates, or ¼ cup of each

3 tablespoons freshly squeezed lemon juice

1½ teaspoons finely grated lemon zest

1 teaspoon ground cinnamon

1 teaspoon ground nutmeg

½ teaspoon ground cloves

¼ teaspoon ground cardamom (optional)

1 box (1.75 ounces) powdered pectin

6¼ cups granulated sugar

¼ teaspoon unsalted butter (optional)

Shirley's great grandma, Granny George, made the "world's best" carrot cake. While this conserve isn't quite as good as Granny George's cake, Shirley says it's darn close! When it's in season, Shirley uses fresh pineapple instead of canned, and she sometimes adds raisins and dates (another throwback to Granny George's carrot cake), lemon zest, cloves, and cardamom to make a very flavorful conserve.

1. In an 8-quart stockpot, combine the carrots, pineapple (including the juice), pears, raisins or dates, lemon juice, lemon zest, cinnamon, nutmeg, cloves, and cardamom, if using. Bring the mixture to a boil over medium-high heat, stirring frequently. Reduce the heat to medium low, cover, and simmer, stirring frequently, until the carrots are tender and the dried fruit is plump, 15 to 20 minutes, stirring every few minutes.

2. Add the pectin and stir until completely dissolved.

3. Bring the mixture to a full rolling boil over medium-high heat, stirring constantly. Add the sugar and the butter, if using, and stir until completely dissolved. Return the mixture to a full rolling boil, stirring constantly. Boil for 1 minute, stirring constantly. Remove the pot from the heat and skim off any foam.

4. Ladle the jam into hot jars, leaving ¼-inch headspace. Remove any air bubbles. Wipe the jar rims and threads with a clean, damp paper towel. Apply hot lids and screw bands.

5. Process 4-ounce, 8-ounce, and pint jars in a water bath canner for 10 minutes (see p. 34 for instructions). Remove from the water bath canner and let cool for 12 to 24 hours. Check the seals and remove the screw bands. Store jars in a cool, dry, dark place for up to 1 year.

VARIATION

Add ½ cup chopped walnuts to the conserve after adding the sugar before the final boil.

Pineapple Rhubarb Strawberry Conserve

CONTRIBUTORS: ROMERO FAMILY, COLORADO

MAKES ABOUT SEVEN 8-OUNCE JARS

1 can (20 ounces) juice-packed crushed pineapple, drained

1½ cups chopped rhubarb (¼-inch pieces, about 3 stalks rhubarb)

1½ cups crushed strawberries (about 2 pints whole strawberries)

2 tablespoons freshly squeezed lemon juice

1 tablespoon finely grated lemon zest

1 box (2 ounces) powdered pectin

½ teaspoon unsalted butter (optional)

6½ cups granulated sugar

½ cup chopped pecans or walnuts

⅓ cup golden raisins

This conserve is so different and so delicious. It is wonderful paired with softened Brie and crackers.

1. In an 8-quart stainless steel stockpot, combine the pineapple, rhubarb, strawberries, lemon juice, and lemon zest. Stir in the pectin and add the butter, if using. Bring the mixture to a full rolling boil over medium-high heat, stirring constantly.

2. Add the sugar and stir until completely dissolved, then stir in the pecans and raisins. Return the mixture to a full rolling boil, stirring constantly. Boil for 1 minute, stirring constantly. Remove the pot from the heat and skim off any foam.

3. Ladle the conserve into hot jars, leaving ¼-inch headspace. Remove any air bubbles. Wipe the jar rims and threads with a clean, damp paper towel. Apply hot lids and screw bands.

4. Process 4-ounce, 8-ounce, and pint jars in a water bath canner for 10 minutes (see p. 34 for instructions). Remove from the water bath canner and let cool for 12 to 24 hours. Check the seals and remove the screw bands. Store jars in a cool, dry, dark place for up to 1 year.

Apple Butter

CONTRIBUTOR: LINDA J. AMENDT, CALIFORNIA

MAKES ABOUT FIVE
8-OUNCE JARS

4 pounds apples, peeled, cored, and chopped

2 cups unsweetened apple juice or water

3 tablespoons freshly squeezed lemon juice

2½ cups granulated sugar

1 teaspoon ground cinnamon

¼ teaspoon ground nutmeg

The aroma of apple butter cooking on the stove makes the whole house smell wonderful and full of happy memories and visions of family holidays. That same feeling returns every time you open a jar of this silky, lightly spiced butter. Cooking the apples in apple juice intensifies the apple flavor.

1. In an 8-quart stainless steel stockpot, combine the apples, apple juice, and lemon juice. Bring the mixture to a boil over medium-high heat. Reduce the heat, cover, and simmer for 30 minutes, stirring frequently to prevent sticking. Remove the pot from the heat.

2. Press the cooked apple mixture through a food mill or a fine-mesh sieve.

3. Return the apple purée to the pot. Stir in the sugar, cinnamon, and nutmeg. Bring the mixture to a boil over medium heat, stirring constantly, until the sugar is completely dissolved. Reduce the heat and simmer, stirring frequently, until the apple butter is very thick and coats the back of a spoon, about 30 minutes. As the mixture thickens, stir constantly to prevent scorching. Remove the pot from the heat.

4. Ladle the butter into hot jars, leaving ¼-inch headspace. Remove any air bubbles. Wipe the jar rims and threads with a clean, damp paper towel. Apply hot lids and screw bands.

5. Process 4-ounce, 8-ounce, and pint jars in a water bath canner for 10 minutes (see p. 34 for instructions). Remove from the water bath canner and let cool for 12 to 24 hours. Check the seals and remove the screw bands. Store jars in a cool, dry, dark place for up to 1 year.

VARIATION: CARAMEL APPLE BUTTER

Make Caramel Apple Butter by substituting 2½ cups firmly packed dark brown sugar for the granulated sugar.

Baked Peach Rum Butter

CONTRIBUTOR: NANCY CHARRON, WASHINGTON

MAKES 4 PINT JARS

8 cups peeled and crushed peaches (6 to 8 pounds peaches)

1 tablespoon molasses

1 teaspoon ground nutmeg

2 cinnamon sticks

1 whole vanilla bean

3 cups firmly packed brown sugar

½ cup freshly squeezed lemon juice

1 cup rum, preferably Jamaican

For a wonderful adult dessert, generously slather this kicked-up butter on gingerbread and then drizzle with cream.

1. Position a rack in the center of the oven and heat the oven to 350°F.

2. In an 8-quart stainless steel stockpot, combine the peaches, molasses, and nutmeg and stir until blended. Add the cinnamon sticks and the vanilla bean. Simmer over medium heat, stirring frequently to keep the mixture from sticking, until the peaches are soft, about 20 minutes. Stir in the brown sugar, lemon juice, and ½ cup of the rum, stirring until the sugar is completely dissolved. Remove the pot from the heat. Remove the cinnamon sticks and vanilla bean.

3. In batches, purée the peach mixture in a food processor or with a potato masher to create a smooth texture. Pour the peach mixture in a 9 x 13 x 2-inch baking pan or roasting pan and spread evenly.

4. Bake for 30 minutes, then stir the butter and check for thickness. The butter is done baking when it forms one large drip off a spoon turned sideways or falls off the edge of the spoon in a sheet. Continue to bake for up to 60 minutes more if needed, checking every 15 minutes for doneness and stirring. Remove the pan from the oven and stir in the remaining ½ cup rum.

5. Spoon the butter into hot jars, leaving ¼-inch headspace. Remove any air bubbles. Wipe the jar rims and threads with a clean, damp paper towel. Apply hot lids and screw bands.

6. Process 4-ounce, 8-ounce, and pint jars in a water bath canner for 10 minutes (see p. 34 for instructions). Remove from the water bath canner and let cool for 12 to 24 hours. Check the seals and remove the screw bands. Store jars in a cool, dry, dark place for up to 1 year.

NANCY CHARRON

YAKIMA, WASHINGTON

NANCY CHARRON grew up in Yakima, Washington, where her family had a large garden. Her mother still cans her garden bounty every year. "Fond childhood memories include the basement canning room full of a year's supply of jams, pickles, and tomatoes; trips to the u-pick farms to pick cucumbers; shucking corn; the smell of ripe orchard fruit; falling out of cherry trees; and the boxes of peaches waiting for jars."

Nancy's garden is now larger than her mom's and it continues to evolve to meet her family's demand for new or better-flavored canned items. "I admit there is some competing with both my mother and a friend, to see who can be the most successful or find that exciting new recipe. It is a very a rewarding challenge and we share the triumphs and the 'not-so-successful' or 'won't do that again' reports."

While the ribbons are nice, the real reward is reading the judge's comments about their entries.

"My husband, Johnny, is the number-one reason there are garden harvests and successful canning results. He is a true professional at weeding and watering. I personally hate watering; weeding is okay. Additionally, Johnny is my chief tomato chopping partner for our salsa production. It may be that he is motivated to help because he is also the main consumer of salsa!"

"Our family eagerly watches for the Central Washington State Fair entry book each year in anticipation of pursuing the unique special awards related to the fair themes that are provided by national or local sponsors." Checking out the awards is the first stop the family makes when they visit the fair. While the ribbons are nice, the real reward is reading the judge's comments about their entries. They also enjoy seeing the clever ideas other exhibitors enter into the fair.

Nancy's blue ribbons number in the hundreds. Each year, she enters about 15 to 20 canned items, made from their homegrown fruits, vegetables, and herbs. Her win ratio is impressive, taking home blue ribbons on 90% of her entries and at least one or two special awards for Best of Show or Best of Category each year. She has also taken home special canning awards from Ball and C&H® Sugar.

Holiday Cranberry Chutney

CONTRIBUTOR: BRENDA BUSTILLOS, TEXAS

**MAKES ABOUT SIX
8-OUNCE JARS**

3 cups fresh cranberries

1¼ cups finely chopped
sweet onions

1¼ cups chopped
candied pineapple

3 cloves garlic, finely
chopped

2 tablespoons finely
chopped crystallized
ginger

1 teaspoon grated orange
zest

¼ cup freshly squeezed
orange juice

1 cup red-wine vinegar

1½ cups granulated
sugar

1 cup golden raisins

1 cup water

1 teaspoon dry mustard

1 teaspoon ground
cinnamon

1 teaspoon ground cloves

½ teaspoon cayenne
pepper

Holidays in the Bustillos family are fun and treasured events, and they love to share unique and festive foods, like this delightful chutney made by Brenda.

1. In an 8-quart stainless steel stockpot, combine the cranberries, onions, pineapple, garlic, ginger, orange zest, orange juice, and vinegar. Bring the mixture to a boil over medium-high heat, stirring occasionally. Reduce the heat, cover, and boil gently until the cranberries soften and burst, about 15 minutes.

2. Add the sugar, raisins, water, mustard, cinnamon, cloves, and cayenne. Boil gently, stirring frequently, for about 15 minutes. The mixture should be slightly runny and will thicken upon cooling. Remove the pot from the heat.

3. Ladle the chutney into hot jars, leaving ½-inch headspace. Remove any air bubbles. Wipe the jar rims and threads with a clean, damp paper towel. Apply hot lids and screw bands.

4. Process 8-ounce jars in a water bath canner for 10 minutes (see p. 34 for instructions). Remove from the water bath canner and let cool for 12 to 24 hours. Check the seals and remove the screw bands. Store jars in a cool, dry, dark place for up to 1 year.

BRENDA D. BUSTILLOS

COLLEGE STATION, TEXAS

BRENDA BUSTILLOS, a captain in the U.S. Army, can trace her earliest memories of canning back to her grandparents' small farmhouse kitchen in Burleson, Texas. Before she ever knew what chow-chow consisted of, and long after the name first made her giggle, she would pull an upturned bucket or wooden chair over by an old gas stove and watch her grandmother as she canned her best garden crops. Her grandfather took great care to produce the most beautiful organic vegetables, peaches, plums, and pecans.

> **"I would watch as my mother and grandmother transformed homegrown, organic harvests into some of my favorite childhood memories."**

Having survived the Great Depression as children, her grandparents placed great value in producing and preserving their own food. "I would watch as my mother and grandmother transformed homegrown, organic harvests into some of my favorite childhood memories. Pickled beets, chow-chow, bread-and-butter pickles, string green beans, stewed tomatoes, spiced peaches…all beautiful, delicious, and seemingly impossible to replicate!"

After she began her undergraduate education in nutrition and food science, Brenda gained a greater interest in the science of canning. She wants to pass on the legacy, as well as share the love and pride she has for producing her own products. "I still smile to myself when I pass by folks in a grocery store who have large jars of commercially produced jam, preserves, jelly, and pickles in their baskets. They could do so much better!"

Brenda began entering fair competitions in 2005. She joined the U.S. Army Medical Specialist Corps in 2007 and, despite spending her first five years of Active Duty service out-of-state, she continued to compete and would exchange stories with her mother and sister of their victories and defeats on the battlefields of competitive canning and cooking. "Though nowhere near as talented in the canning arena as my mother and sister, I always know that we have something unique and special in common—and someone to call when I run out of jars."

In addition to canning, Brenda has won a number of baked goods special awards where she used her homemade preserves, chutneys, jellies, jams, and barbecue sauce as ingredients in cakes, pies, sweet breads, and savory foods. "I have won local titles in national competitions such as Fleishmann's Yeast Baking for a Cure and Spam® by incorporating some of my home canned goods!"

Mango Chutney

CONTRIBUTORS: ROMERO FAMILY, COLORADO

MAKES ABOUT SEVEN 8-OUNCE JARS

2 quarts peeled and chopped firm mangos (8 to 10 mangos)

½ cup raisins

½ cup chopped onions

1 small hot red pepper, seeded and finely chopped

2½ cups cider vinegar

1½ cups firmly packed dark brown sugar

2 tablespoons mustard seeds

1 tablespoon ground ginger

1 teaspoon table salt

The bright color of the mangos makes this chutney a feast for the eyes. You can vary the heat to suit your personal taste by choosing your favorite hot pepper. Try the chutney spooned over roast pork.

1. In an 8-quart stainless steel stockpot, combine the mangos, raisins, onions, and red pepper. Stir in the vinegar, brown sugar, mustard seeds, ginger, and salt.

2. Bring the mixture to a boil over medium-high heat, stirring frequently. Reduce the heat and simmer, stirring frequently, until thickened, 25 to 30 minutes. Remove the pot from the heat.

3. Ladle the chutney into hot jars, leaving ½-inch headspace. Remove any air bubbles. Wipe the jar rims and threads with a clean, damp paper towel. Apply hot lids and screw bands.

4. Process 8-ounce jars in a water bath canner for 10 minutes (see p. 34 for instructions). Remove from the water bath canner and let cool for 12 to 24 hours. Check the seals and remove the screw bands. Store jars in a cool, dry, dark place for up to 1 year.

Strawberry Syrup

CONTRIBUTORS: ROMERO FAMILY, COLORADO

MAKES ABOUT 3 PINT JARS

3 quarts whole strawberries, stemmed and crushed

3 cups water

1 tablespoon grated lemon zest

2½ cups granulated sugar

3½ cups light corn syrup

2 tablespoons freshly squeezed lemon juice

Jeremiah Romero loves any and all fruit syrups. According to him, pancakes cannot be eaten without homemade fruit syrup. Serve with fresh berries or cut bananas on the side.

1. In an 8-quart stainless steel stockpot, combine the strawberries, 1½ cups of the water, and the lemon zest. Bring the mixture to a boil over medium-high heat, stirring frequently. Reduce the heat and simmer, stirring frequently, for 6 minutes. Remove the pot from the heat.

2. Strain the strawberry mixture through a fine-mesh sieve lined with several layers of damp fine-knit cheesecloth. Set the juice aside and discard the seeds and pulp.

3. In a large saucepan, combine the sugar and the remaining 1½ cups water. Bring the mixture to a boil over medium-high heat, stirring until the sugar is completely dissolved. When the syrup reaches 230°F on an instant-read thermometer or candy thermometer, stir in the strawberry juice and corn syrup. Return the syrup to a boil and boil for 5 minutes, stirring occasionally. Stir in the lemon juice. Remove the pan from the heat.

4. Ladle the syrup into hot jars, leaving ½-inch headspace. Remove any air bubbles. Wipe the jar rims and threads with a clean, damp paper towel. Apply hot lids and screw bands.

5. Process 8-ounce and pint jars in a water bath canner for 10 minutes (see p. 34 for instructions). Remove from the water bath canner and let cool for 12 to 24 hours. Check the seals and remove the screw bands. Store jars in a cool, dry, dark place for up to 1 year.

Apricot Syrup

CONTRIBUTOR: LINDA J. AMENDT, CALIFORNIA

MAKES ABOUT SIX 8-OUNCE JARS OR 3 PINT JARS

6 cups pitted and chopped fresh apricots (4 to 5 pounds apricots)

4½ cups granulated sugar

3 tablespoons freshly squeezed lemon juice

This syrup is fabulous served on pancakes and waffles, or as a topping for pound cake or over ice cream for apricot sundaes.

1. In a 6-quart stainless steel stockpot, combine the apricots and sugar. Cover and let stand for 3 hours.

2. Cook the mixture over medium-low heat, stirring constantly, until the sugar is completely dissolved. Increase the heat to medium high, stirring frequently, and bring the mixture to a boil. Reduce the heat, cover, and simmer gently for 15 minutes. Remove the pot from the heat and skim off any foam. Let cool for 15 minutes.

3. Strain the apricot mixture through a fine-mesh sieve. Discard the pulp. Rinse the sieve and line it with 3 layers of clean, damp fine-knit cheesecloth. Strain the syrup through the cheesecloth.

4. In a 4-quart stainless steel stockpot, combine the apricot syrup and lemon juice and bring to a boil over medium-high heat. Reduce the heat and boil gently, stirring frequently, until the syrup starts to thicken, 10 to 15 minutes. Remove the pot from the heat.

5. Ladle the syrup into hot jars, leaving ½-inch headspace. Wipe the jar rims and threads with a clean, damp paper towel. Apply hot lids and screw bands.

6. Process 8-ounce and pint jars in a water bath canner for 10 minutes (see p. 34 for instructions). Remove from the water bath canner and let cool for 12 to 24 hours. Check the seals and remove the screw bands. Store jars in a cool, dry, dark place for up to 1 year.

Berry Syrup

CONTRIBUTOR: SHIRLEY ROSENBERG, UTAH

MAKES 3 TO 4 PINT JARS

2 quarts fresh or thawed
frozen whole berries,
crushed

6¾ cups granulated
sugar

¼ teaspoon unsalted
butter (optional)

TIP

For a chunky syrup,
include some of
the fruit pulp in the
juice.

This syrup is delicious made from any unsweetened berry juice. Try raspberry, blackberry, or blueberry. In addition to a variety of berry syrups, Shirley also has made spiced apple syrup and spiced pear syrup. This recipe is as versatile as your imagination and taste buds!

1. In a 4-quart stainless steel stockpot, bring the crushed berries to a boil over medium-high heat, stirring frequently. Reduce the heat and simmer, stirring frequently, until the berries are very soft, about 10 minutes. Remove the pot from the heat and let cool for a few minutes. Strain the mixture through a fine-mesh sieve to separate the juice from the pulp. Discard the pulp. For a clearer syrup, line the sieve with a few layers of damp fine-knit cheesecloth and strain the juice again. Measure out 5 cups of berry juice.

2. Pour the berry juice into an 8-quart stainless steel stockpot. Stir in the sugar and add the butter, if using. Bring the mixture to a boil over medium-high heat, stirring constantly, until the sugar is completely dissolved. Reduce the heat to medium and boil, stirring frequently, until the syrup is thickened, 5 to 8 minutes. The longer the mixture boils, the thicker the syrup will be. Remove the pot from the heat.

3. Ladle the syrup into hot jars, leaving ½-inch headspace. Remove any air bubbles. Wipe the jar rims and threads with a clean, damp paper towel. Apply hot lids and screw bands.

4. Process 8-ounce and pint jars in a water bath canner for 10 minutes (see p. 34 for instructions). Remove from the water bath canner and let cool for 12 to 24 hours. Check the seals and remove the screw bands. Store jars in a cool, dry, dark place for up to 1 year.

Blueberry Pie Filling

CONTRIBUTORS: ROMERO FAMILY, COLORADO

MAKES ABOUT 5 PINT JARS

3 cups granulated sugar

¾ cup ClearJel powder

12 cups fresh or thawed frozen whole blueberries

1 tablespoon finely grated lemon zest

¼ cup bottled lemon juice

A pie filling that's never been used for a pie? This one is too good, so the Romero family never has any left. They love this on waffles and pancakes—with whipped cream.

1. In an 8-quart stainless steel stockpot, combine the sugar and ClearJel powder and stir until well blended. Add the blueberries and stir to combine. Cover and let stand for 30 minutes.

2. Add the lemon zest and lemon juice to the blueberry mixture. Bring the mixture to a gentle boil over medium heat, stirring constantly, and cook until the mixture thickens, 5 to 10 minutes. Remove the pot from the heat.

3. Ladle the pie filling into hot jars, leaving ½-inch headspace. Remove any air bubbles. Wipe the jar rims and threads with a clean, damp paper towel. Apply hot lids and screw bands.

4. Process pint and quart jars in a water bath canner for 30 minutes (see p. 34 for instructions). Remove from the water bath canner and let cool for 12 to 24 hours. Check the seals and remove the screw bands. Store jars in a cool, dry, dark place for up to 1 year.

TIP

If using fresh blueberries, lightly crush some of them to release a bit of the juice before adding them to the sugar mixture. Be careful not to mash the blueberries.

Basil Vinegar

CONTRIBUTOR: LINDA J. AMENDT, CALIFORNIA

MAKES ABOUT FOUR 8-OUNCE JARS OR 2 PINT JARS

2 cups loosely packed fresh basil leaves, chopped

1 large clove garlic, sliced

4½ cups white- or red-wine vinegar

Basil vinegar makes a delicious base for salad dressings and a delightful addition to sauces and gravies. This recipe can be used to make a variety of herb-infused vinegars.

1. Place the basil leaves and the garlic in a 1½- to 2-quart glass jar or other glass container.

2. In a large stainless steel saucepan, over medium-low heat, heat the vinegar just until hot. Do not bring to a simmer. Remove the pan from the heat.

3. Carefully pour the hot vinegar over the basil leaves in the jar and gently swirl the jar to combine. Cover the jar with two layers of plastic wrap, then apply the lid or secure the plastic wrap to the sides of the container. Place in a paper bag and let steep in a cool, dark, dry place for 2 to 4 weeks. Gently swirl the jar or container every few days. Start tasting the vinegar after 2 weeks. For a stronger flavor, allow the vinegar to steep for up to 4 weeks.

4. Line a fine-mesh sieve with cheesecloth and strain the vinegar. Discard the basil and garlic. Line the sieve with 3 layers of clean, damp fine-knit cheesecloth and strain the vinegar again into a clean container. Cover the vinegar and let stand overnight to allow any sediment to settle to the bottom.

5. Slowly pour the vinegar into a large saucepan, being careful not to disturb any sediment in the bottom of the container (discard the sediment). Heat the vinegar to 180°F over medium-low heat. Remove the pan from the heat.

6. Ladle the hot vinegar into hot jars, leaving ½-inch headspace. Wipe the jar rims and threads with a clean, damp paper towel. Apply hot lids and screw bands.

7. Process 8-ounce and pint jars in a water bath canner for 10 minutes (see p. 34 for instructions). Remove from the water bath canner and let cool for 12 to 24 hours. Check the seals and remove the screw bands. Store jars in a cool, dry, dark place for up to 1 year.

Pear Topping

CONTRIBUTOR: DOROTHY HALTIWANGER, SOUTH CAROLINA

MAKES ABOUT 10 PINT JARS

12 pounds pears, peeled, cored, and coarsely ground

4 or 5 oranges, peeled, seeded, and coarsely ground

2 teaspoons fruit preservative crystals

5 pounds granulated sugar (about 11¾ cups)

1 can (20 ounces) juice-packed crushed pineapple, drained

This is a delicious topping for ice cream or simply spread on toast or hot biscuits. If the oranges are large, use the smaller number of fruit; if the oranges are small, use the larger amount.

1. In an 8-quart stainless steel stockpot, combine the ground pears and oranges. Sprinkle the fruit preservative over the fruit and stir gently to blend. Pour the sugar over the fruit, cover, and let stand for about 1 hour.

2. Bring the mixture to a boil over medium-high heat, stirring frequently. Reduce the heat and simmer, stirring frequently, until the fruit is tender and the mixture starts to thicken, 10 to 15 minutes. Stir in the pineapple. Return the mixture to a full boil, stirring frequently. Remove the pot from the heat and skim off any foam.

3. Ladle the topping into hot jars, leaving ½-inch headspace. Remove any air bubbles. Wipe the jar rims and threads with a clean, damp paper towel. Apply hot lids and screw bands.

4. Process 8-ounce and pint jars in a water bath canner for 10 minutes (see p. 34 for instructions). Remove from the water bath canner and let cool for 12 to 24 hours. Check the seals and remove the screw bands. Store jars in a cool, dry, dark place for up to 1 year.

Mémère Doyon's Vegetarian Mincemeat

CONTRIBUTOR: STELLA DOYON, MAINE

MAKES 6 TO 7 QUART JARS

½ peck green tomatoes, roughly chopped (about 5 pounds)

3 quarts peeled, cored, and chopped apples (4 to 5 pounds apples)

2 pounds dark raisins

3 pounds granulated sugar (about 6 cups)

1 cup white vinegar

1 cup grape jelly

2 tablespoons kosher salt

1 tablespoon unsalted butter

1 tablespoon ground cinnamon

1½ teaspoons ground nutmeg

This Franco-American mincemeat recipe has been a favorite among the Doyon clan for generations. Soon after Stella's parents married in 1956, this recipe was handed down to her mother from Stella's Mémère (Grandmother) Doyon.

1. Using a food processor or a meat grinder, grind the green tomatoes, apples, and raisins.

2. In an 8-quart stainless steel stockpot, combine the ground green tomatoes, apples, and raisins. Add the sugar, vinegar, grape jelly, salt, butter, cinnamon, and nutmeg. Bring the mixture to a boil over medium-high heat, stirring constantly, until the sugar and jelly are completely dissolved. Reduce the heat and simmer, stirring occasionally, until the mincemeat is tender, 30 to 45 minutes. Remove the pot from the heat.

3. Ladle the mincemeat into hot jars, leaving ½-inch headspace. Remove any air bubbles. Wipe the jar rims and threads with a clean, damp paper towel. Apply hot lids and screw bands.

4. Process pint jars and quart jars in a water bath canner for 30 minutes (see p. 34 for instructions). Remove from the water bath canner and let cool for 12 to 24 hours. Check the seals and remove the screw bands. Store jars in a cool, dry, dark place for up to 1 year.

SERVING SUGGESTION

Make mincemeat pie: Combine ¼ cup cold water with 2 tablespoons cornstarch and whisk until smooth. Pour 1 quart Vegetarian Mincemeat into a large saucepan, add ¾ cup chopped walnuts and ½ cup dark raisins, and bring to a boil over medium heat, stirring frequently. Stir in the cornstarch mixture. Return to a boil, stirring constantly. Cook until the filling is thick, remove from the heat, and cool for 10 to 15 minutes. Spoon into the bottom of a double-crust pie shell, add the top crust, and bake at 350°F until golden brown, 45 to 50 minutes.

✻ Blue Ribbon Canning ✻ for Fair Competitions

For those of you who would like to enter your canned goods into a fair competition for the first time, and for those who already enter but would like to improve your entries and increase your win ratio, I'm happy to share with you my expert canning competition advice, garnered from years as a successful exhibitor and experienced preserved foods judge.

Fair Entry Requirements

The first step toward success at a fair competition is to read through and familiarize yourself with the rules and entry requirements found in the fair's competition or premium handbook. The entry requirements can vary from one fair to another. Precisely following these rules and requirements means your entry will be accepted for judging and won't be disqualified on a technicality.

These are some important items to pay careful attention to when you submit your entries.

- Be sure to submit your entry form before the entry deadline.
- Provide all the information required on the entry form and include the entry fees.
- Make note of entry delivery dates and times.
- Deliver your entries on time (many fairs are very strict about delivery times and won't accept entries even a few minutes late). Be sure to allow plenty of time to deliver your entries (allow extra time for traffic on the way to the fair and at the fairgrounds).
- Submit the number and size of jars required for each entry.
- Submit any additional information, such as recipes, when required.

Judging Systems

There are two systems of judging that are used to determine placings and awards for fair entries. These are the American System of Judging and the Danish System of Judging.

✻ AMERICAN SYSTEM OF JUDGING ✻

In the American System of Judging, the system used by most fairs, all entries within a class are judged against each other. The judges award only one first place, one second place, and one third place within the class. Some fairs award down through fifth place or encourage the judges to give honorable mention awards to deserving entries. While there may be several entries in a class that are worthy of winning first place, only one entry can receive the blue ribbon under the American System.

❋ DANISH SYSTEM OF JUDGING ❋

In the Danish System of Judging, each entry in a class is judged against a standard for that particular type of preserve, and awards are given based on individual merit. Judges can award as many first place awards as the quality of the entries warrants. Any entry earning 90 to 100 points wins first place. Between 80 and 89 points, the entry is awarded second place. For scores from 70 to 79 points, the entry earns third place. If an entry is scored lower than 70 points, then no award is given. The American System of Judging is then used to determine special awards for Best of Class, Best of Division, and Best of Show, where only one entry can win the top prize. The Danish System of Judging is used by most fairs for judging youth and kids' entries, and some fairs also use it to judge the adult entries.

Closed and Open Judgings

Most fairs conduct a closed judging, meaning the judging is done in private and is not open to the public. Canning entries are often delivered to the fair a week or more before the fair opens. The judging can take place the same day or several days later. The entries and awards are then arranged in the display cases before the fair opens. Closed judgings are often seen as shrouded in secrecy and exhibitors are left to wonder why one entry won over another.

If you're lucky, your fair will conduct an open judging where the entries are judged in front of an audience and the judges will explain why an entry did or didn't win a ribbon. Open judgings are usually held during the fair, with entries delivered the morning of the judging. They are very educational events. Open judgings allow the exhibitors to see how the judging process works and what it really takes to bring home the top awards.

The highlight of my judging year is the California State Fair. All of the canning and baked goods competitions are conducted with open judgings. We discuss each entry and offer advice for improvement. The audience has the opportunity to ask questions and receive answers from the judges. It is a great experience for all. If your fair conducts open judgings, I strongly encourage you to attend.

What Judges Look for in Canning Entries

Understanding the judging process and how and why judges pick one entry out of dozens to receive first place can sometimes be mystifying. So let me take away some of that mystery, pull back the curtain, and explain what the judges look for in an entry.

There are four basic criteria that judges use to evaluate a canning entry—container, appearance, texture, and flavor. The best entries score high in all of these areas.

✳ CONTAINER ✳

The rules will specify the size and number of jars that are required to be submitted per entry. If you are required to submit two jars per entry and the rules state the jars must be identical, this means everything about the two jars must be identical—the size and shape of the jar, the brand of jar, and even any embossed pattern or logo on the outside of the jar. Make sure the lids, screw bands, and even the labels and label placement are identical. The jars should be mirror images of each other.

The judges will also check to make sure the jar is clean, that there is no product under the screw band and no rust on the band or lid, that the label contains all required information and is attached to the jar according to the rules, and that the lid is tightly sealed. Product under the band and rust indicate that the screw bands were not removed and the jars were not washed and thoroughly dried after being canned.

DID YOU KNOW?

AMERICA'S FIRST COUNTY FAIR

Gentleman farmer and businessman Elkanah Watson of Albany, New York, organized America's first agricultural fair, the Berkshire County Fair in Pittsfield, Massachusetts, in 1811. To spark local and national pride, he invited area farmers to enter their livestock, crops, and produce into competitions to select the best farm-raised products in the county.

Two years later, he encouraged women to enter their needlework, tatting, and homespun cloth in an effort to encourage interest in American-made products. By 1819, he had convinced the New York legislature to contribute $10,000 a year for six years to provide premium awards for exhibitors of agricultural and home products, including preserved foods.

The container normally accounts for 5% to 10% of an entry's score. It can count for as much as 25% of the score if the entries are judged on appearance only, where the judges don't open the jars to test the texture and flavor of the canned products.

✳ APPEARANCE ✳

First impressions are important. When an entry comes before a judge, the first thing he or she notices is how the jar and contents look. Is it attractive and appealing? Does it look like it would taste good? The judge also looks at the size and shape of the pieces. Are they all about the same size? Do they look like they came from the same batch of produce? The color of the preserves is also important. Does the canned item have a bright, pretty, uniform color, or is the color too pale, too dark, or appears to have faded? Are there any trapped air bubbles or floating fruit? All of these elements determine the appearance of the canning entry.

The amount of headspace in the top of the jar is a major consideration. Some judges will bring out a ruler to measure the exact headspace while others have a good eye for accurately judging the headspace in a jar. Headspace is a safety concern, and using the correct headspace, as specified by the USDA, demonstrates the canner's skill and canning knowledge.

Jams, conserves, and preserves should have a translucent, jewel-tone color with no separation of the mixture or fruit floating in the top of the jar. Marmalades should have a bright color with pieces of citrus peel and fruit evenly suspended throughout the jar. Jellies should be crystal clear and shimmering. Spreads with pale, dark, or oxidized colors will have low appearance scores.

Fruits, vegetables, and pickles should be neatly packed and fill the entire jar with no floating produce or clear space at the bottom of the jar. The produce should be properly trimmed and free of defects. Both whole produce and cut pieces should be of reasonably uniform size and shape. The color should be attractive, characteristic of the type of produce, and as near as possible to that of the standard for a cooked product. The liquid should just cover the top of the product and be clear and free of small particles, cloudiness, or air bubbles.

The appearance or pack of the canned item can account for 20% to 75% of an entry's score. Some fairs judge entries on appearance only without opening the jars to judge the texture and flavor of the canned product, making this category absolutely critical to winning awards. Entries that are judged on appearance only are all about the look, color, and artistry of the pack rather than the art and science of safe and delicious food preservation.

If your fair judges on appearance only, look closely at the winning entries when you visit the fair. Chances are the winning fruit, vegetable, and pickle entries will have an artisanal pack. This means the produce is carefully arranged in the jars in a highly decorative manner. If this is the case, you will need to creatively pack your jars to have a chance to take home the top awards.

❋ TEXTURE ❋

Each type of preserve has its own texture. For example, jams should be smooth on the palate, not grainy, and should mound up in a spoon and spread easily, while pickles should be firm, crisp, and tender. Judges look for these specific characteristics when they judge a particular type of preserves. If canned goods don't have the appropriate texture, they won't score well. Texture usually accounts for 25% to 35% of an entry's score.

Jams and conserves should contain small pieces of crushed or chopped fruit evenly distributed throughout the jar. It should mound up in a spoon without any separation of the fruit and jelly. The best marmalades will have thin, soft pieces of citrus peel and fruit suspended in a tender jelly. Preserves should contain whole small fruits or uniform pieces of fruit that are tender and hold their shape, and are uniformly distributed throughout the jar. Jellies should quiver, cut easily, and hold their shape. They should be tender with no sugar crystals. Butters should be smooth and silky without any graininess, stickiness, or separation of the fruit and juice when spooned onto a plate.

Canned fruit should be tender, easy to cut, and hold its shape without being too firm, too soft, or mushy. Pickles should be plump, tender, firm, and crisp, and not limp, shriveled, or overcooked. Relishes should contain tender vegetable pieces of uniform size and texture.

Because of safety concerns with pressure canned foods, many fairs do not offer judging classes for vegetables. At fairs that do accept vegetables, most judge the entries on appearance only without opening the jars. When opened for judging, vegetables should be tender and hold their shape without being overcooked or mushy.

❋ FLAVOR ❋

Flavor is the most important element in judging canned items. An entry may be attractive and have a nice texture, but if it doesn't taste good, it won't win a blue ribbon. Judges look for canned goods with a pleasing, balanced flavor that retains strong flavor elements of the fresh produce. The flavor may be complex, bold, or delicate. If the preserve tastes overcooked or the flavor of one ingredient overpowers the others, the entry won't score well. Impress the judges with great tasting, canned goods to take home those blue ribbons.

Jams, jellies, and other soft spreads should have a strong, fully ripe flavor characteristic of the type of fruit or other ingredients. They should not be bland, too tart or sour, overly sweet, or taste overcooked. The best flavor compliment I ever received was at an open judging at the California State Fair when a highly respected judge tasted my strawberry preserves during the Best of Show open judging and exclaimed, "Wow! Some of those strawberries are still alive!"

Fruits should have a strong flavor of ripe fruit, not bland, underripe, or overripe. Pickles and relishes should have a matured, balanced flavor, appropriate for the type of preserve, without too strong of a tart vinegar taste or being too sour or salty. Vegetables, if tasted by the judge, should have a pleasing flavor, not bland or overcooked.

REASONS FOR DISQUALIFICATION

- » Jars not identical
- » Incorrect size of jars
- » Use of unapproved canning jars or lids
- » Paraffin wax seals
- » Label incorrectly placed on jars
- » Information missing from label
- » Preserves entered in wrong class or division
- » Unsealed jars
- » Screw bands unable to be removed from jars
- » Rust on lids or screw bands
- » Jars not processed according to USDA guidelines
- » Incorrect processing method or insufficient processing time
- » Preserves containing unsafe ingredients for canning
- » Hair or foreign object in jar
- » Mold, spoilage, or rising air bubbles in jars

BIGGEST CANNING MISTAKES

These are the most common mistakes that fair competitors make, reducing their entry's score and taking their preserves out of consideration for the awards. To give yourself the best chance of winning a ribbon, make sure your canned goods don't have any of these issues.

- » Incorrect or incomplete label information
- » Jars not identical
- » Entering preserves in the wrong class or division
- » Dirty or sticky jars; not washing jars before delivery
- » Product under screw bands; bands hard to remove
- » Rust on lids or screw bands
- » Weak seals
- » Incorrect headspace
- » Jars inverted after processing—product stuck on underside of lid
- » Preserves are too dark or show signs of oxidation
- » Low-quality or underripe ingredients used
- » Mild or bland flavor
- » Spreads are too stiff and rubbery
- » Spreads are overcooked and developed a scorched flavor
- » Spreads are too thin or unset
- » Fruit in spreads is undercooked
- » Fruit pieces in jams are too large
- » Jam made with puréed fruit rather than small crushed pieces of fruit
- » Foam not skimmed from soft spreads before filling jars
- » Separated spreads with fruit floating in the top of jar and clear jelly in the bottom of jar
- » Stale nuts used in conserves
- » Fruit or vegetables floating in jars
- » Uneven pack or uneven sizes of fruits, vegetables, or pickles
- » Soft or mushy fruit, vegetables, or pickles
- » Poor or faded color of fruit, vegetables, or pickles
- » Shriveled pickles from too much vinegar or the vinegar acidity is too strong
- » Uneven sizes of vegetables in relish
- » Adding too much spice, particularly cloves, and overpowering the flavor of other preserve ingredients

* Fair Directory *

Here is contact information for each state's largest fairs and, where available, the website for the state's fair association, which provides a list of fairs throughout the state. At the end of the list are websites for Canadian fair associations.

NATIONAL FAIR ASSOCIA-TION WEBSITES
International Association of Fairs and Expositions
www.fairsandexpos.com

US Fairs and Festivals
www.usfairsandfestivals.com

ALABAMA
Alabama State Fair
www.alstatefair.com

Alabama National Fair
www.alnationalfair.org

Association of Alabama Fairs
www.alabamafairs.com

ALASKA
Alaska State Fair
www.alaskastatefair.org

Tanana Valley State Fair
www.tananavalleystatefair.com

Alaskan Fairs and Festivals
www.usfairsandfestivals.com/alaska

ARIZONA
Arizona State Fair
www.azstatefair.com

Arizona Fairs Association
www.arizonafairs.com

ARKANSAS
Arkansas State Fair
www.arkansasstatefair.com

Arkansas Fair Managers Association
arkansasfairs.com

CALIFORNIA
California State Fair
www.castatefair.org

OC Fair
www.ocfair.com

L. A. County Fair
www.lacountyfair.com

California Fairs and Festivals
www.californiafairsandfestivals.com

COLORADO
Colorado State Fair
www.coloradostatefair.com

Colorado Association of Fairs and Shows
www.coloradofairs.org

CONNECTICUT
Durham Fair
www.durhamfair.com

North Haven Fair
www.northhaven-fair.com

Orange Country Fair
www.orangectfair.com

Connecticut Agricultural Fairs
www.ctagfairs.org

DELAWARE
Delaware State Fair
www.delawarestatefair.com

Delaware Fairs and Festivals
www.usfairsandfestivals.com/delaware

FLORIDA
Florida State Fair
www.floridastatefair.com

Citrus County Fair
www.citruscountyfair.com

Florida Fairs and Festivals
www.usfairsandfestivals.com/florida

GEORGIA
Georgia State Fair
www.georgiastatefair.org

Georgia National Fair
www.georgianationalfair.com

North Georgia State Fair
www.northgeorgiastatefair.com

Georgia Association of Agricultural Fairs
www.georgiafairs.org

HAWAII
Hawaii State Farm Fair
www.hfbf.org

IDAHO
Eastern Idaho State Fair
www.funatthefair.com

Western Idaho State Fair
www.idahofair.com

Rocky Mountain Association of Fairs
www.rmaf.net

ILLINOIS
Illinois State Fair
www.agr.state.il.us/isf

Illinois Association of Agricultural Fairs
www.illinoiscountyfairs.org

INDIANA
Indiana State Fair
www.indianastatefair.com

Marion County Fair
www.marioncountyfair.org

Indiana Association of Fairs
www.indianafairsandfestivals.org

IOWA
Iowa State Fair
www.iowastatefair.org

Association of Iowa Fairs
www.iowafairs.com

KANSAS
Kansas State Fair
www.kansasstatefair.com

Kansas Fairs Association
www.kansasfairsassociation.com

KENTUCKY
Kentucky State Fair
www.kystatefair.org

Kentucky Association of Fairs
www.kafs.net

LOUISIANA
The State Fair of Louisiana
www.statefairoflouisiana.com

Louisiana Association of Fairs &
Festivals
www.laffnet.org

MAINE
Cumberland Fair
www.cumberlandfair.com

Skowhegan State Fair
www.skowheganstatefair.com

Fryeburg Fair
www.fryeburgfair.org

Topsham Fair
www.topshamfair.net

Maine Association of
Agricultural Fairs
www.mainefairs.org

MARYLAND
Maryland State Fair
www.marylandstatefair.com

MASSACHUSETTS
The Big E
www.thebige.com/fair

Topsfield Fair
www.topsfieldfair.org

Massachusetts Agricultural Fairs
Association
www.mafa.org

MICHIGAN
Fifth Third Bank Michigan
State Fair
michiganstatefairllc.com

Michigan Association of Fairs &
Exhibitions
www.michiganfairs.org

MINNESOTA
Minnesota State Fair
www.mnstatefair.org

Minnesota Federation of County
Fairs
www.mfcf.com

MISSISSIPPI
Mississippi State Fair
www.msfair.net

MISSOURI
Missouri State Fair
www.mostatefair.com

Ozark Empire Fair
www.ozarkempirefair.com

Missouri Association of Fairs and
Festivals
www.missourifairsandfestivals.org

MONTANA
Montana State Fair
www.montanastatefair.com

MontanaFair
www.montanafair.com

Montana Association of Fairs
www.montanafairs.org

NEBRASKA
Nebraska State Fair
www.statefair.org

Nebraska Association of
Fair Managers
www.nebraskafairs.org

NEVADA
Elko County Fair
www.elkocountyfair.com

Clark County Fair & Rodeo
www.ccfair.com

Nevada Fairs and Festivals
www.usfairsandfestivals.com/
nevada

NEW HAMPSHIRE
Hopkinton State Fair
www.hsfair.org

Rochester Fair
Rochester Fair Grounds
www.RochesterFair.com

New Hampshire Association of
Fairs & Expositions
nhfairs.yolasite.com

NEW JERSEY
New Jersey State Fair
www.njstatefair.com

Hunterdon County 4H &
Agricultural Fair
www.co.hunterdon.nj.us/4hagfair.
htm

Agricultural Fair Association of
New Jersey
www.njagfairs.com

NEW MEXICO
New Mexico State Fair
www.exponm.com

Southern New Mexico
State Fair
www.snmstatefairgrounds.net

NEW YORK
The Great New York State Fair
www.nysfair.org

New York State Association of
Agricultural Fairs
www.nyfairs.org

NORTH CAROLINA
North Carolina State Fair
www.ncstatefair.org

Dixie Classic Fair
www.dcfair.com

North Carolina Association of
Agricultural Fairs
www.ncagfairs.org

NORTH DAKOTA
North Dakota State Fair
www.ndstatefair.com

North Dakota Association
of Fairs
www.ndfairs.org

OHIO
Ohio State Fair
www.ohiostatefair.com

Canfield Fair
www.canfieldfair.com

Ohio Fair Managers Association
www.ohiofairs.org

OKLAHOMA
Oklahoma State Fair
www.okstatefair.com

Tulsa State Fair
www.tulsastatefair.com

OREGON
Oregon State Fair
www.oregonstatefair.org

Marion County Fair
www.mcfair.net

Lane County Fair
www.atthefair.com

Oregon Fairs Association
www.oregonfairs.org

PENNSYLVANIA
Bloomsburg Fair
www.bloomsburgfair.com

Big Butler Fair
www.bigbutlerfair.com

South Mountain Fair
www.southmountainfair.com

Pennsylvania State Association of
County Fairs
www.pafairs.org

RHODE ISLAND
Washington County Fair
www.washingtoncountyfair-ri.
com

Rhode Island Fairs and
Festivals
www.usfairsandfestivals.com/
rhode_island

SOUTH CAROLINA
South Carolina State Fair
www.scstatefair.org

Coastal Carolina Fair
www.coastalcarolinafair.org

South Carolina Association of
Fairs
www.scfairs.org

SOUTH DAKOTA
South Dakota State Fair
www.sdstatefair.com

Sioux Empire Fair
www.siouxempirefair.com

South Dakota Association of Fairs
www.southdakotafairs.com

TENNESSEE
Tennessee State Fair
www.tnstatefair.org

Tennessee Association of Fairs
www.tnfairs.com

TEXAS
State Fair of Texas
www.bigtex.com

North Texas State Fair
www.ntfair.com

Texas Association of Fairs &
Events
texasfairs.com

UTAH
Utah State Fair
www.utahstatefair.com

Iron County Fair
www.ironcountyfair.net

Utah Association of Fairs &
Events
www.utahfairsandevents.org

VERMONT
Vermont State Fair
www.vermontstatefair.net

Champlain Valley Fair
www.champlainvalleyfair.org

Vermont Agricultural Fairs
Association
gmfairs.org

VIRGINIA
State Fair of Virginia
www.statefairva.org

Prince William County Fair,
Virginia
www.pwcfair.com

Virginia Association of Fairs
www.vafairs.us

WASHINGTON
Washington State Fair
www.thefair.com

Evergreen State Fair
www.evergreenfair.org

Central Washington State Fair
www.fairfun.com

Northwest Washington Fair
www.nwwafair.com

Washington State Fairs
Association
www.wastatefairs.com

WEST VIRGINIA
The State Fair of West Virginia
www.statefairofwv.com

West Virginia Association of
Fairs & Festivals
www.wvfairsandfestivals.org

WISCONSIN
Wisconsin State Fair
www.wistatefair.com

Wisconsin Association of Fairs
www.wifairs.com

WYOMING
Wyoming State Fair
www.wystatefair.com

Wyoming Association of Fairs
www.wyomingfairs.org

CANADA
Canadian Association of Fairs &
Exhibitions
www.canadian-fairs.ca

BRITISH COLUMBIA
British Columbia Association
of Agricultural Fairs &
Exhibitions
www.bcfairs.ca

NOVA SCOTIA
Exhibitions Association of Nova
Scotia
www.eans.ca

ONTARIO
Ontario Association of
Agricultural Societies
www.ontariofairs.org

PRINCE EDWARD ISLAND
Prince Edward Island Association
of Exhibitions
peiae.ca

SASKATCHEWAN
Saskatchewan Association
of Agricultural Societies &
Exhibitions
www.saase.ca

* Metric Equivalents *

LIQUID/DRY MEASURES

U.S.	METRIC
¼ teaspoon	1.25 milliliters
½ teaspoon	2.5 milliliters
1 teaspoon	5 milliliters
1 tablespoon (3 teaspoons)	15 milliliters
1 fluid ounce (2 tablespoons)	30 milliliters
¼ cup	60 milliliters
$^1/_3$ cup	80 milliliters
½ cup	120 milliliters
1 cup	240 milliliters
1 pint (2 cups)	480 milliliters
1 quart (4 cups; 32 ounces)	960 milliliters
1 gallon (4 quarts)	3.84 liters
1 ounce (by weight)	28 grams
1 pound	454 grams
2.2 pounds	1 kilogram

OVEN TEMPERATURES

°F	GAS MARK	°C
250	½	120
275	1	140
300	2	150
325	3	165
350	4	180
375	5	190
400	6	200
425	7	220
450	8	230
475	9	240
500	10	260
550	Broil	290

✳ Index ✳